GW01606974

THE ILLUSTRATED MOTORCAR LEGENDS

JAGUAR

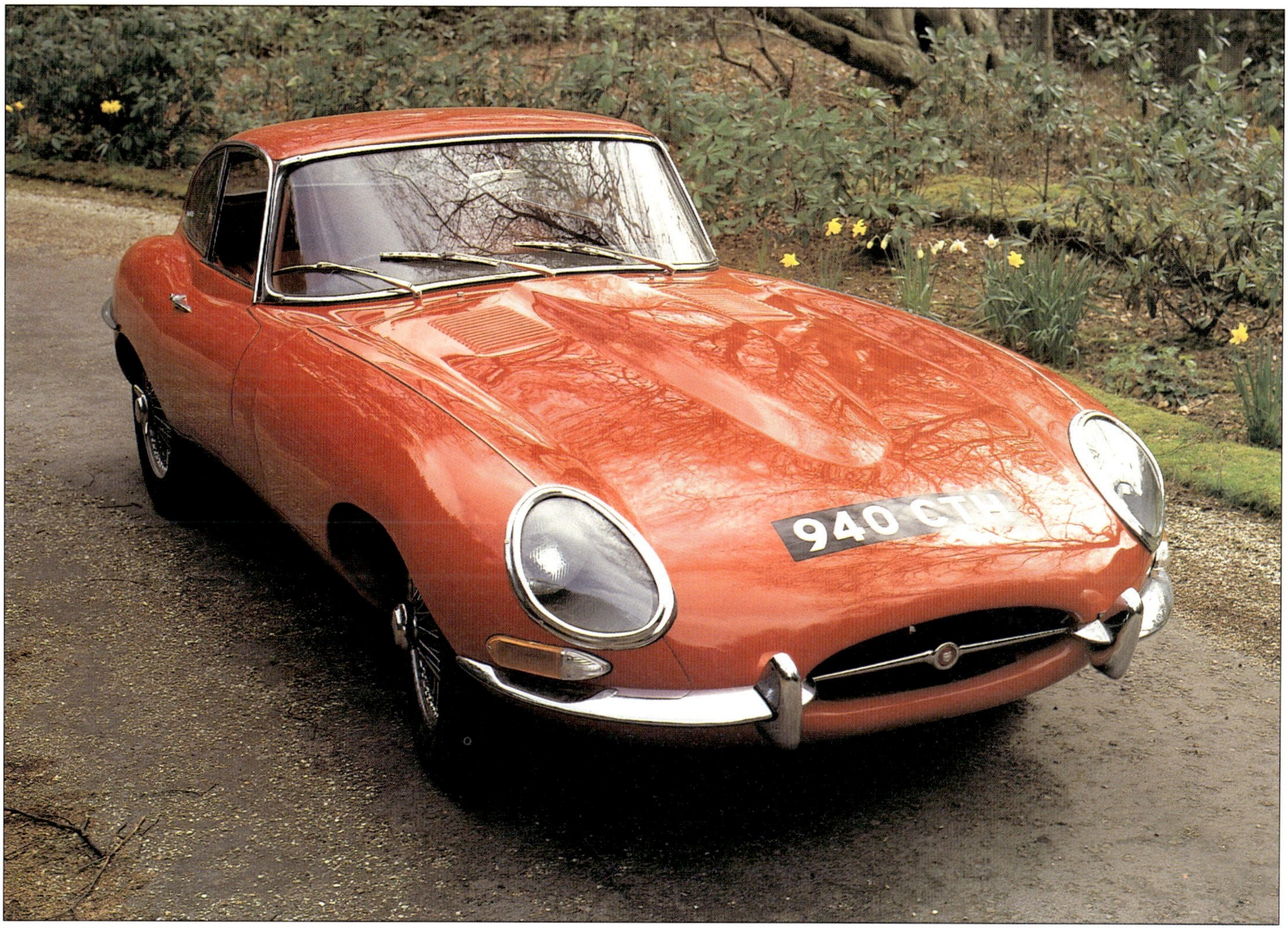

ROY BACON

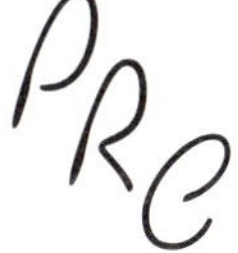

Acknowledgements
The author and publishers wish to acknowledge their debt to all who loaned material and photographs for this book. The bulk of the pictures came from the extensive archives of the National Motor Museum at Beaulieu, and we had kind assistance from Jaguar itself while a picture or two came from the author's camera. Thanks to all who helped.

Published 1996 by Promotional Reprint Company, Kiln House, 210 New Kings Road, London SW6 4NZ.

ISBN 1 85648 361 4
Printed and bound in China

CONTENTS

SIDECARS, SWALLOWS & SS

1922-1939

JAGUAR - 'Grace...Space...Pace' - said the postwar advertisements and they surely summed up the marque with the grace of its distinctive lines, so easy to pick out from the crowd both then and now. Space came in the big saloons, built to carry their occupants in style, silence and comfort, while Pace reflected the five wins at Le Mans in the 1950s, the successful return in the 1980s, and the fabled XK series of sports cars.

Before Jaguar there was SS, before SS there was Swallow and that name was first used for a motorcycle sidecar. It was in the early days after World War 1 that Bill Walmsley set up in the motorcycle trade and built a sidecar with a smart, Zeppelin-shaped, polished aluminium body, a style that proved popular for many years. In 1922 his 20-year old neighbour, William Lyons, saw the commercial possibilities of that sidecar and together they formed the Swallow Sidecar

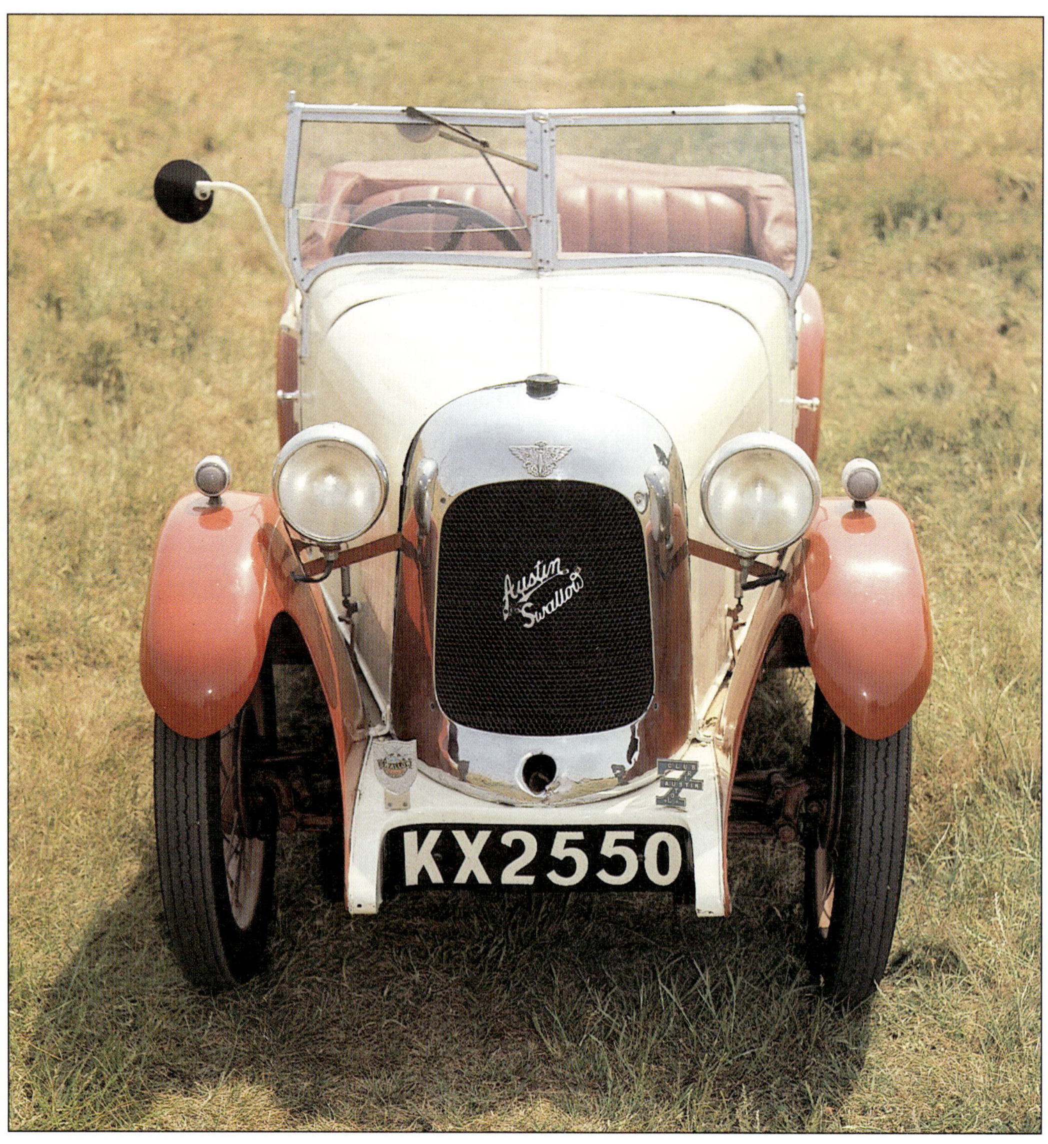

The Austin Seven was the first car to have a Swallow body, demonstrating William Lyons's style and line right from the start.

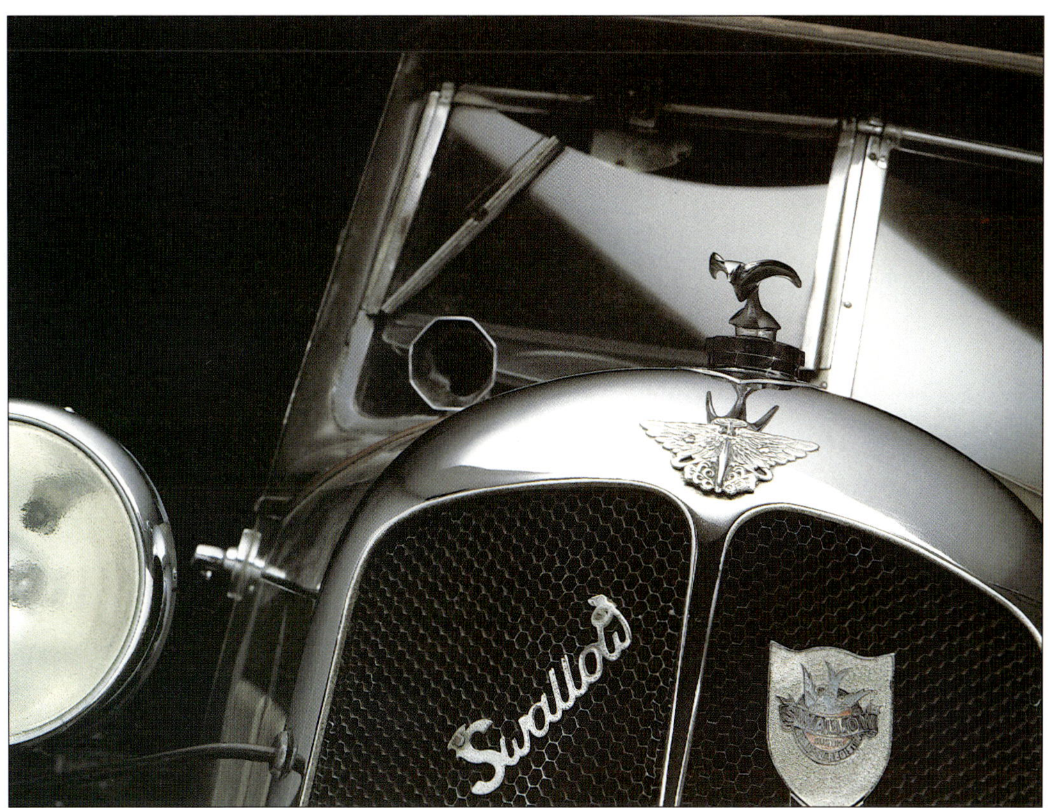

LEFT: Close-up of the radiator and bonnet motif of a 1929 Austin Seven Swallow showing the Austin and Swallow register badges.

BELOW: This is a 1931 Swift Swallow, just one of several makes rebodied by Lyons in those early days.

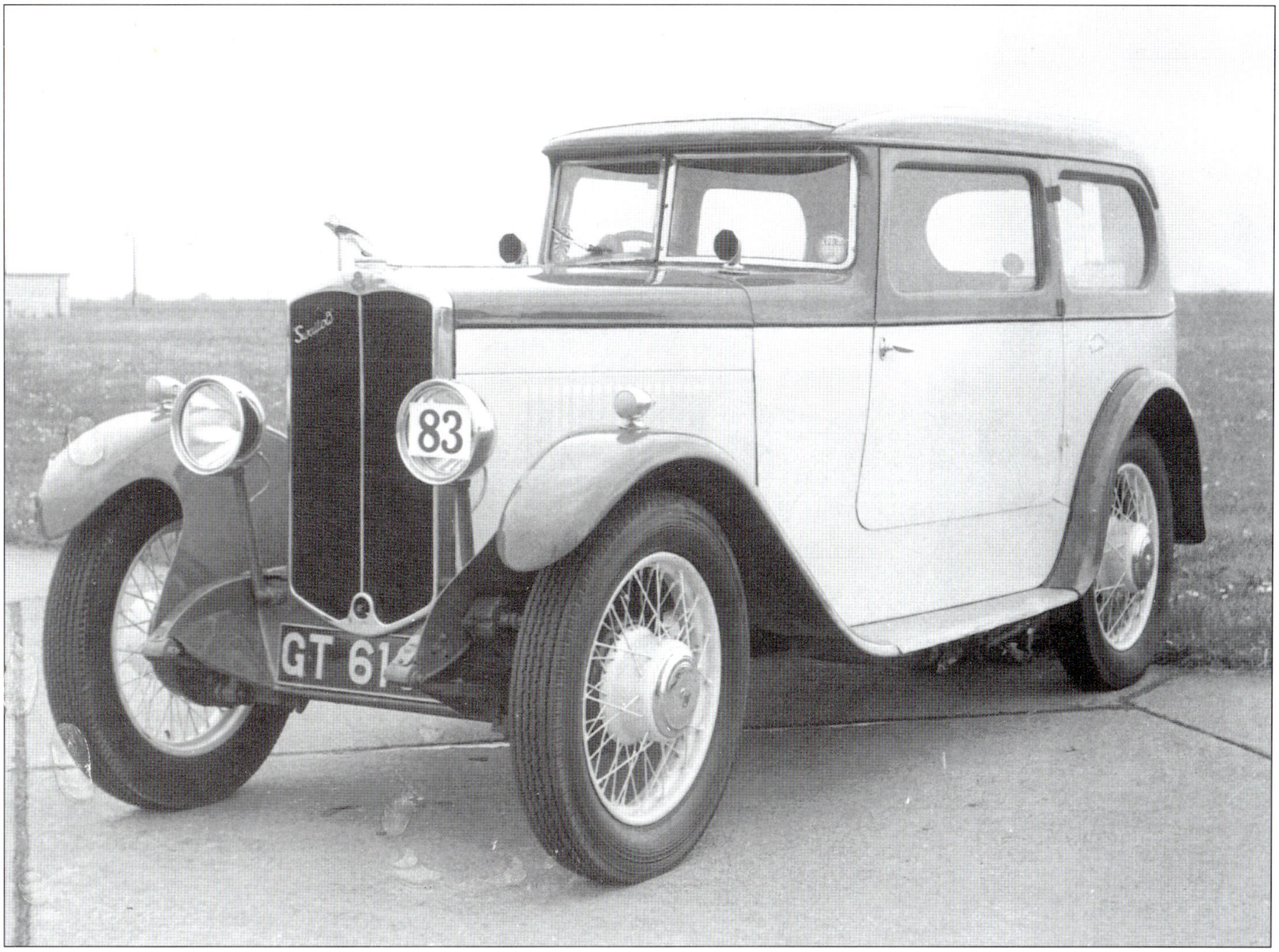

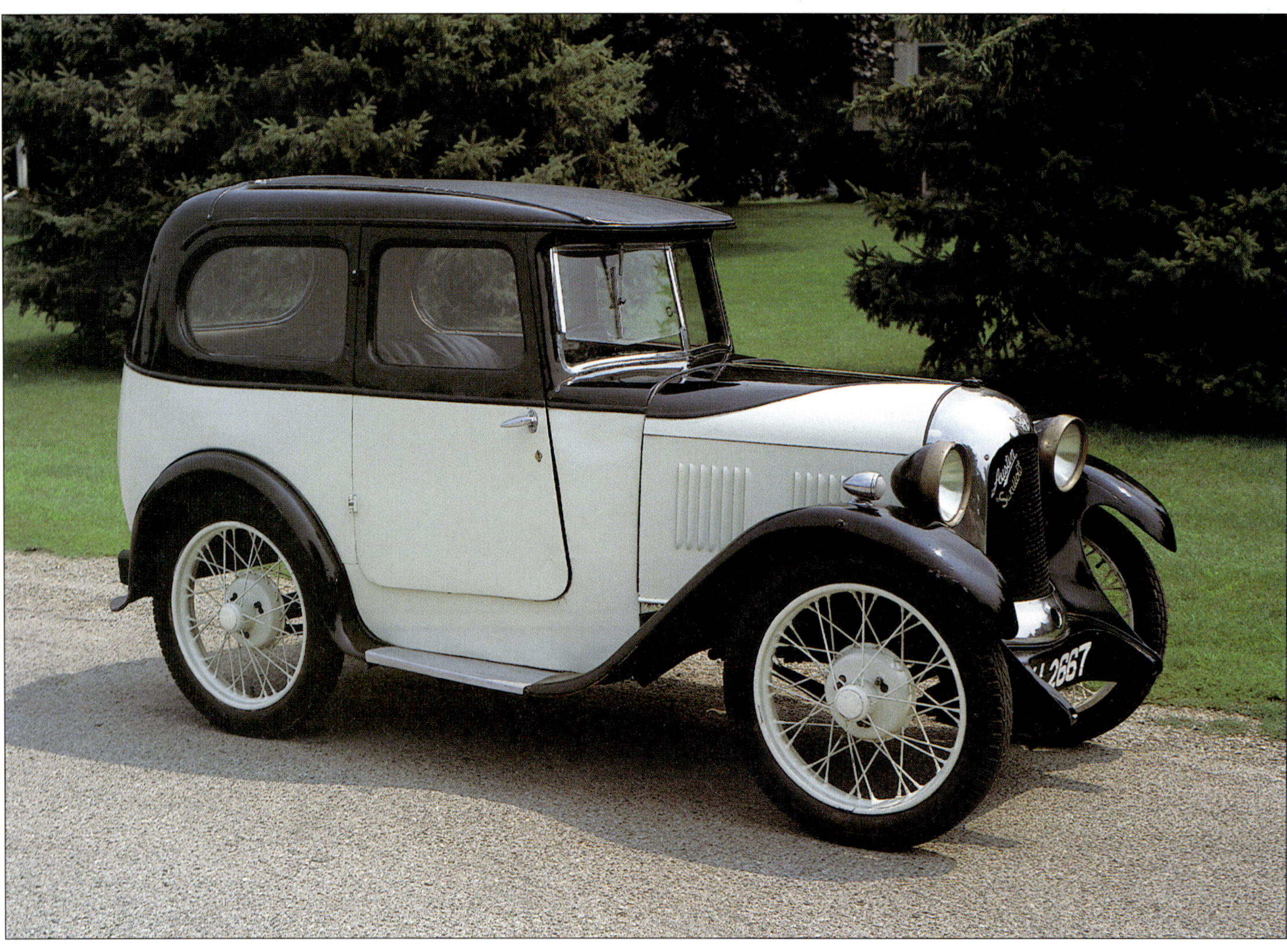

This 1931 Austin Seven Swallow has the pen-nib style of two-tone paint for the bonnet, common to the saloons and a marked contrast to the standard finish.

Company. William Lyons proved to be a remarkable man who combined a real flair for the line and style of bodies with a fine business sense. It was to take him to the top and it is remarkable that his distinctive personal stamp remained on his many successful designs down the years. The elegant sweep of the Jaguar was not to be lost, nor his ability to build stunning cars at prices that offered remarkable value for money.

The small sidecar firm, based in Coker Street, Blackpool, soon expanded and by 1926 had become the Swallow Sidecar & Coachbuilding Company. One of the first results of this came in 1927 with the rebodying of Austin Sevens as the Austin Swallow. This gave the car much more sporting lines and was listed as a saloon-coupé for the rigid top could be removed and replaced by a fabric one. The first was finished in cream with dark crimson wings and top to give the car much improved looks.

The Swallow Austin continued in production to 1932 in saloon and sports two-seater forms, being joined by a Morris Cowley Swallow, Fiat Swallow and Swift Swallow during that period. Of more long-term importance was the Standard Swallow which brought a link to that firm that lasted to the early postwar years.

The Standard Swallow was based on the four-cylinder Nine, at first with the stock Standard radiator but this was soon altered. In 1931 the body was revamped and moved onto the six-cylinder Standard Ensign chassis. That year also brought the Wolseley Hornet Swallow, an open car with an overhead-camshaft and six-cylinder engine.

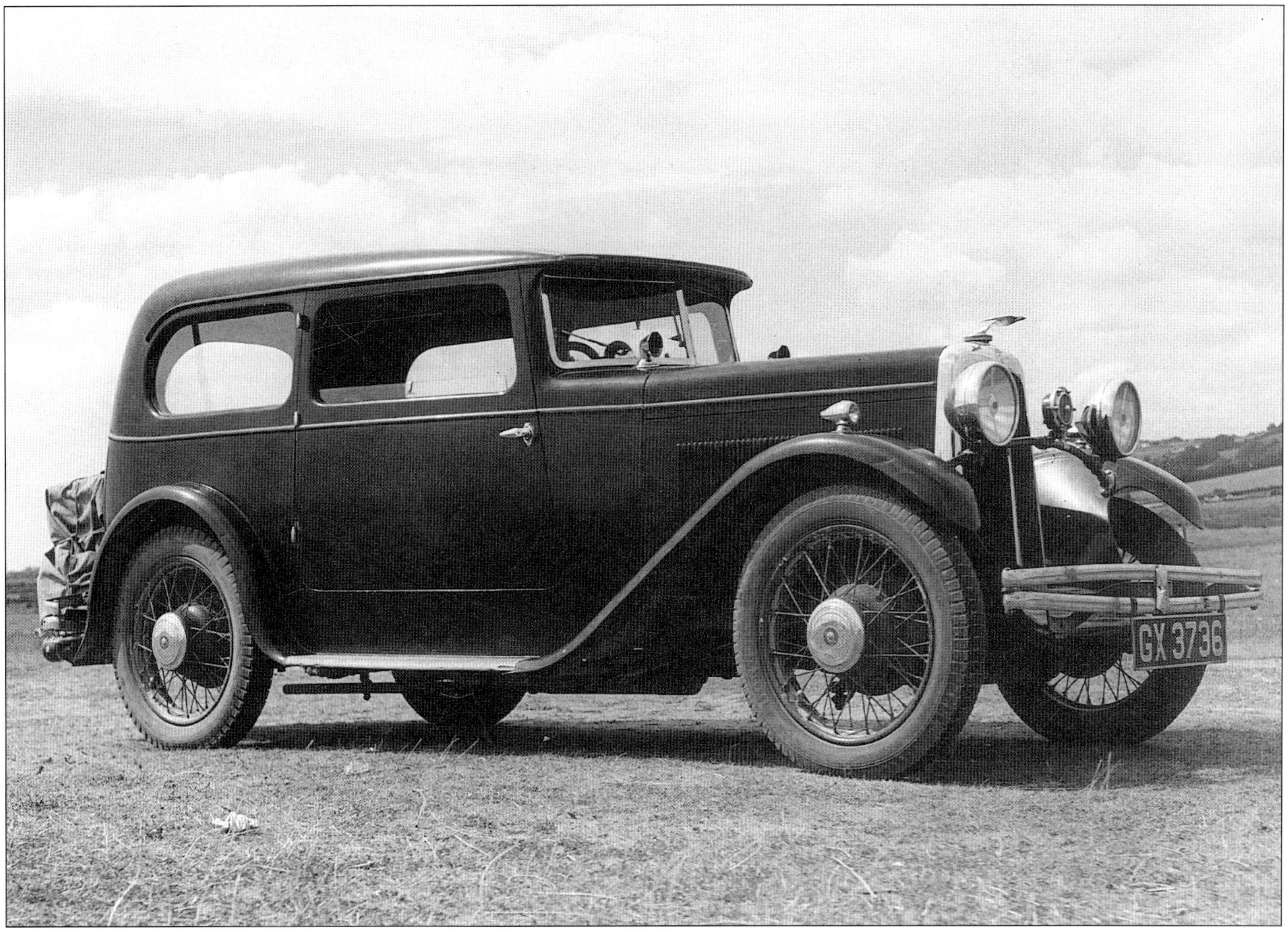

ABOVE: A 1932 Standard Big Nine with the Swallow body and improved line.

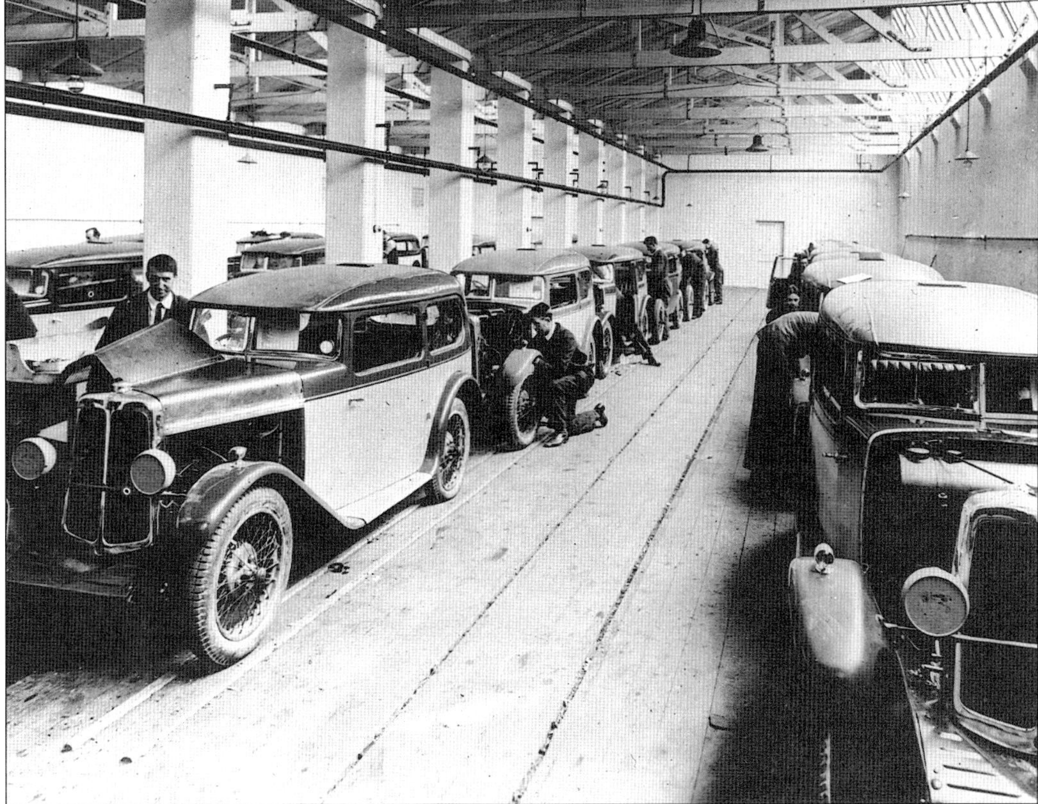

LEFT: Taken early in the 1930s, this picture shows lines of Big Nine Standard Swallows being assembled at the firm's works.

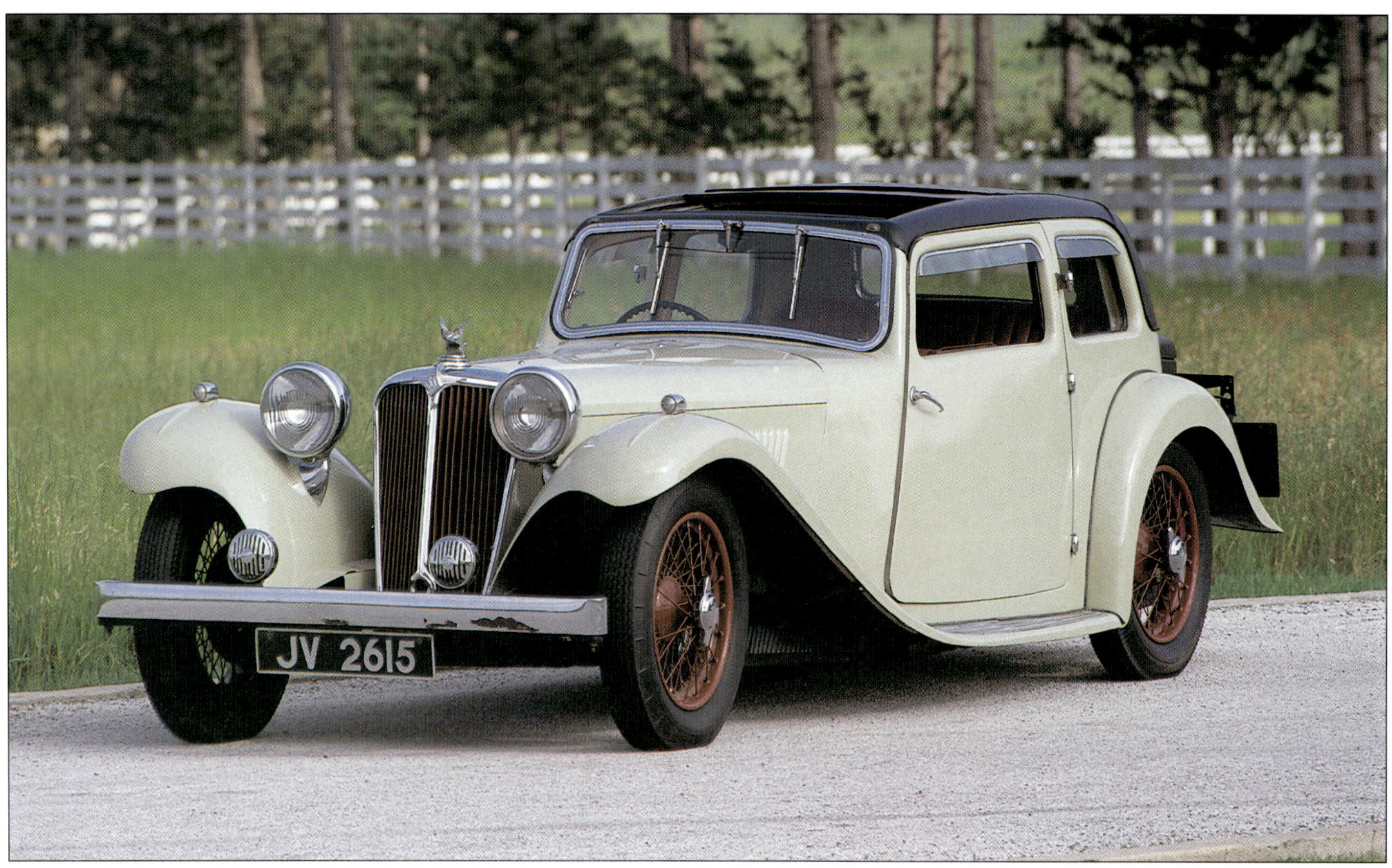

For 1933 the original SS1 had new wings and running boards flowing along the body to enhance the lines for coupé and tourer.

Up to that point all the Swallow bodies went onto stock chassis and engines to give more style and better fittings. If there was a performance improvement, it came from some weight reduction alone. What came next was the start of the Lyons line for it had a chassis especially made by Standard for Lyons, underslung at the rear, and powered by the Standard 2,054cc side-valve, six-cylinder engine, with a 2,552cc version as an option. Onto this went a close-coupled coupé body with a lengthy bonnet ahead of the cramped occupants' quarters.

Thus was born the SS1, first seen at the 1931 Motor Show and highly praised by the press, for it had the looks of a £1,000 car but was priced at £310. Performance was limited to around 70mph from the stock engine and it was dubbed the 'cad's car' by some, but it demonstrated William Lyons's ability to produce down to a price by using clever production methods without sacrificing quality. Design it simple, get it right and then leave it alone have always been key factors in this, and the firm kept to them.

The SS1 was revised for 1933 when production rose from 500 to 1,200 plus. The mechanics remained as they were but the body was built as a four-seater coupé or tourer with sweeping new wings, running boards and a lower roof line. An alloy cylinder head helped the top speed up to 75mph, the car was well made and the looks better. That year, the firm became SS Cars Ltd, but just what 'SS' stood for was not made clear. Standard, Sports, Super and Swallow could be combined in any way to taste.

From 1932 there had also been an SSII listed as a close-coupled coupé in the style of the SS1, but struggling a little with just 1,005cc of side-valve Standard Little Nine engine to pull it along. Around 60mph was its best, but it cornered well and the style made it look so much faster.

There were changes to both models for 1934 when the SS1 engine was

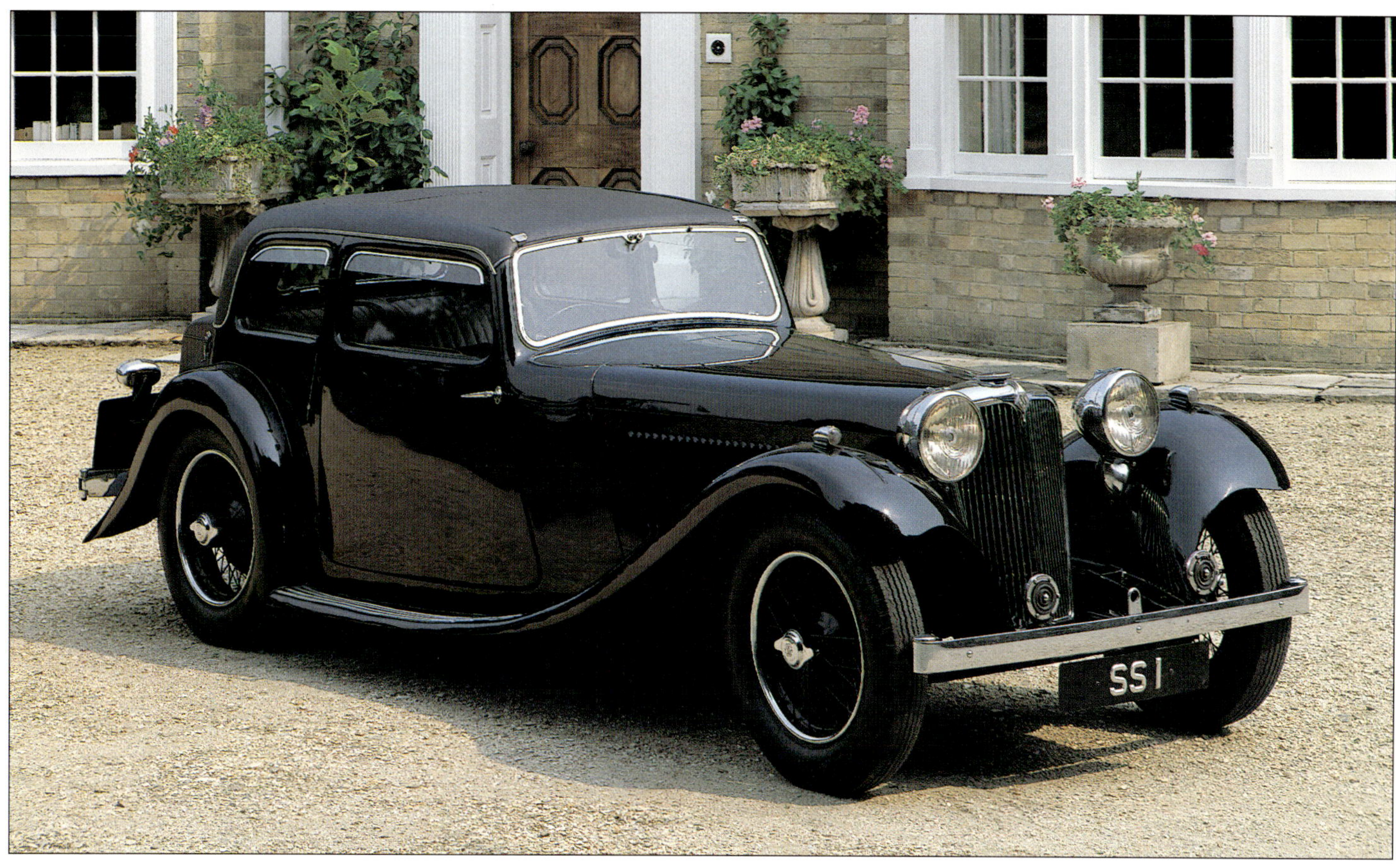

ABOVE: By 1935 the SS1 had evolved to a new frame, a larger Standard engine and this fine saloon joined the coupé and tourer models.
BELOW: Early SSII that had the form and style of the SS series but only the Little Nine engine to push it along.

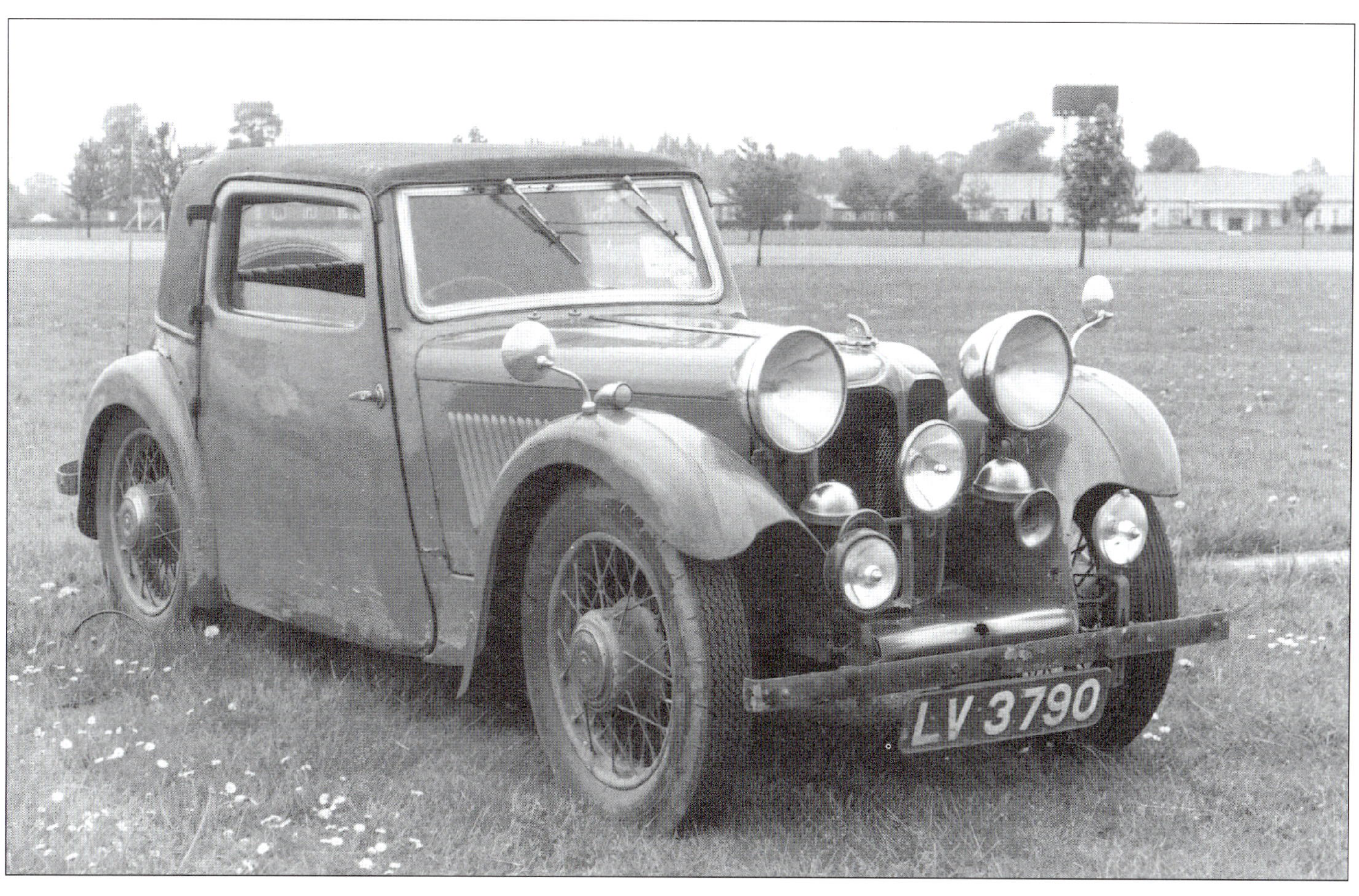

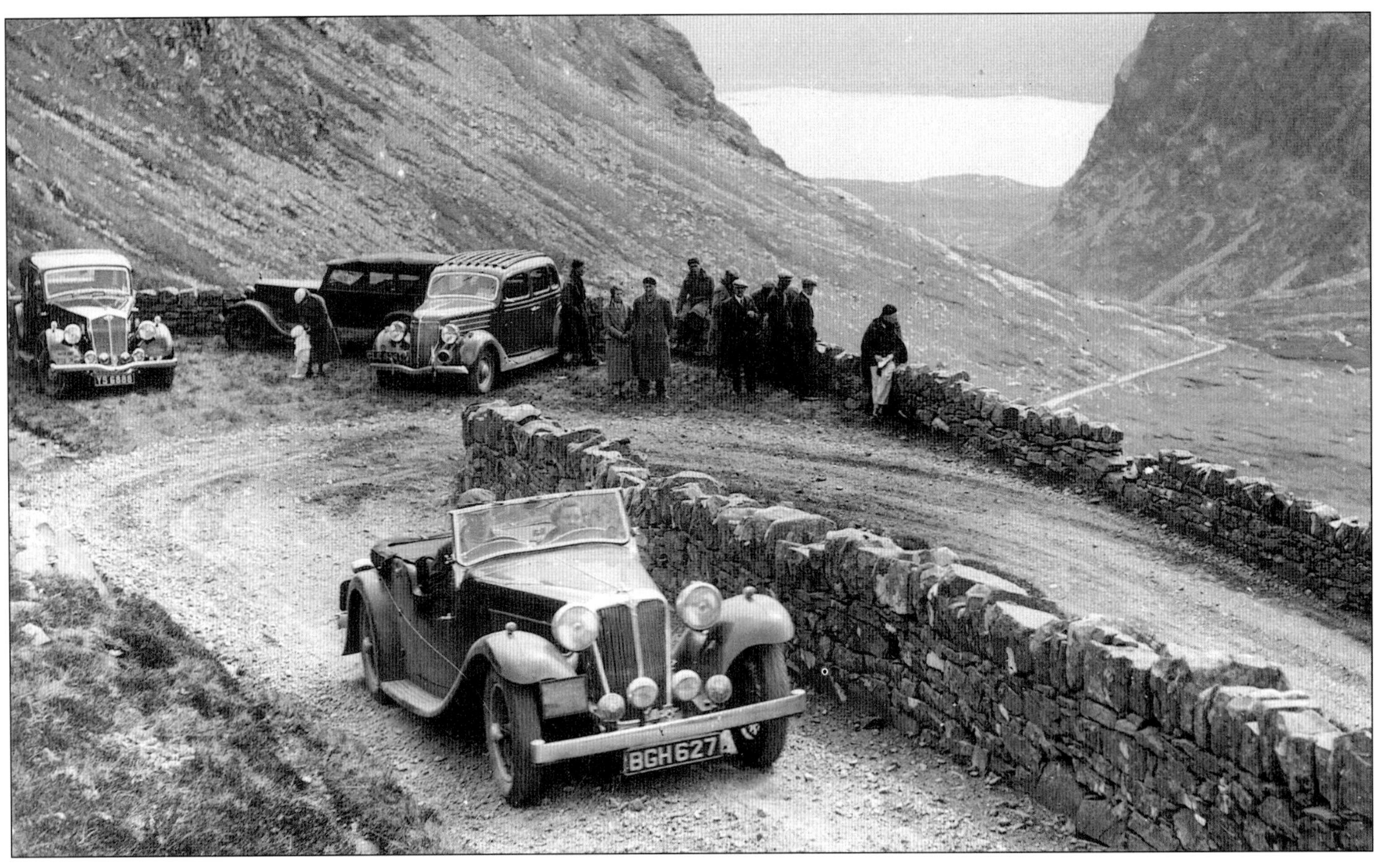

Scottish Rally section with a 1934 SS1 tourer making its ascent against a fine background.

enlarged to 2,143cc, or 2,663cc for the option, kept its side valves, but went into a new chassis. Saloon, drophead coupé and tourer bodies were available, joined by the Airline saloon for 1935. The flamboyance remained in the style and the price was still only £340.

The SSII also had a larger engine, 1,343cc as stock and 1,608cc as the option, these coming from the Standard 10 and 12 models. The wheelbase increased and the styling was revised for the coupé, saloon and four-seater tourer bodies, but it lacked the charisma of the SS1 and had limited success selling against cars from several other British firms.

Both the SS1 and SSII were dropped after 1936 but before then, in 1935, there appeared the SS90. It was only built that year and there were few of them, just 23 in total, but it was a great sports car and the first of a long line that would extend for decades. The SS90 was a sports two-seater whose body had the long bonnet, flowing wings and special style that was the hallmark of William Lyons's work. It also performed, for the 2,663cc engine was modified, although it kept its side valves, and was able to propel the car to the 90mph the model code suggested while the price remained a modest £395.

Up to 1935 the SS cars were from one mould, but this all changed for 1936 when the firm introduced sporting saloons, the Jaguar name and began to turn to the use of overhead-valve engines. The saloons were built in two sizes - as the Jaguar 1½-litre and 2½-litre, the larger as a tourer as well. The smaller had the 1,608cc side-valve four-cylinder engine in a new frame, with better brakes, on which went a four-door saloon body with simple, elegant lines that stood up against the best of the late-1930s. The 2½-litre had the 2,663cc of the SS90 but with overhead valves for its Standard-based bottom half. Twin SU carburettors helped the power, there was a new frame and the fine saloon body. It made for an

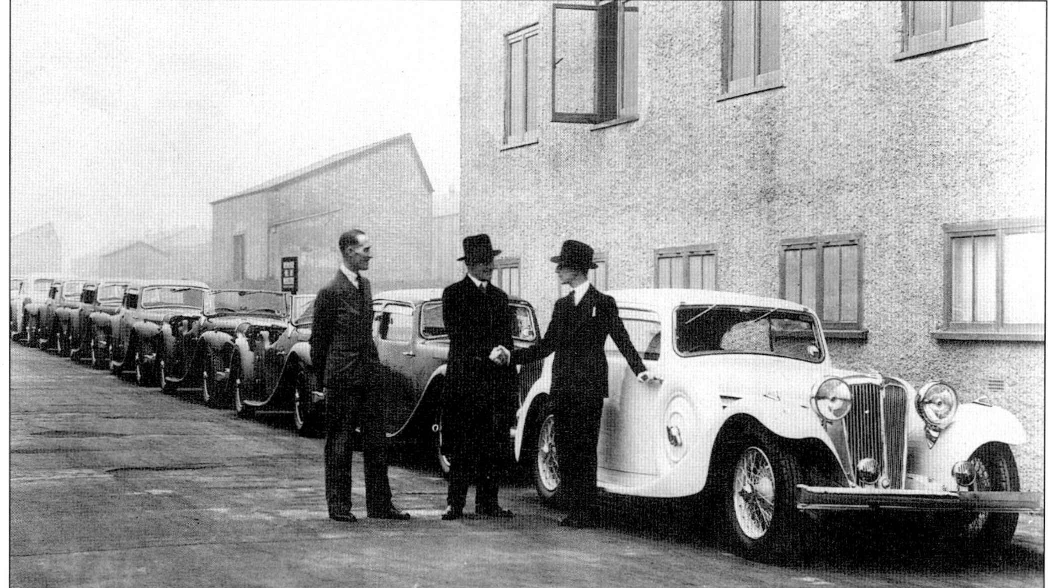
Late in 1934 and the first batch of SS1 cars for the USA is ready to roll, the lead car with an Airline saloon body.

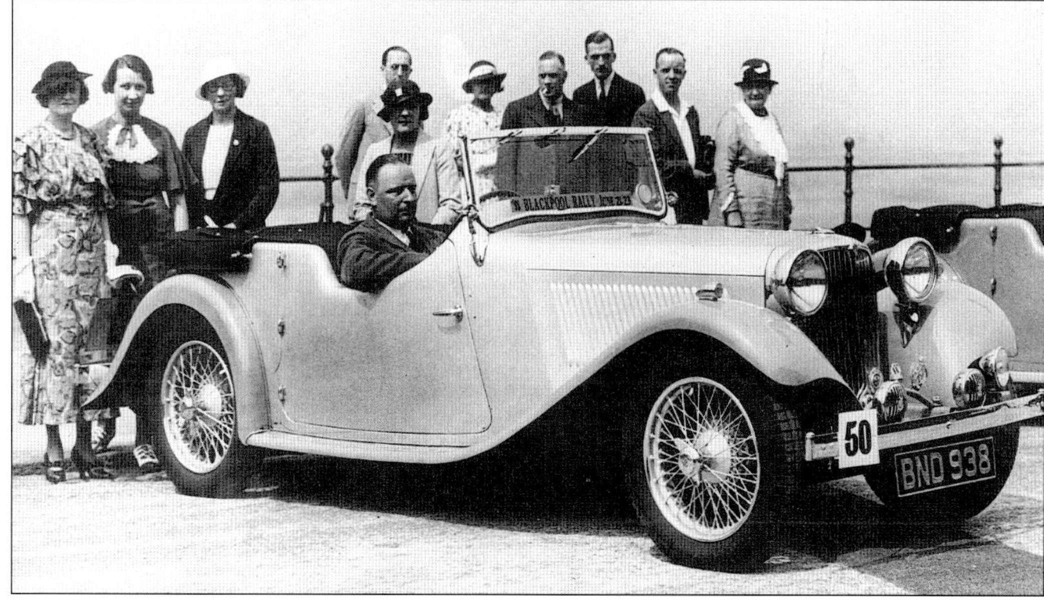

An SSII tourer taking part in the Blackpool Rally in June sometime in the mid-1930s.

excellent car; smooth, comfortable and easy to drive.

If the saloons had one of the best styles of their type for the period, the SS90 developed into the archetypal 1930s sports car. It became the Jaguar 2½-litre '100' with long flowing wings, low lines, cutaway doors and slab tank tail, better known as the SS100. It used the 2,663cc overhead-valve, six-cylinder engine from the saloon, could run close to 95mph and the price was kept to £395. Purists may have called it the 'Soda Squirt', but it gave real performance in style.

The saloons were revised for 1938 when the 1½-litre model changed to a 1,775cc engine having overhead valves; a drophead coupé joined the saloon, and a Jaguar 3½-litre model was added, this having a 3,485cc overhead-valve, six-cylinder engine. To gild the lily, the 2½-litre sports model was joined by the Jaguar 3½-litre '100', the fabulous 104mph SS100 with all that any enthusiast of the time could wish for - including a pair of massive Lucas P100 headlamps to light the way - and all for £445.

This brought the firm up to the war when car production stopped, all manner of other things were made, including sidecars, and plans for the postwar era laid.

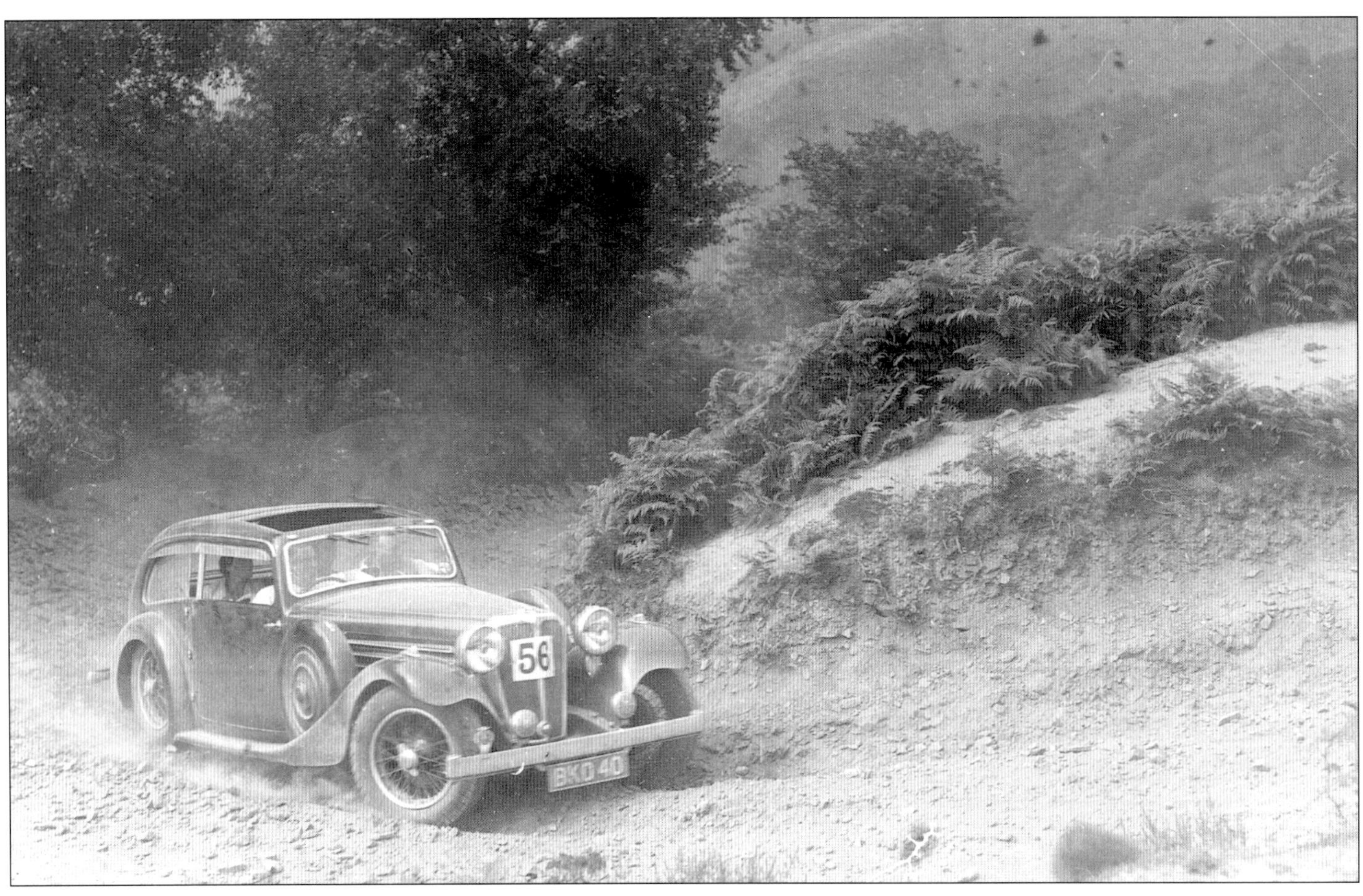

ABOVE: Barnstaple Trial with a 1935 Airline SS1 saloon storming a hill with dust and stones flying as it fights for grip.
BELOW: Improved 1936 SSII saloon with larger engine for better performance and longer wheelbase to allow a revised style.

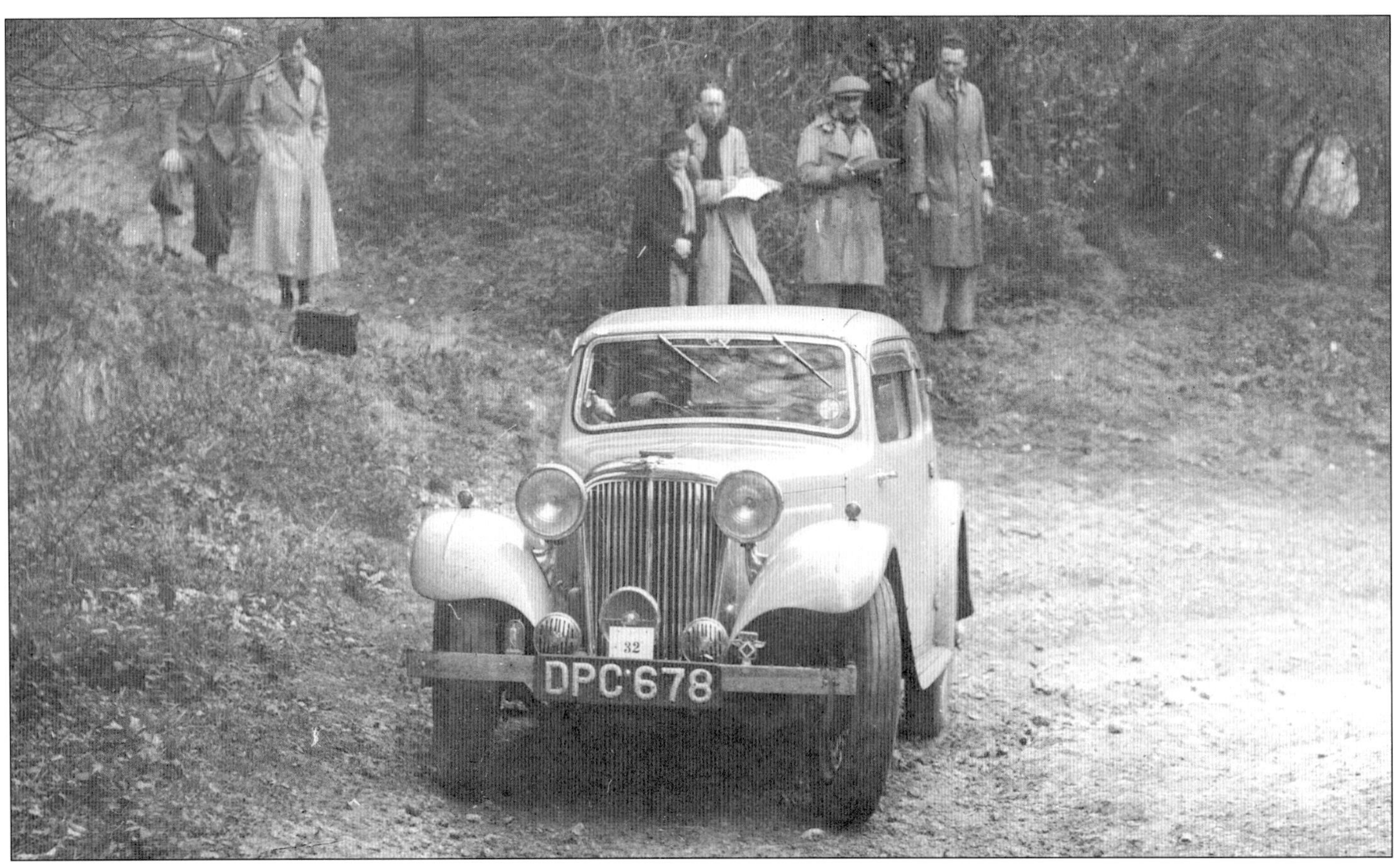

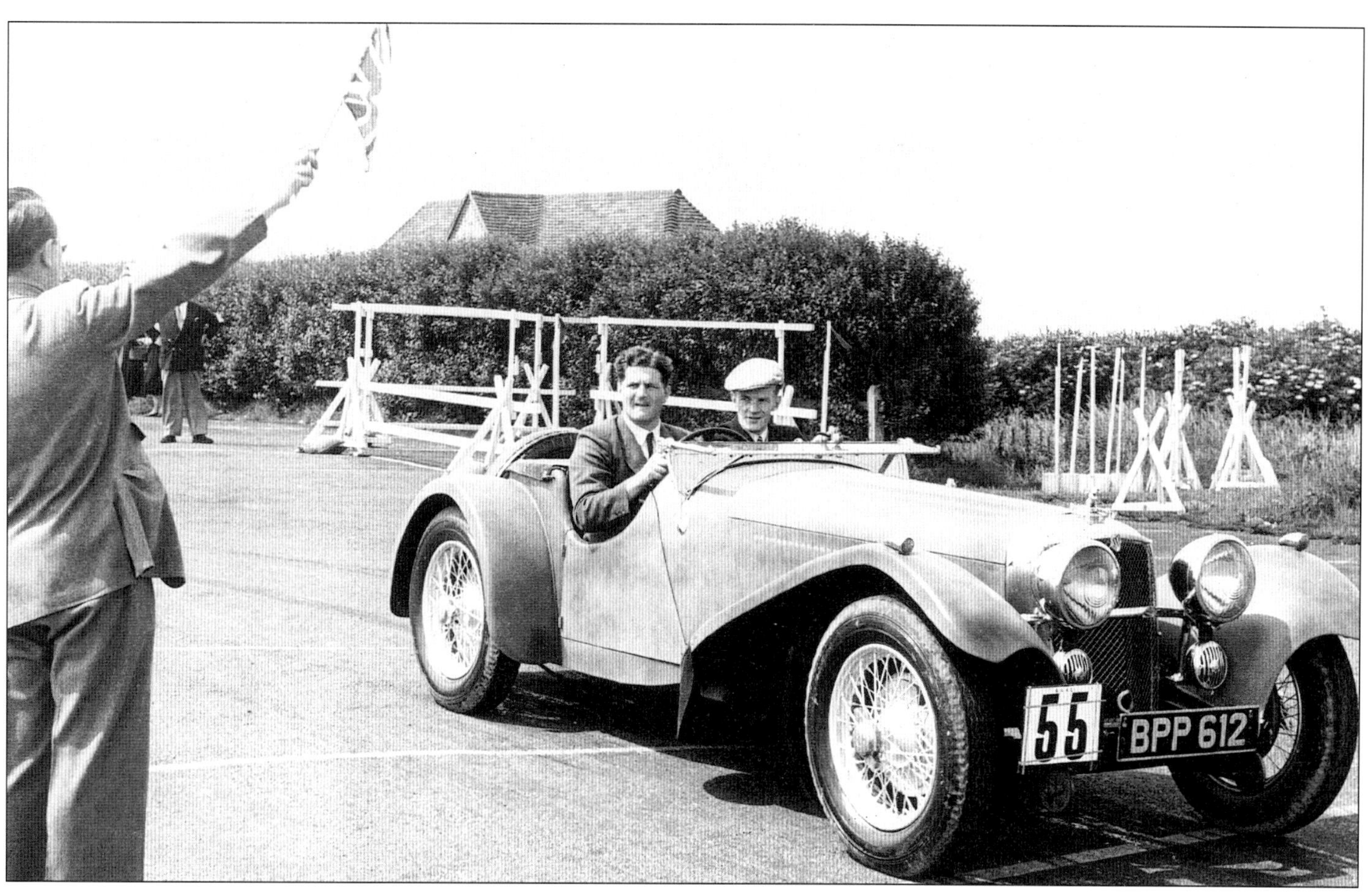

ABOVE: Rare SS90 from 1935 that had lost the part of its flowing wing that should run into the rear mudguard by the time this 1953 picture was taken.
BELOW: Open tourer SS Jaguar 2½ of 1936, its body a stage between the SS1 and SS100, but built mainly as a saloon.

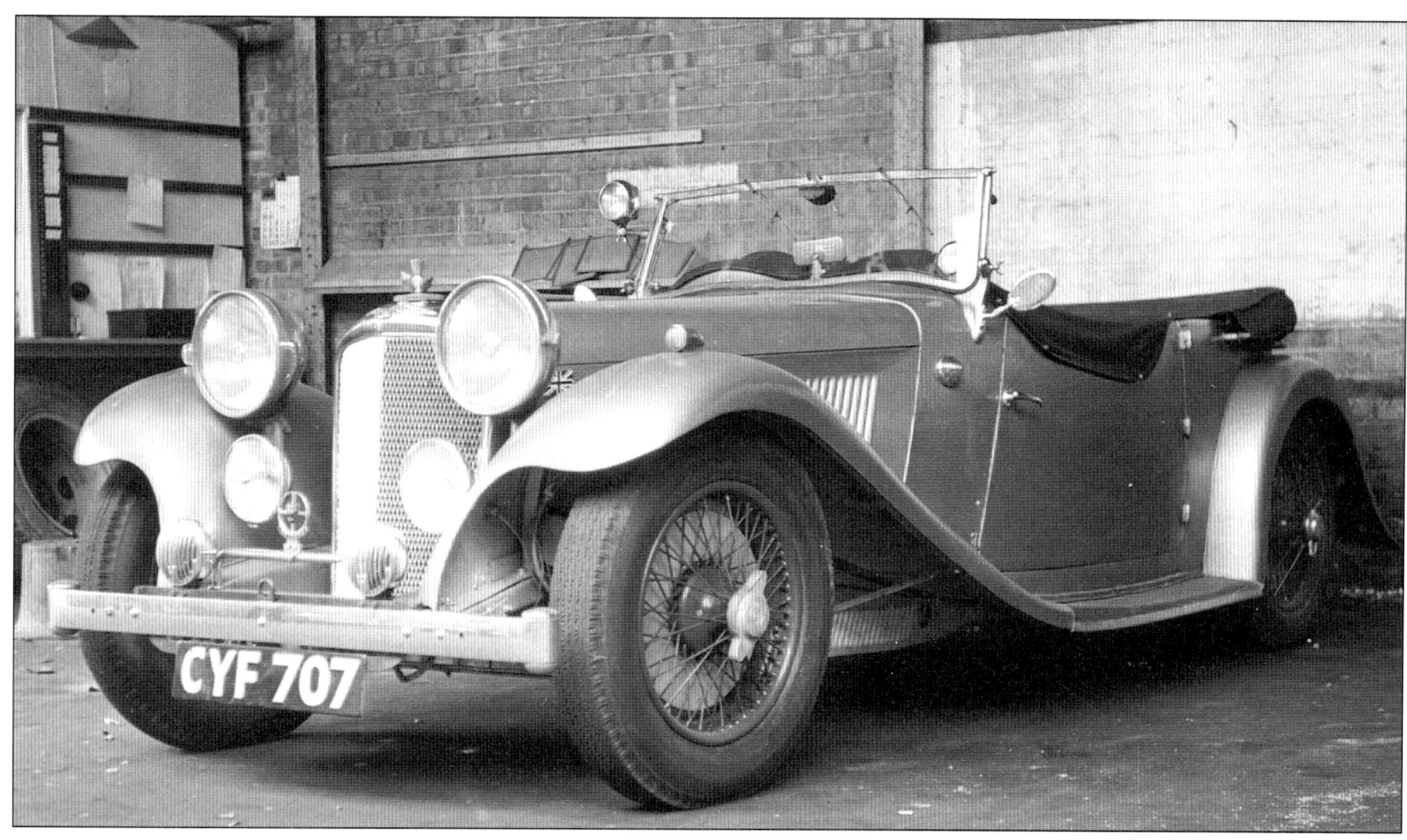

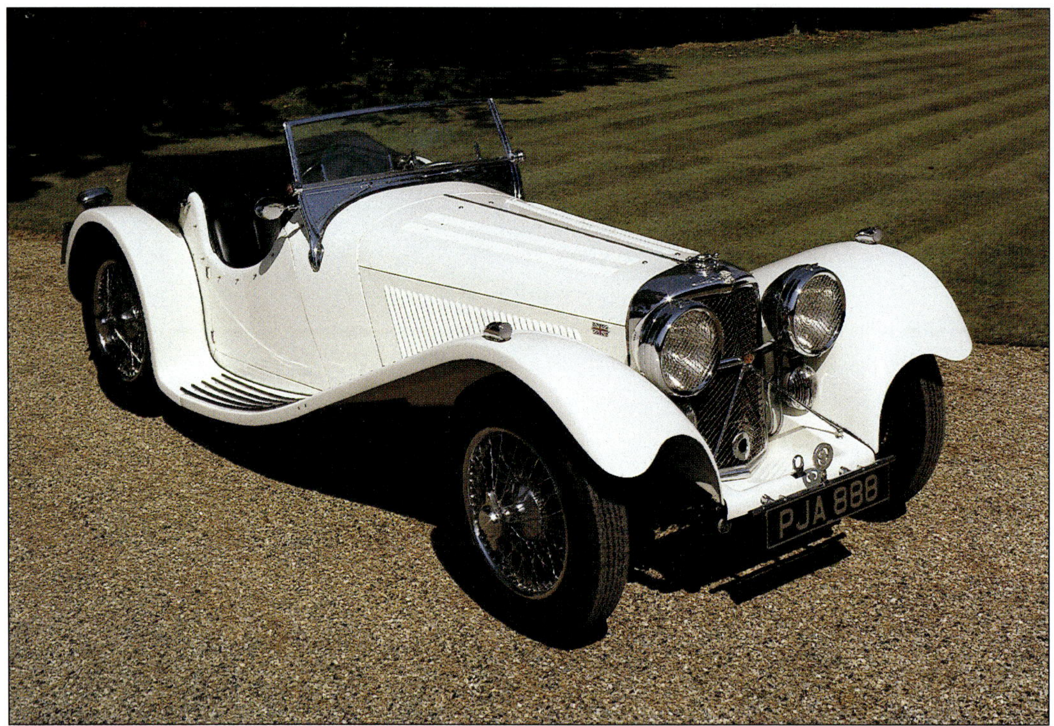

The car that confirmed William Lyons's great ability to style a car and build it at an affordable price, the SS100 with 2.6-litre engine.

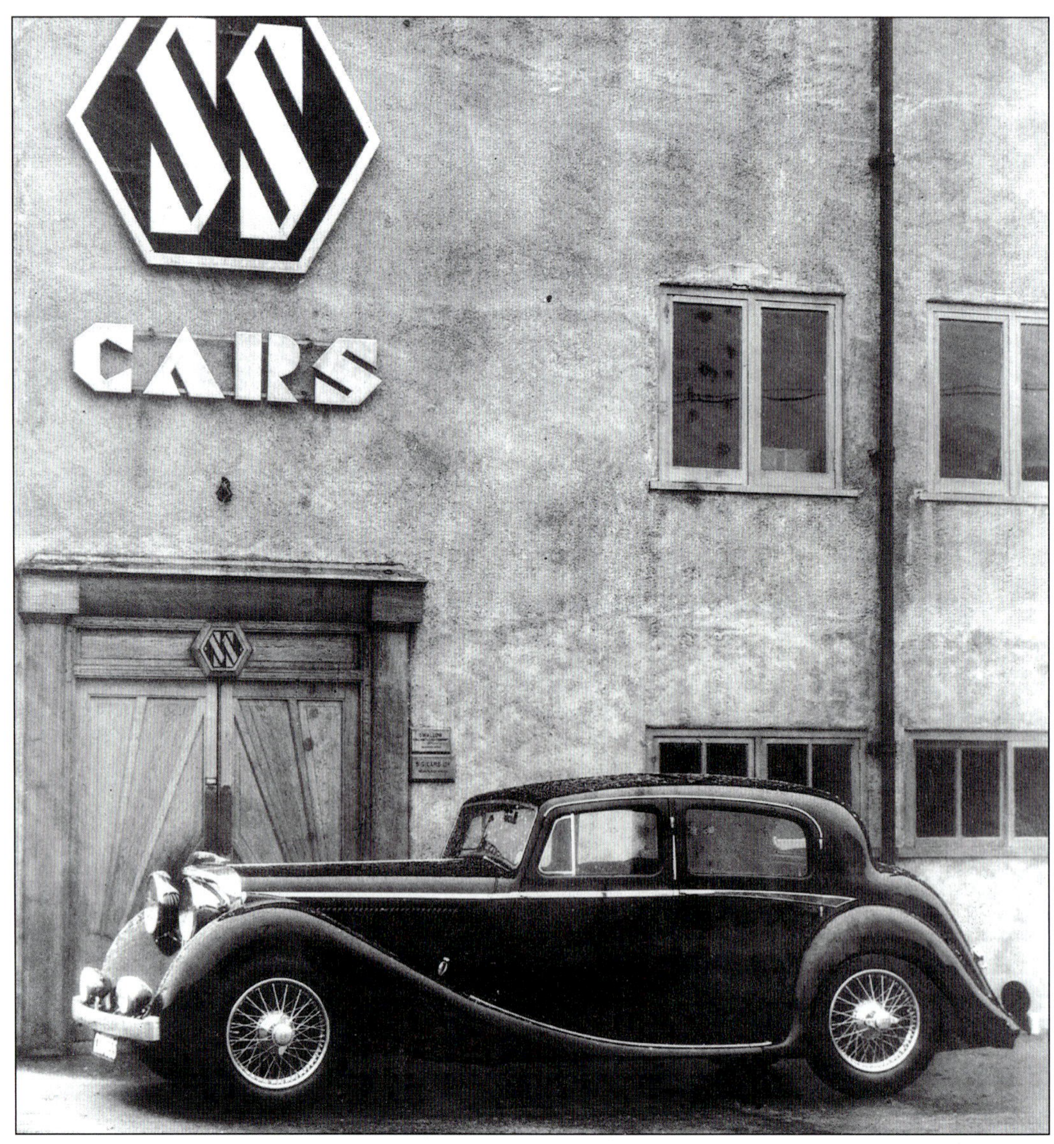

The first cars to carry the Jaguar name were 1936 saloons that grew into this 1939 example parked outside the factory.

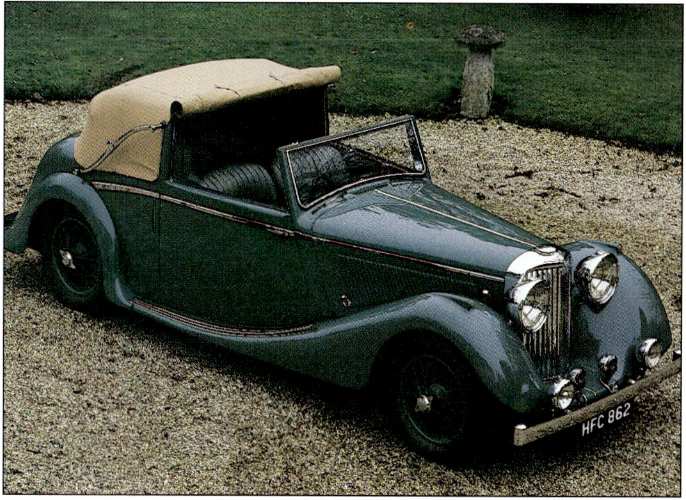

Fine drophead coupé demonstrating the great lines the firm developed in the late-1930s, among the best of the period, here for a 3½-litre of 1938.

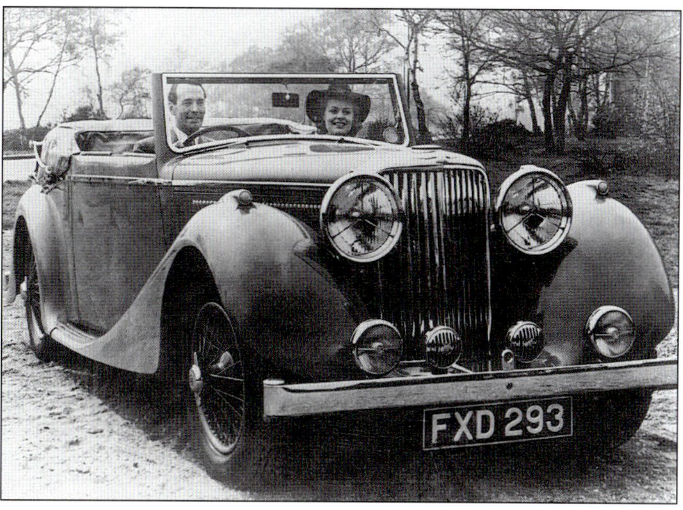

A 1939 3½-litre Jaguar drophead coupé with the top down for the couple to enjoy their drive in a fine car.

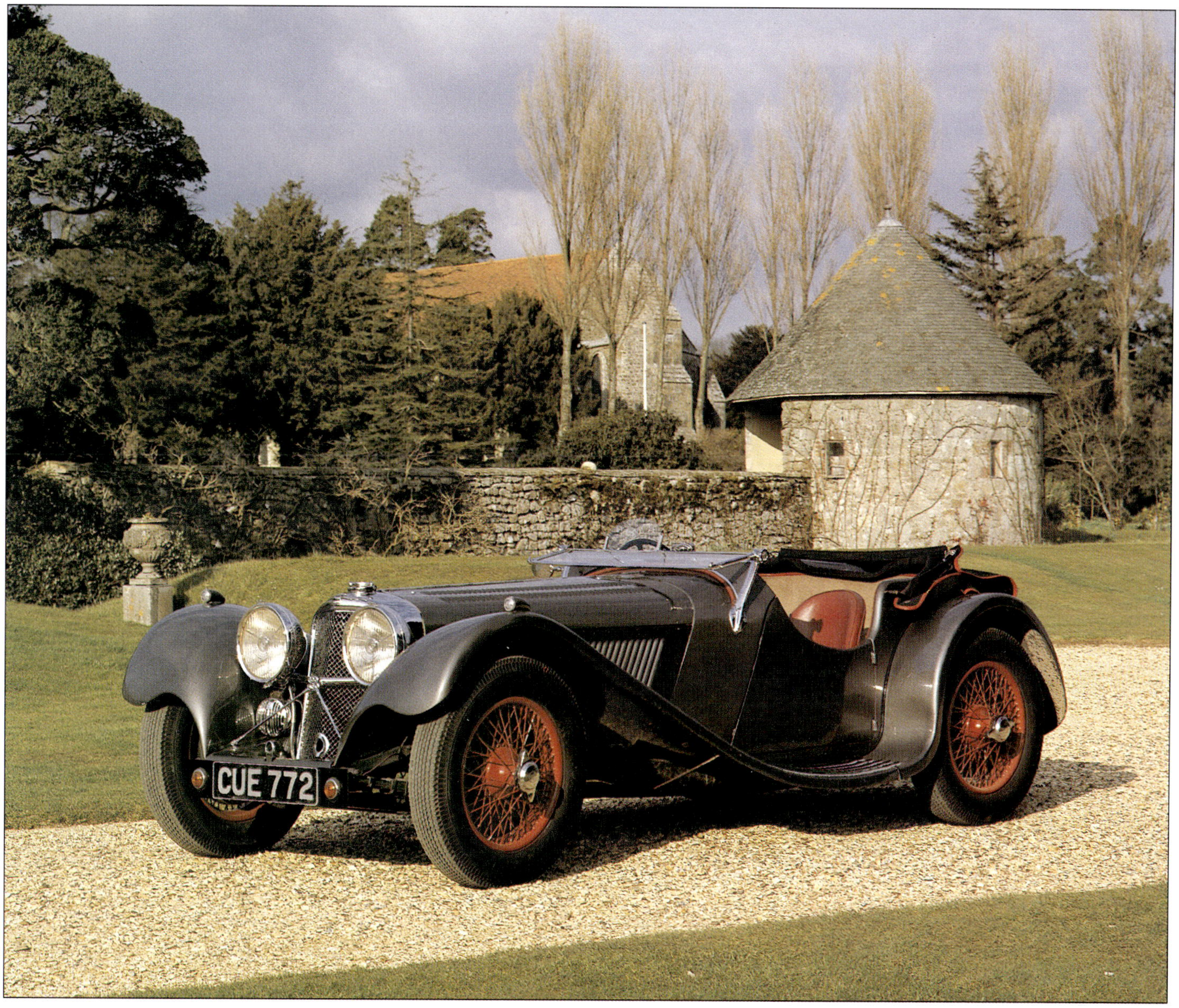

Archetypal British sports car of the time, the 3½-litre SS100 of 1939 with its fine Lucas headlamps and real performance.

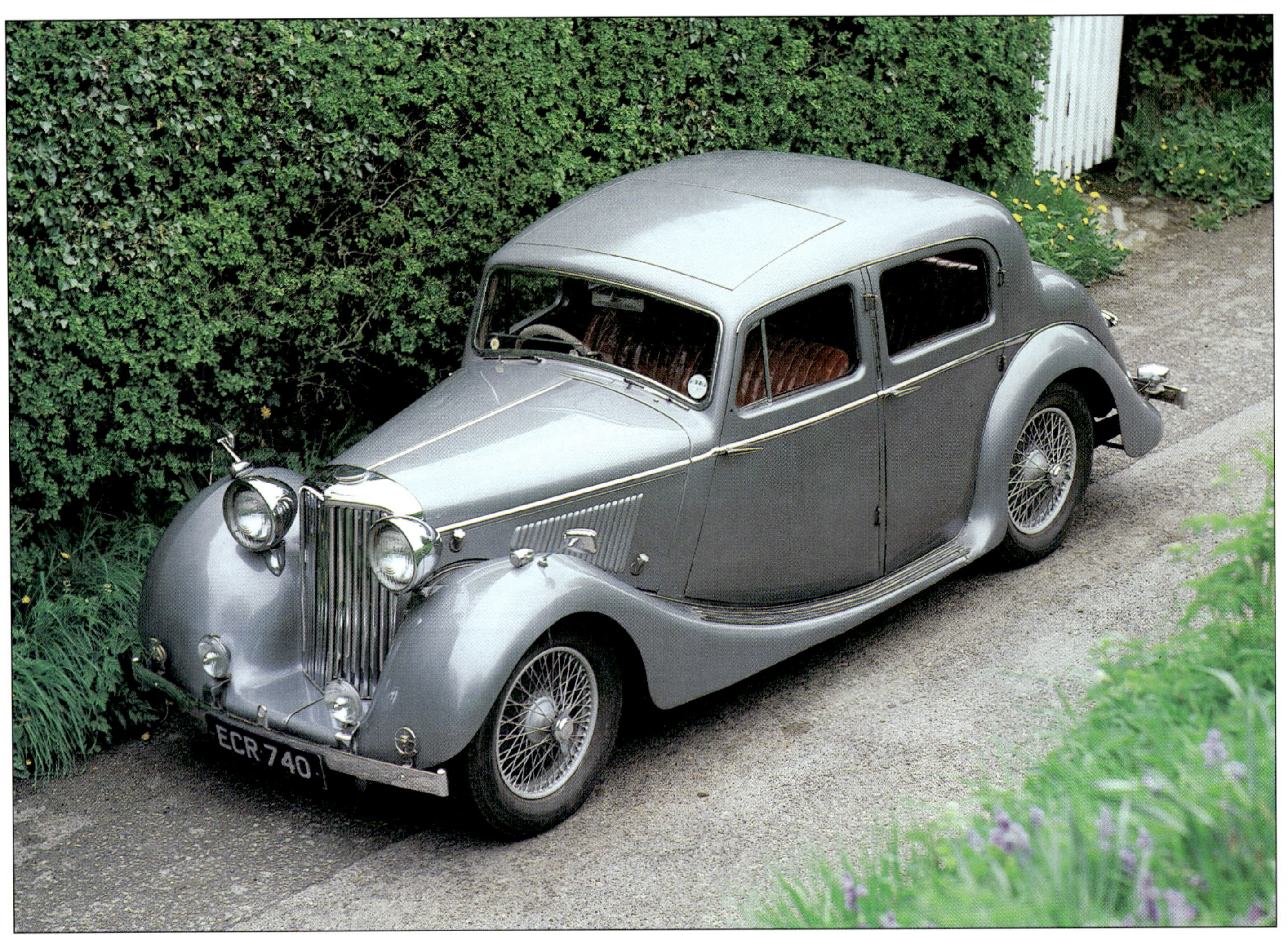

POSTWAR AND XK

1945-1950

Postwar 1½-litre saloon that was a prewar stop-gap, albeit a pleasant one, using the overhead-valve, four-cylinder engine.

IN 1945 William Lyons founded Jaguar Cars Limited and the 'SS' initials were dropped as they were naturally far from popular at that time. The open sports cars were abandoned for, while exciting, they had only ever been built in small numbers, around 300 SS100s in all. The saloons and coupés had sold in much larger quantities so it was these in the 1½, 2½ and 3½-litre capacities that the firm produced.

Behind the scenes work concentrated on a new engine, intended to power a new line of saloons, but in the end it was launched at the 1948 Motor Show installed in the famous XK120 Roadster sports car. There were new saloons as well that year, but as transitional cars using the old engines.

What set the new engine apart from the common herd was not its six cylinders but its twin overhead camshafts in an era when side valves were still common and overhead sporting twin camshafts were for expensive exotica only and seen as complex, hard to maintain and often none too reliable. Jaguar changed all that for its twin-cam engine was to power models into the 1980s, be built in a variety

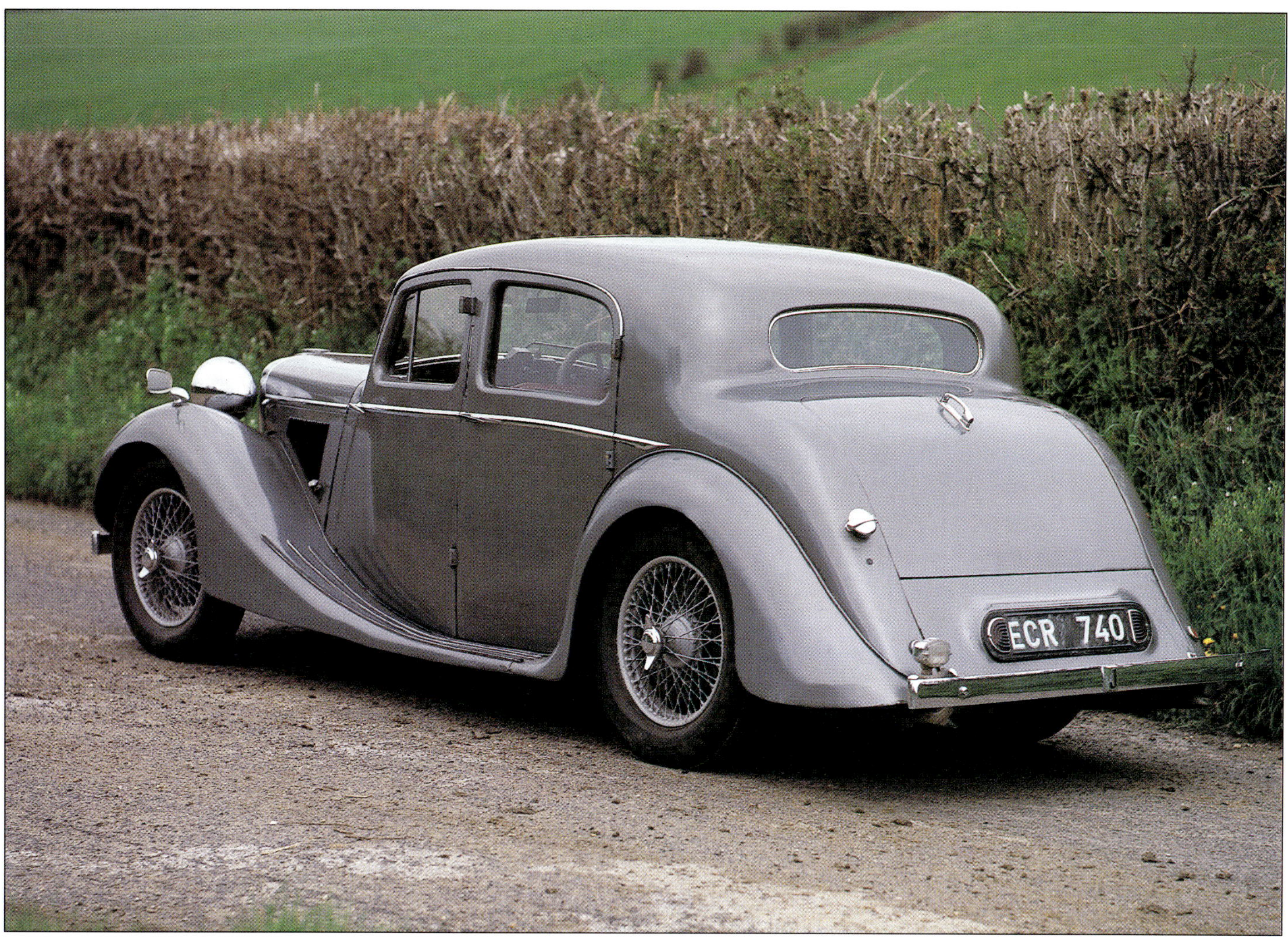

Rear quarter view of the 1946 1½-litre saloon showing its fine line and typical quality construction.

of sizes and prove well able to satisfy the needs of a mass-produced car.

The new engine was required to propel a saloon to 100mph without tuning and for this a 5,000rpm peak speed was selected. In addition to all the technical requirements involved, it was also laid down that the assembled unit should be styled to convey high-speed efficiency to the layman when the car bonnet was raised.

Twin overhead camshafts and a hemispherical head were the classic way to performance from the early days and Jaguar first built a series of four-cylinder engines to develop its ideas. These were the XF, XG and XJ, the first and last with twin cams, the XG with pushrods in the style of the prewar BMW. Next came the XJ six and finally the 3,448cc XK six.

The engine was conventional in many ways, but well thought out and detailed for long life and capable of further development. The camshafts were driven by chain in two stages, one from the crankshaft to an idler at the top of the block, the other from this to the camshafts via a tensioning sprocket. Single chain was tried, but produced a persistent whine that proved impossible to eradicate so it was not used.

If the new engine was a sensation, it was nothing compared to the car it was first seen in, the XK120. Suddenly, in those dreary, restricted postwar days there was this exotic, two-seater sports car well able to run at its suggested 120mph. And all for a modest £1,263 including the iniquitous purchase tax.

The XK120 was built to try the engine out and its chassis based on that being

RIGHT: Largest of the immediate postwar saloons was the 3½-litre model that shared the body style but had a six-cylinder engine.

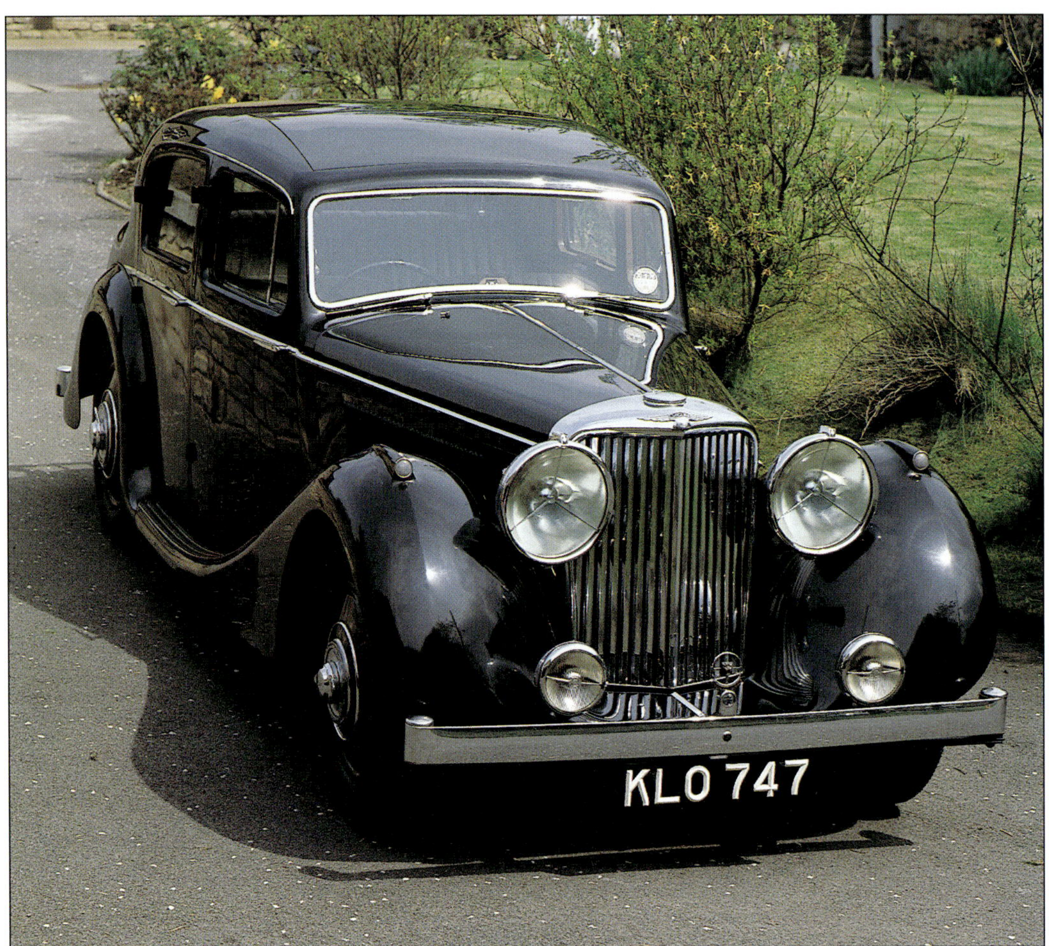

BELOW: The postwar saloons were also built in drophead coupé form for 1948, their last year, and this is the largest.

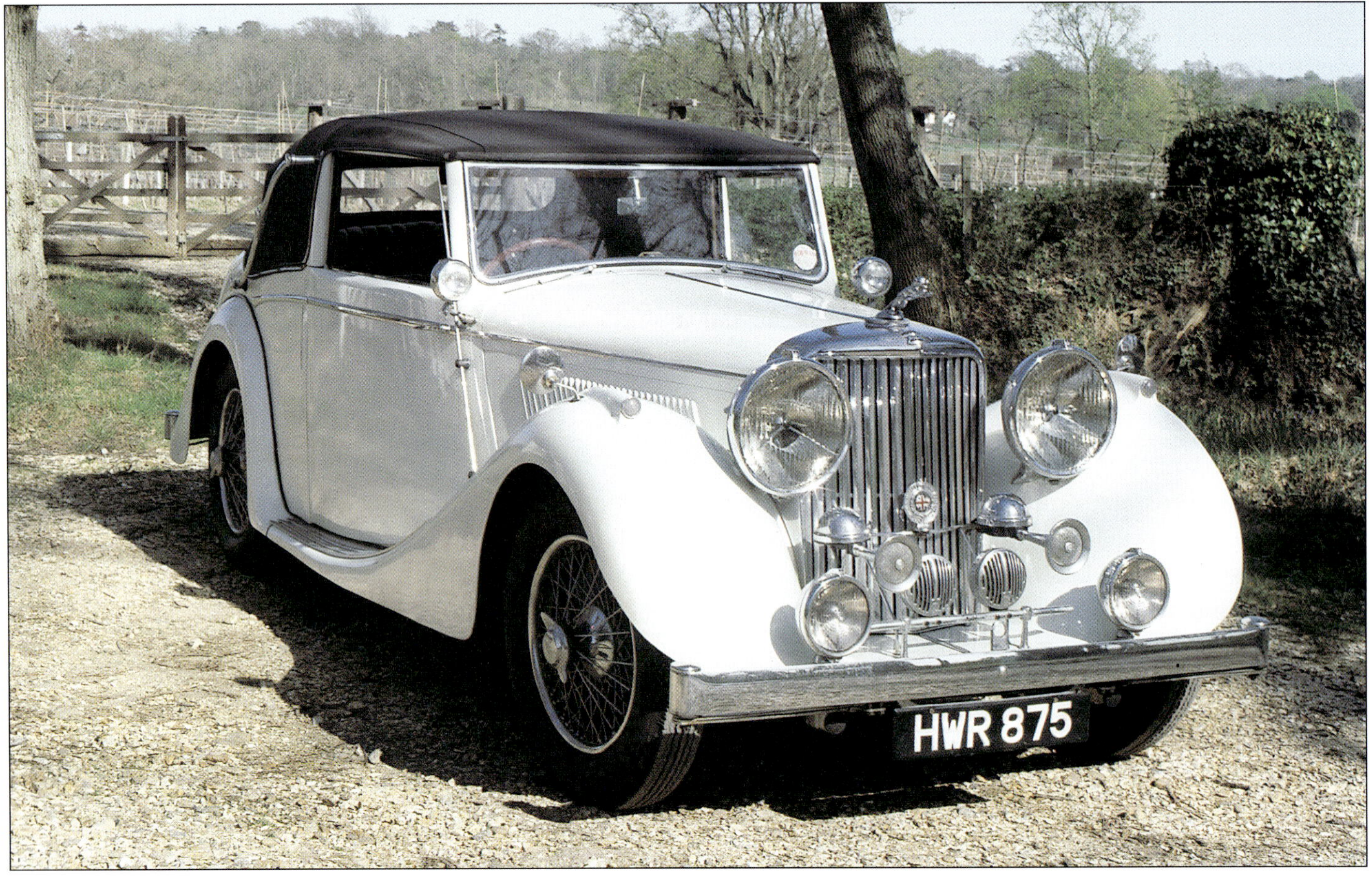

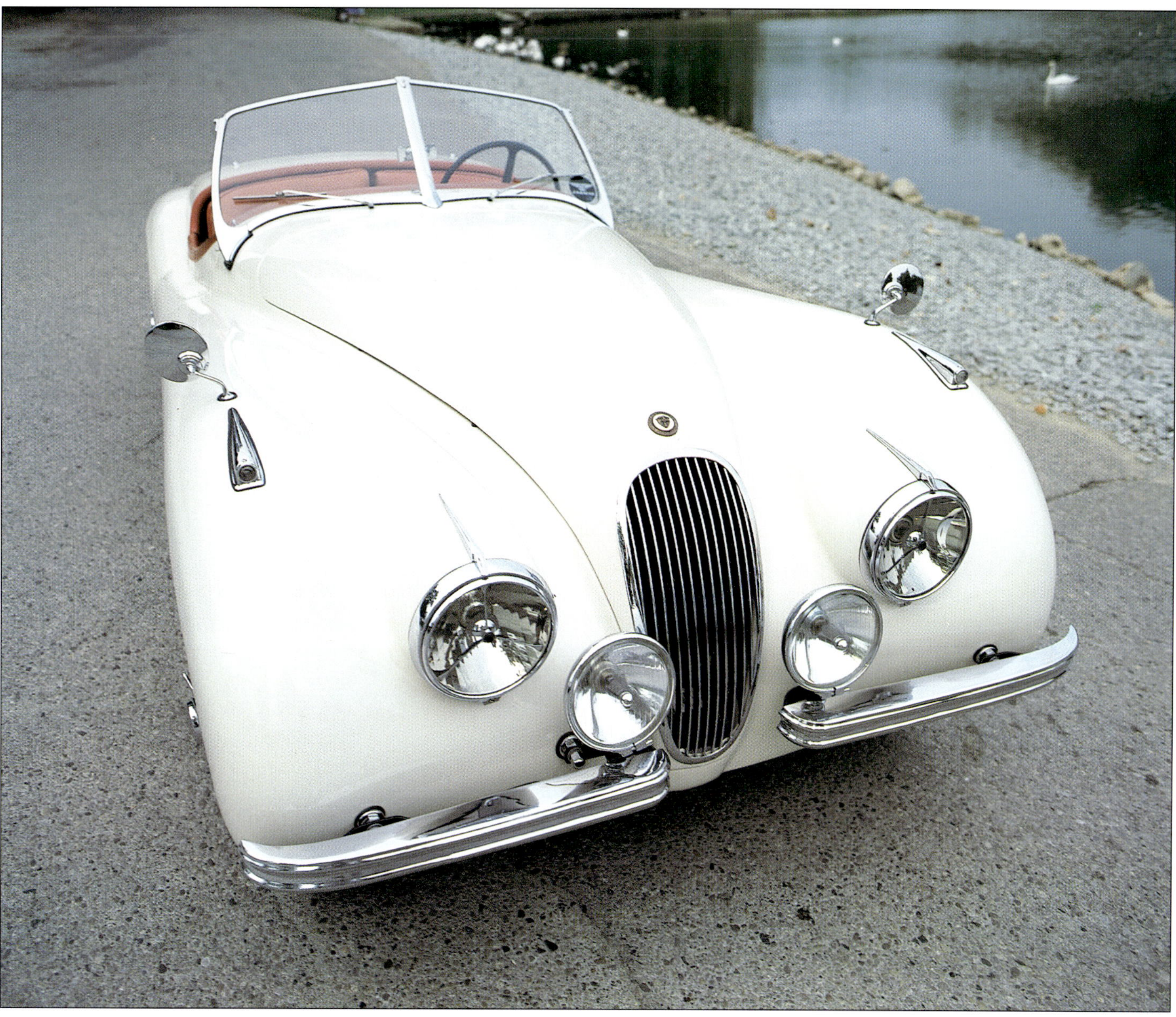

developed for the new saloons. This was shortened to suit and had independent front suspension, semi-elliptic rear and drum brakes that were to be hard pressed to cope with the car's performance. The body was, at first, in aluminium and the prototype constructed by a skilled sheet-metal man working under William Lyons's direction, the line being styled to his satisfaction as they went along. This was his usual method and one to which his great talent was suited, for it resulted in some wonderful designs. Aluminium was intended for the production cars, being more readily available at that time and easier to handwork, for only a small quantity of cars was envisaged.

Fabulous XK120 Roadster launched late in 1948 and a sensation in looks and performance even before the low price was taken into account.

Once the car was seen the orders flooded in - so much so that Jaguar had to go over to a pressed-steel body to meet the demand. Thus, aluminium-bodied cars are rare; but it was one of them that was taken to Jabbeke in Belgium where it was timed at 132mph over a flying mile in both directions, assisted by an added undertray, and then pottered past those watching at 5mph in top gear.

Along with the XK120 came the Mk V saloon in 2½- and 3½-litre forms. These kept to the older overhead-valve, six-cylinder engines, but had the same suspension as on the sports car and hydraulic brakes. The Mk V was built in drophead

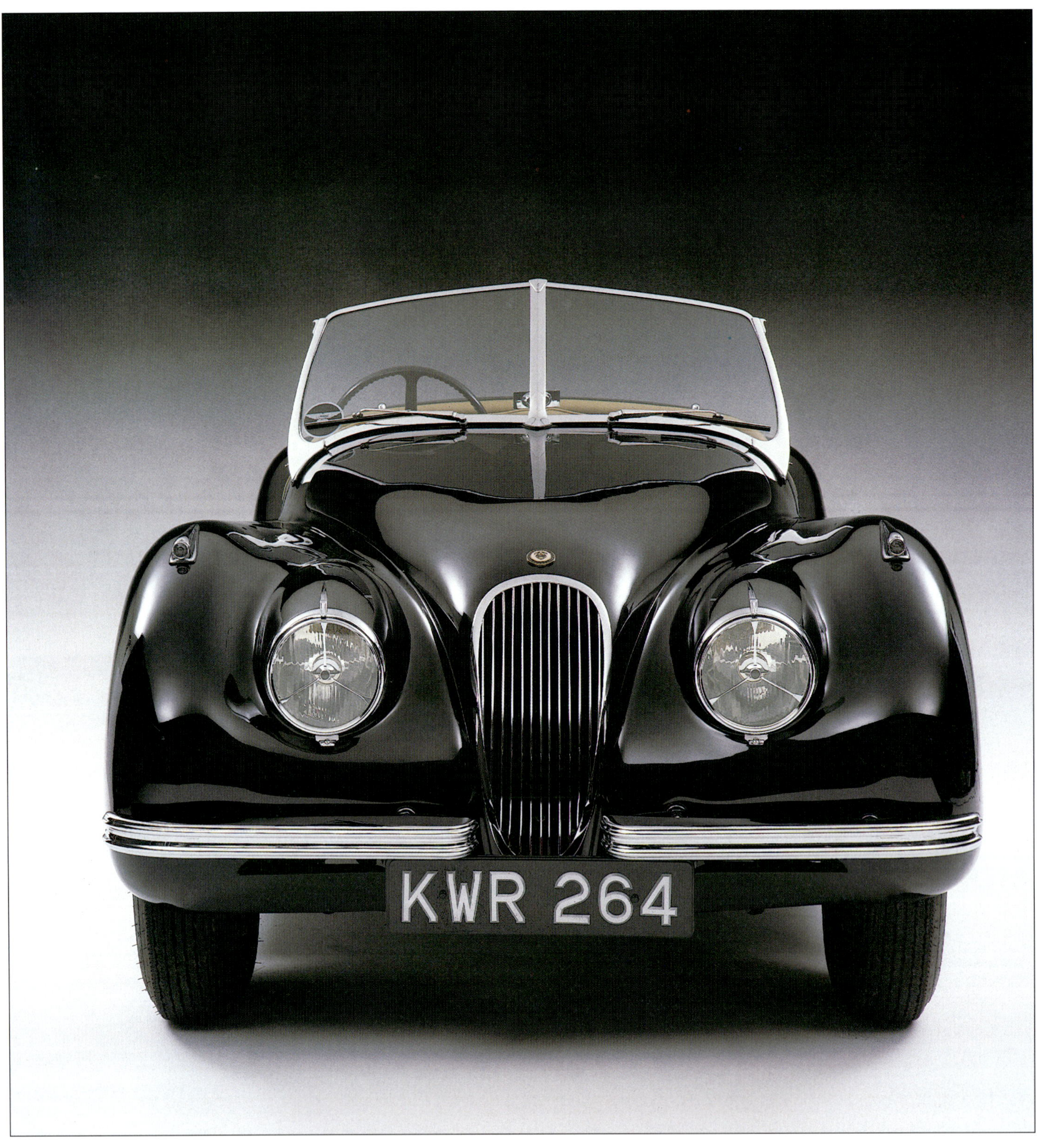

Front aspect of the XK120, clean and uncluttered; in the image of the SS100 but even better.

coupé form as well as the saloon up to 1951 but was effectively replaced for 1950 by the Mk VII.

The new saloon brought together the chassis improvements, the twin-cam engine and another great body style that most certainly had space and grace. It was a big car, over 16ft long, and quite heavy at around 4,000lb, so its 16mpg was to be expected, especially if its 100mph performance was used to any extent. An overdrive, on top gear only, was an option from 1954 and there was an earlier two-speed automatic transmission that was less popular.

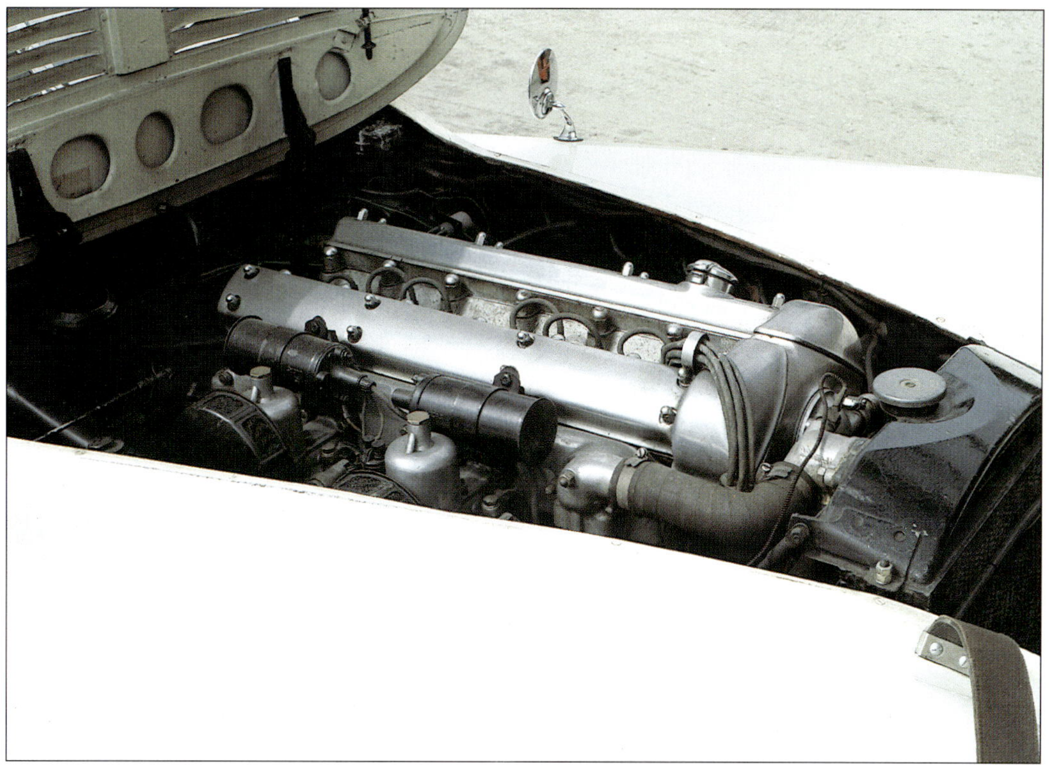

LEFT: The wonderful XK six-cylinder, twin-cam engine installed in the XK120 car, a power unit destined for a long life in many models.

BELOW: Further view of the lovely lines of the XK120, the footwell vent between front wheel and door indicating a 1951 car.

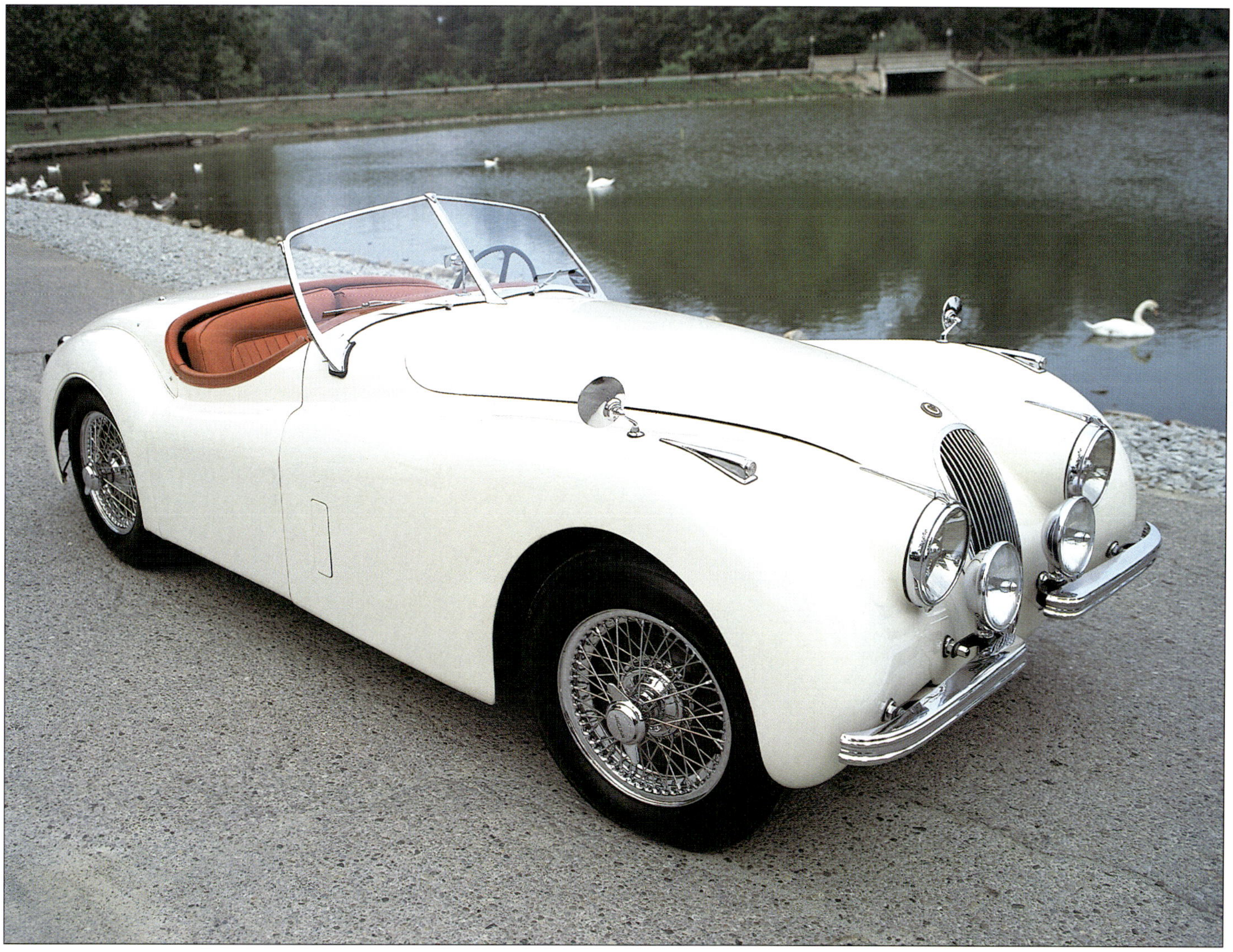

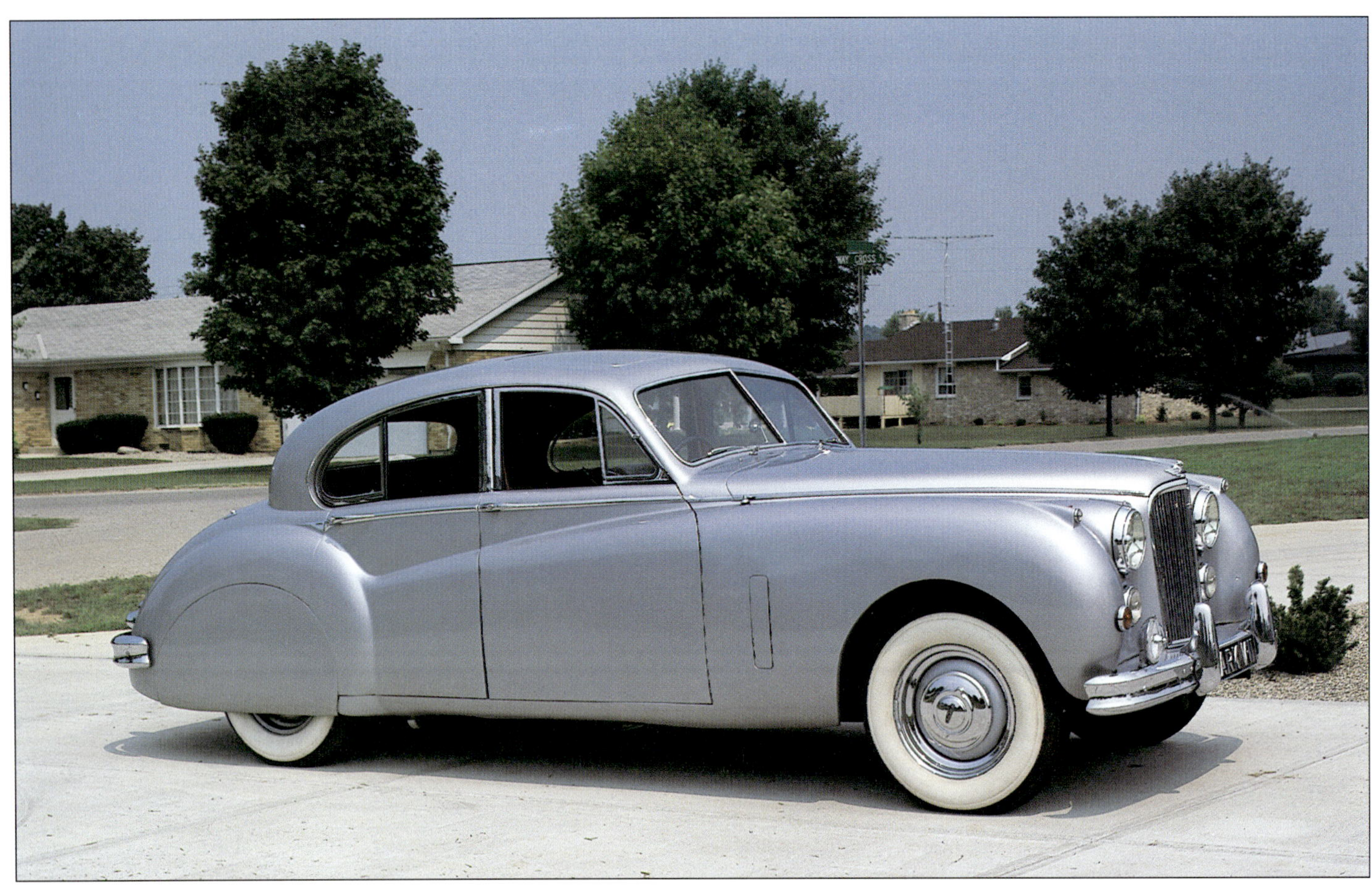

ABOVE: The saloon line moved on to the Mk VII for 1950, combining the Mk V body with the twin-cam engine.

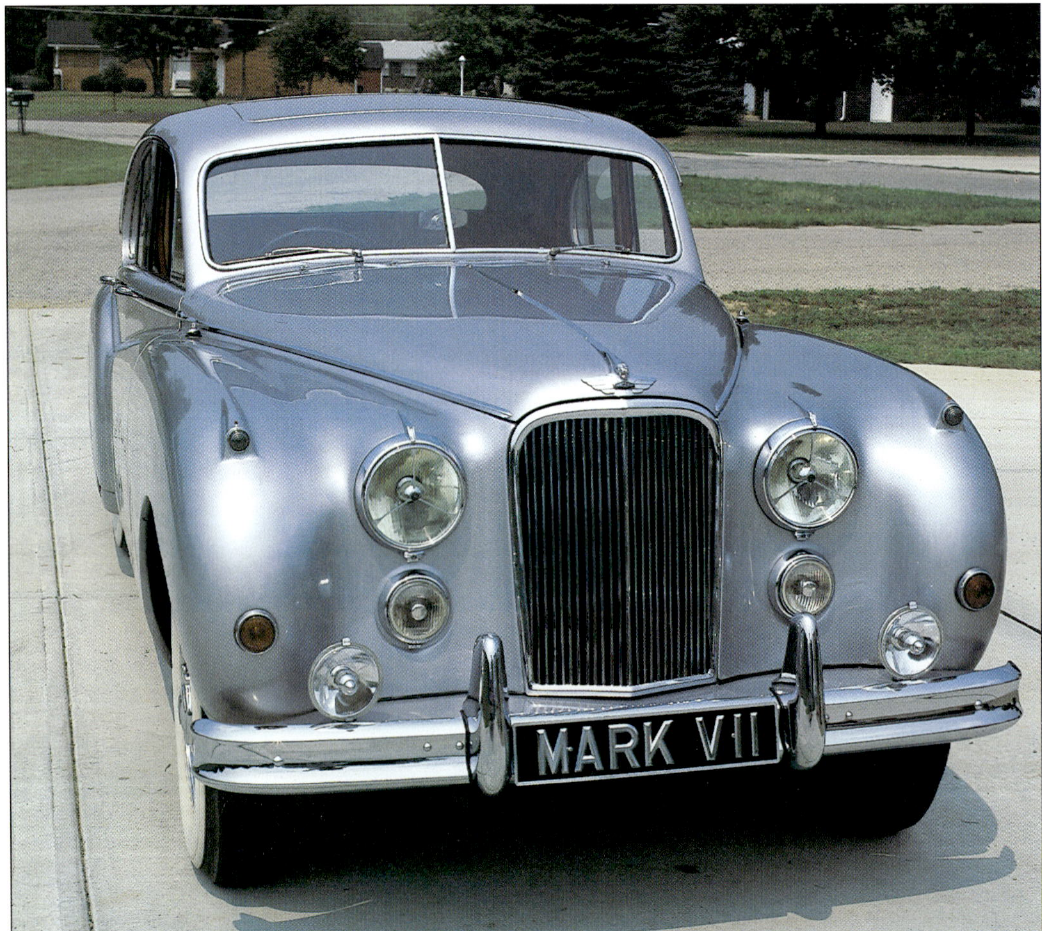

RIGHT: A big and thirsty car, but the Mk VII could run to 100mph and handled well thanks to chassis improvements.

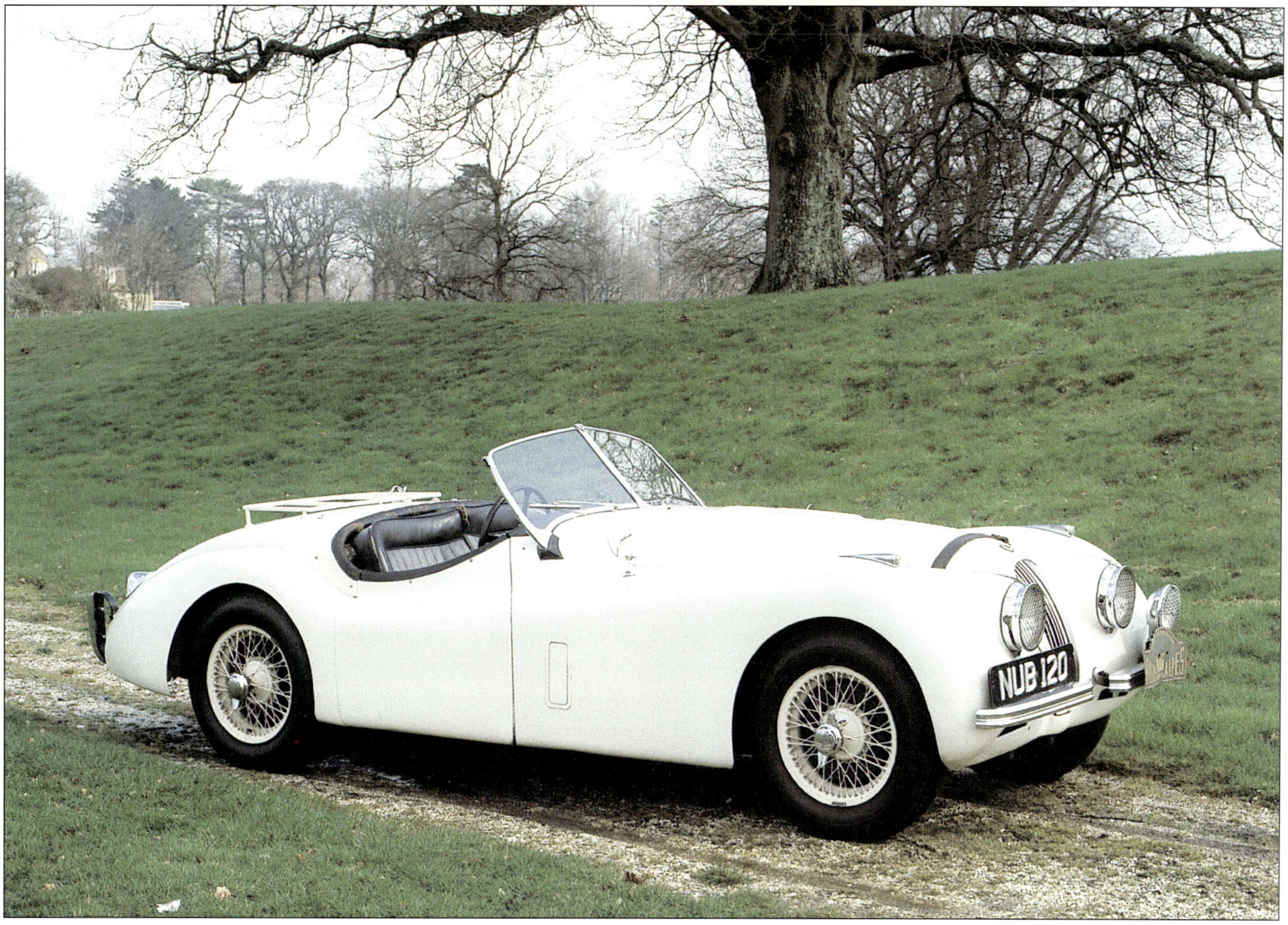

ABOVE: Famous and most successful XK120 driven by Ian Appleyard in many rallies and production races.

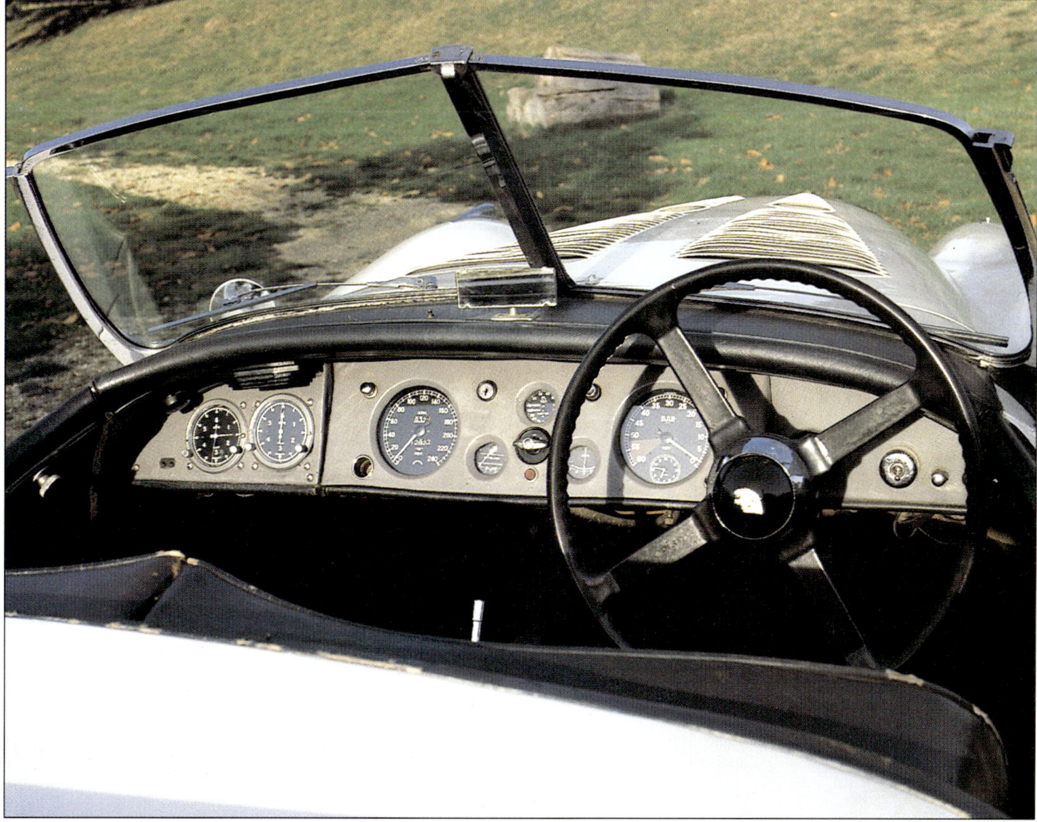

LEFT: Fascia of the Appleyard XK120, hence the special rally clock on the left, non-standard rev-counter, and kph speedometer to its left.

XK, LE MANS & SALOONS

1951-1960

IN 1951 a fixed-head coupé XK120 joined the Roadster, housing just two people in the cockpit, and the factory ran a works team at Le Mans. Up to then the XK120 had had a number of racing and rally successes but with limited works involvement. However, some good results in 1950 brought about the XK120C and three cars at Le Mans. The C-type, as it was always known, had a space frame chassis and a tuned engine producing around 210bhp in place of the stock 160.

During the race two of the Jaguars dropped out while heading the field due to oil pipe breakages, but the third ran on to the end to win by a handsome margin. It was the first of the Le Mans victories and from it came a modified cylinder head, carburettors to suit and alternative camshafts, all of which went on to a limited production run of the XK120C, and also were an option for the XK120 and, in some areas, the Mk VII saloon.

There was also a Special Equipment specification that produced the XK120SE, and this comprised higher-lift camshafts, lighter flywheel, stiffer suspension and wire wheels amongst its items. For 1953 a drophead coupé XK120 was added to the model list and the firm returned once more to Le Mans. The team had retired due to overheating in 1952 but there were no problems in 1953 with first, second

An XK120 Roadster of 1954, still with the clean body lines of six years before and about to move on to become the XK140.

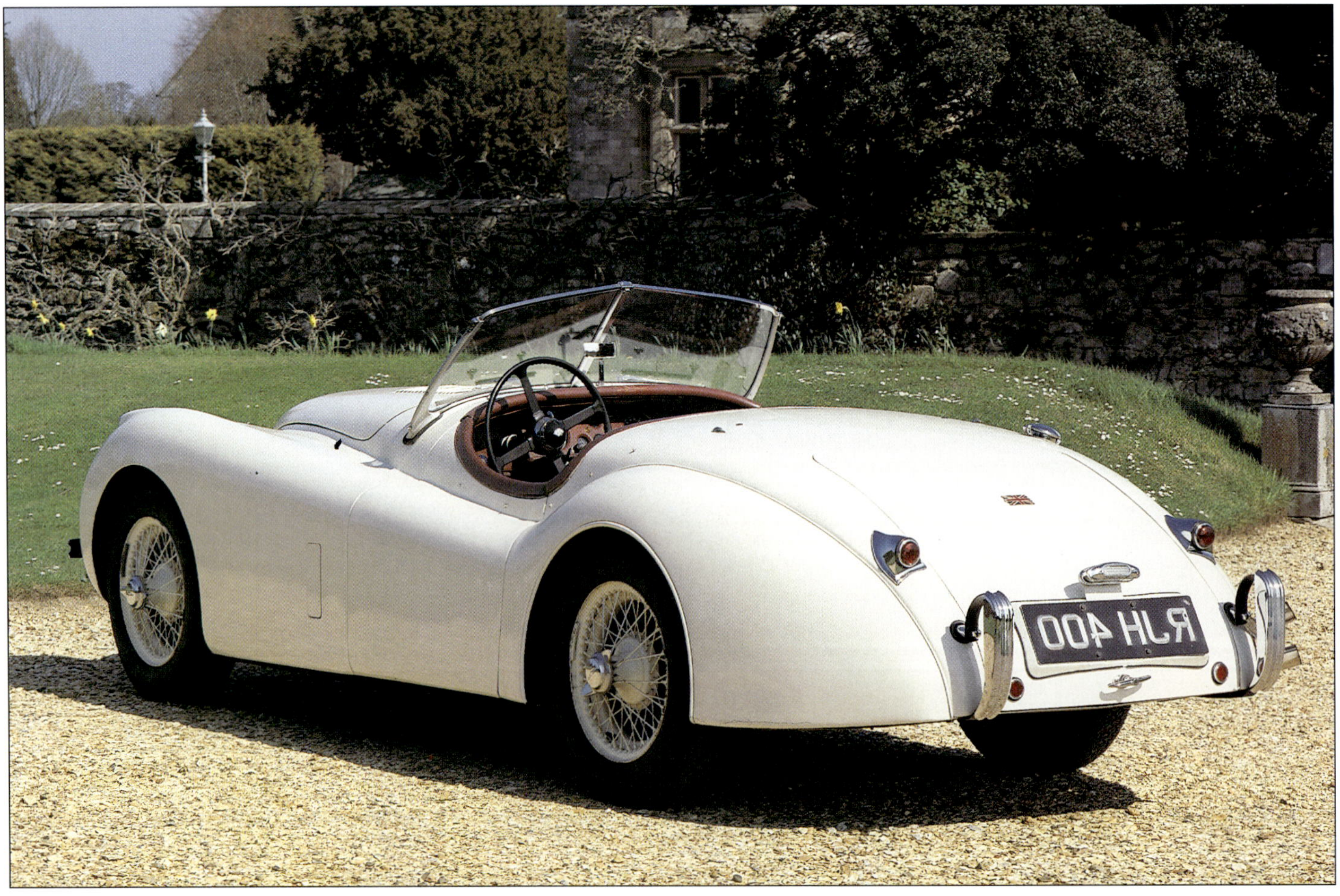

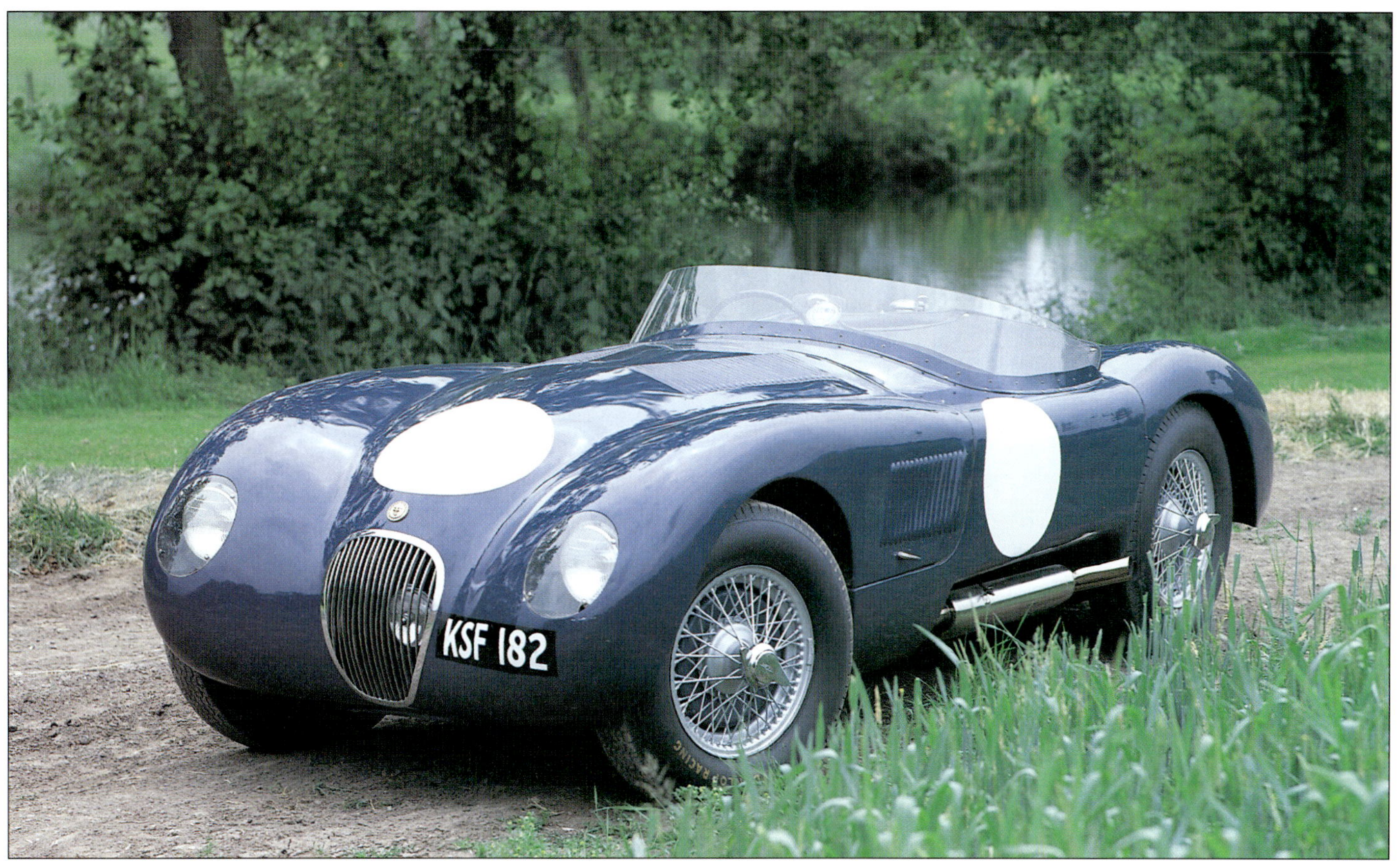

ABOVE: The C-type that the works raced at Le Mans in 1951-53, winning twice, and also built in limited numbers for sale.
BELOW: D-type, the car developed from the C-type and which won at Le Mans in 1955, 1956 and 1957 after a close second in 1954, and was also built as a limited-production model.

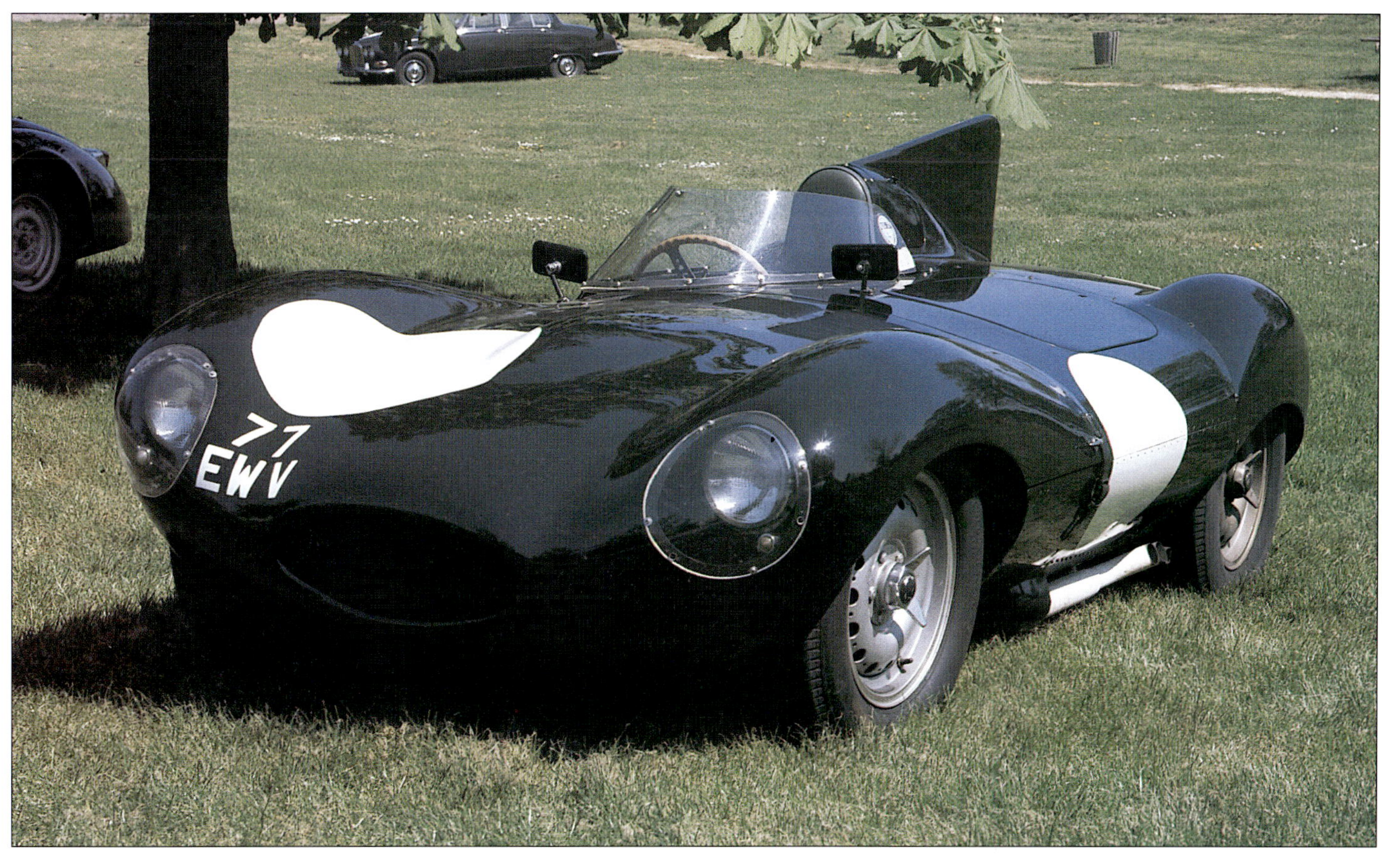

and fourth places, all helped by the adoption of disc brakes.

For the 1954 Le Mans race Jaguar built the D-type, lighter, faster and with a dry-sump engine in a monocoque body on the space frame, usually with a fairing behind the driver's head, but teething troubles kept it back to finish a close second. As with the C-type, the D-type was built as a production model from 1954 to 1956 in some numbers, about 70 compared with 50 C-types.

The XK120 trio was replaced late in 1954 by the XK140 built in the same three styles. Changes were limited but there was rack-and-pinion steering and the engine output went up to 190bhp with 210bhp for the special equipment version. The coupé body, in fixed and drophead forms, had an extended roof line to allow the fitting of rear occasional seats or a little more luggage space. The result was a better equipped series of cars, although the inevitable weight increase kept the top speed to around 120mph, unless overdrive was fitted when 130mph was there on a good day. Finally, the big saloon became the Mk VIIM with the 190bhp engine and a close-ratio gearbox plus some changes to the body style that included wrap-around rear bumpers.

The team won at Le Mans in 1955 but the event was overshadowed by the carnage of the Mercedes crash; in 1956 the works cars were all eliminated for minor

Engine room of the D-type with its three twin-choke carburettors on one side matched by the oil tank on the other.

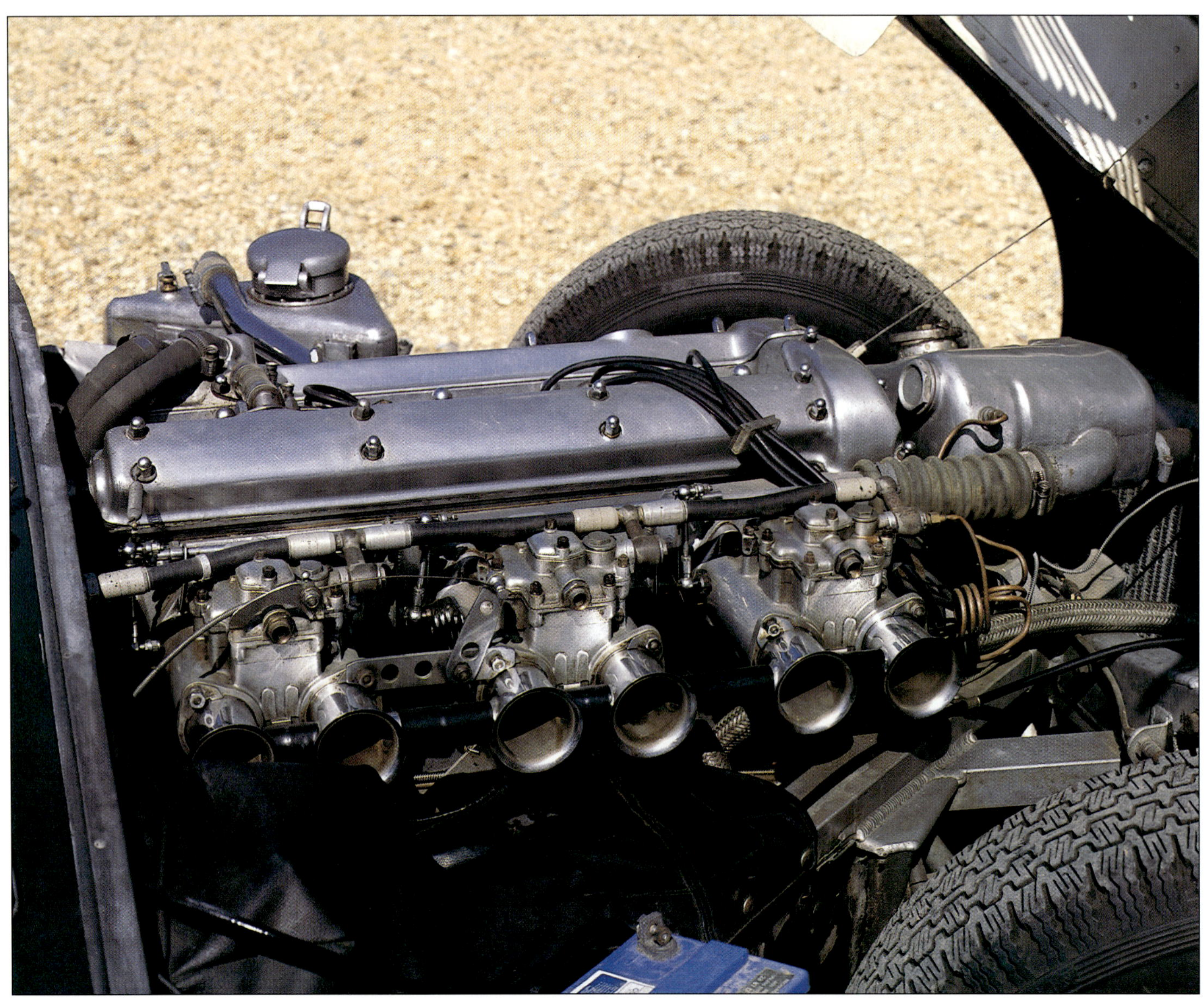

reasons but Ecurie Ecosse took a D-type to the win. That year also saw plain Mr Lyons become Sir William in recognition of all that he had accomplished.

For the driver, 1956 brought a new and more compact Jaguar saloon, the 2.4-litre Mk I. It was the first from the firm to have unitary construction and its fine body lines accommodated four people in style. The engine remained the faithful twin-cam six but its capacity was reduced to 2,483cc and the power to 112bhp so that the top speed was close to 100mph. It was the start of another highly successful series and there was an immediate call for a version using the larger engine. Early in 1957 this was answered by the 3.4-litre Mk I able to run to 120mph and, fortunately, offered with the option of disc brakes.

The big saloon had further refinements for 1957 to become the Mk VIII with a little more power, a new grill and a one-piece curved windscreen. Manual, overdrive and automatic transmissions were listed and a two-tone finish introduced.

Never one to waste anything, the firm built a few XK-SS models in 1957, these using spare D-type bodies minus the tail fin but plus some domestic furnishings for road use. Into this went the dry-sump engine and the running gear from the D-type including disc brakes. Only 16 were produced.

In the middle of the year the sports cars moved on to the XK150 series, pro-

Further view of the D-type with its monocoque body, driver's headrest and metal tonneau cover over the passenger seat area.

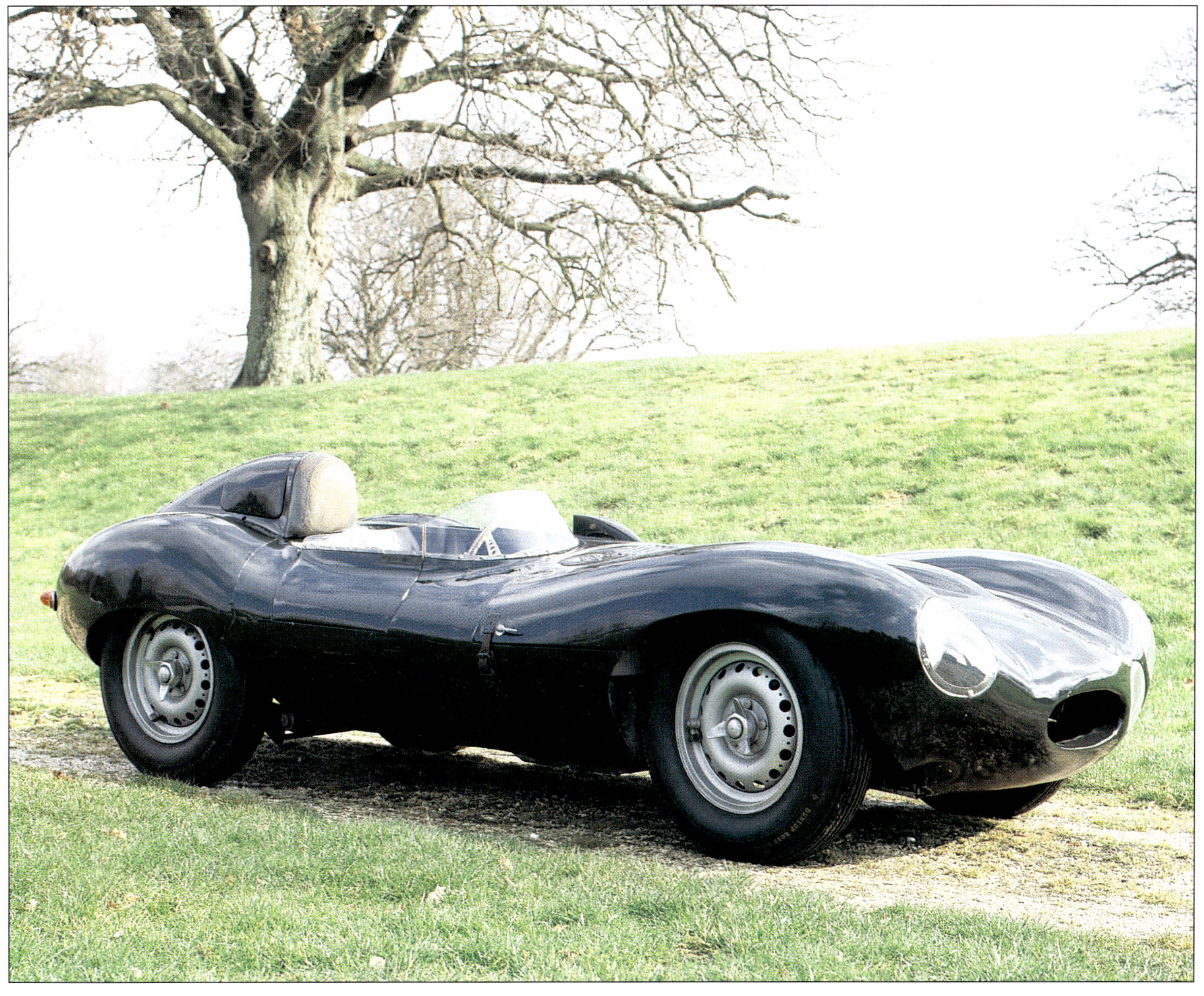

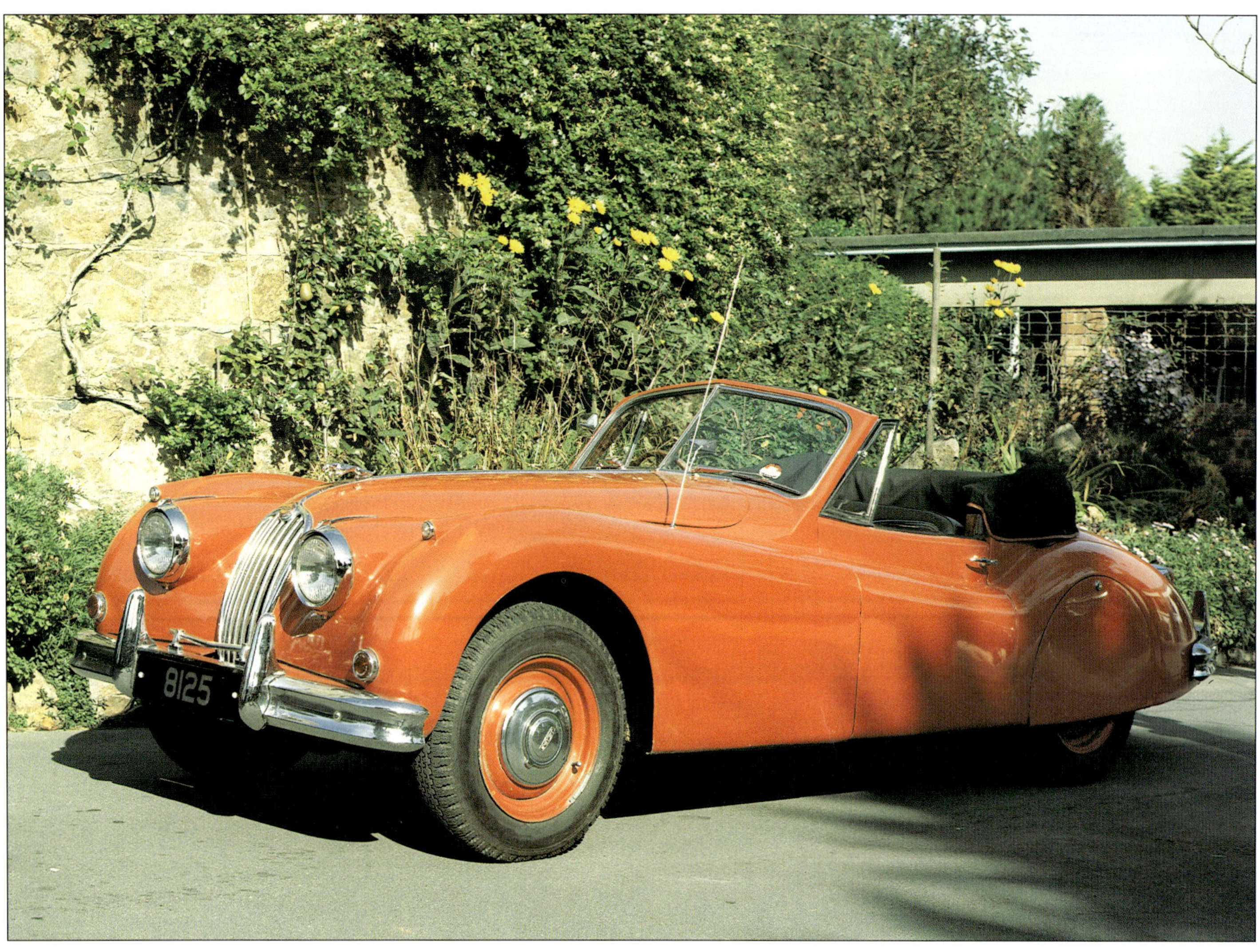

ABOVE: The XK140 that replaced the earlier car late in 1954 had the engine moved forward for more interior room; this is a 1956 drophead coupé.

OPPOSITE: There was more chrome on the XK140, as this 1957 fixed-head coupé shows, but the fine lines remained.

duced at first in fixed and drophead coupé forms. They followed the concept but had a wider body with a higher wing line, while the major mechanical advance was the adoption of much needed disc brakes all round. The engine was the 190bhp unit from the XK140 with the special equipment models fitted with a 210bhp engine incorporating a new cylinder head. Thus, although the power was as before, it came at a lower engine speed as did the increased torque.

In the middle of 1958 a Roadster XK150 joined the other two models and an 'S' version of each appeared, this fitted with an engine having yet another cylinder head and other changes to raise its power to 250bhp. For those seeking even more urge the engine was stretched to 3,781cc and this 3.8-litre unit listed in 220bhp stock and 265bhp 'S' forms. The end result was therefore three body styles - each available with four engine choices - plus three transmissions in most cases.

While the sports cars were adding their variations the big saloon became the Mk IX for 1959, using the 220bhp version of the 3.8-litre engine, disc brakes all round and power-assisted steering. It remained a large, fast but thirsty car.

The 1960 range saw the compact saloons in Mk II form with disc brakes, wider rear track and larger rear window. The 2.4-litre had a little more power while the 3.4 was joined by a version fitted with the 3.8-litre engine. This was also the year when Jaguar bought Daimler and in time this was to lead to the expected badge engineering.

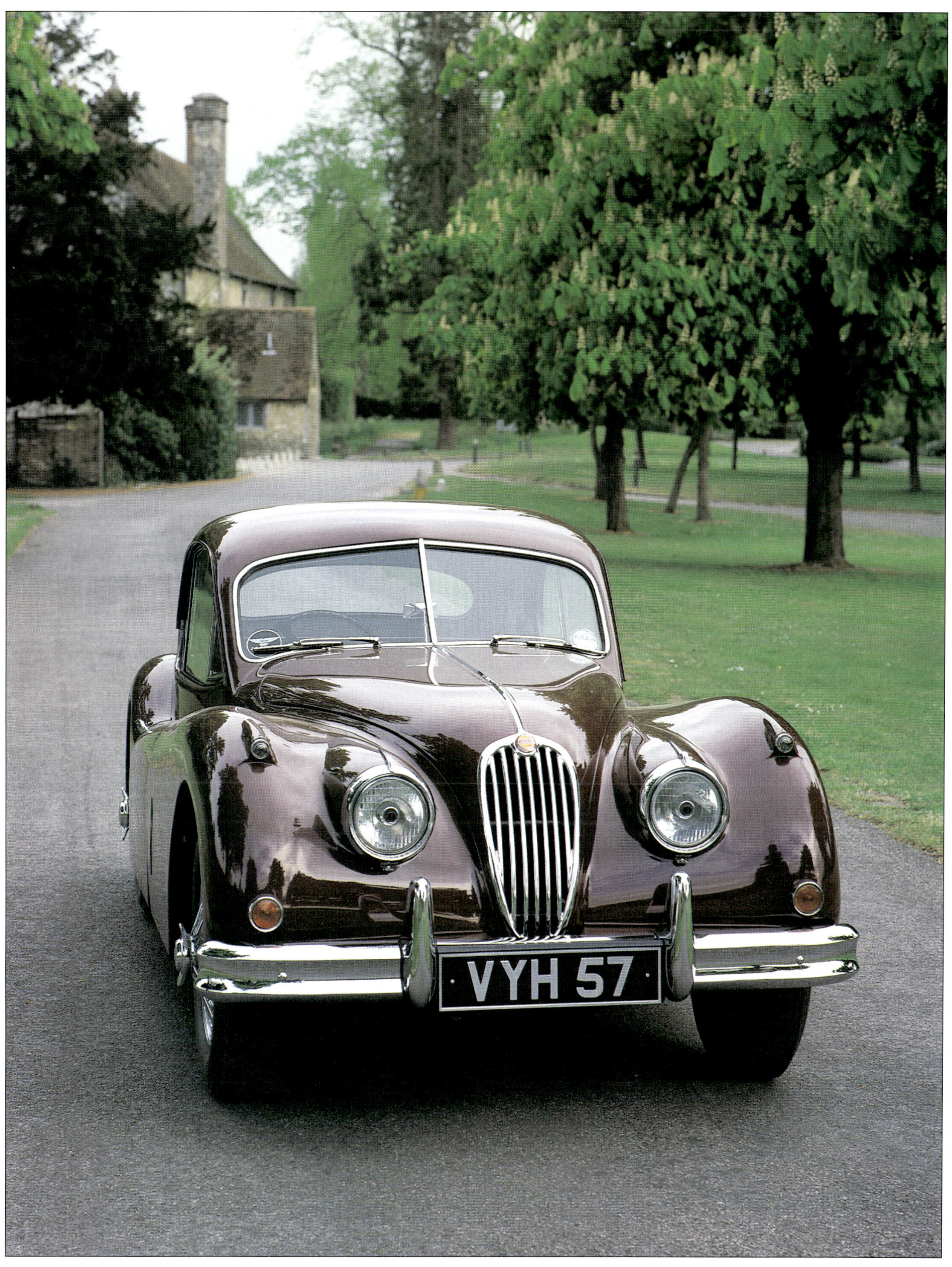
VYH 57

RIGHT: Famous leaping Jaguar mascot was not an option until the XK150 but is often added to earlier cars, sadly later to be banned by the safety lobby.

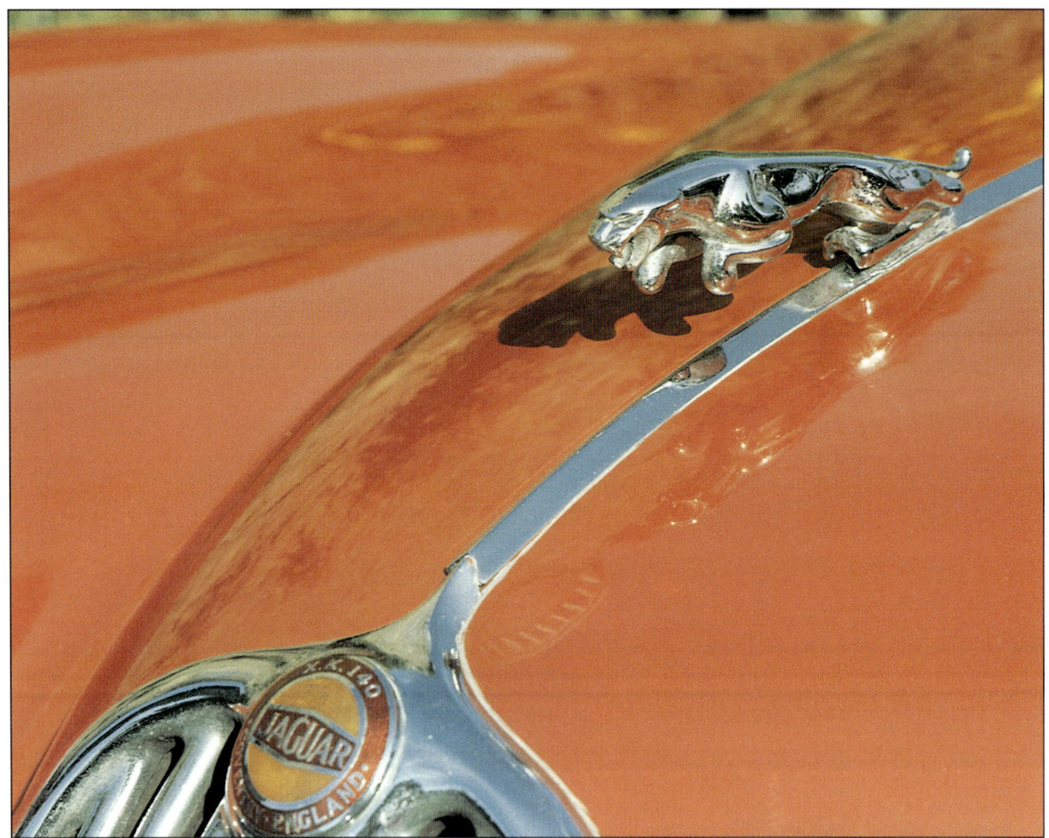

BELOW: Further view of a 1956 XK140 drophead coupé, the top down and the car ready to enjoy the sunshine.

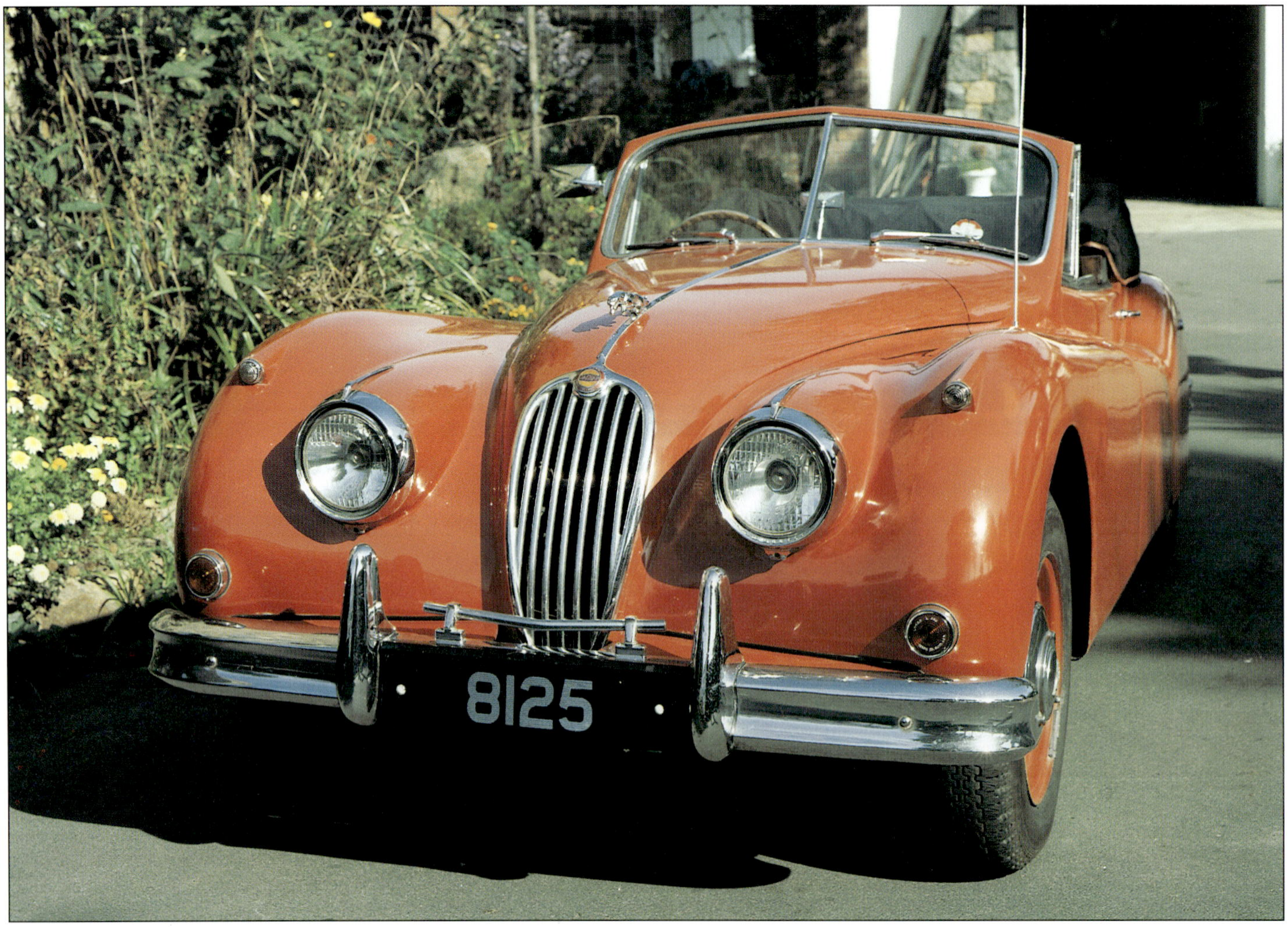

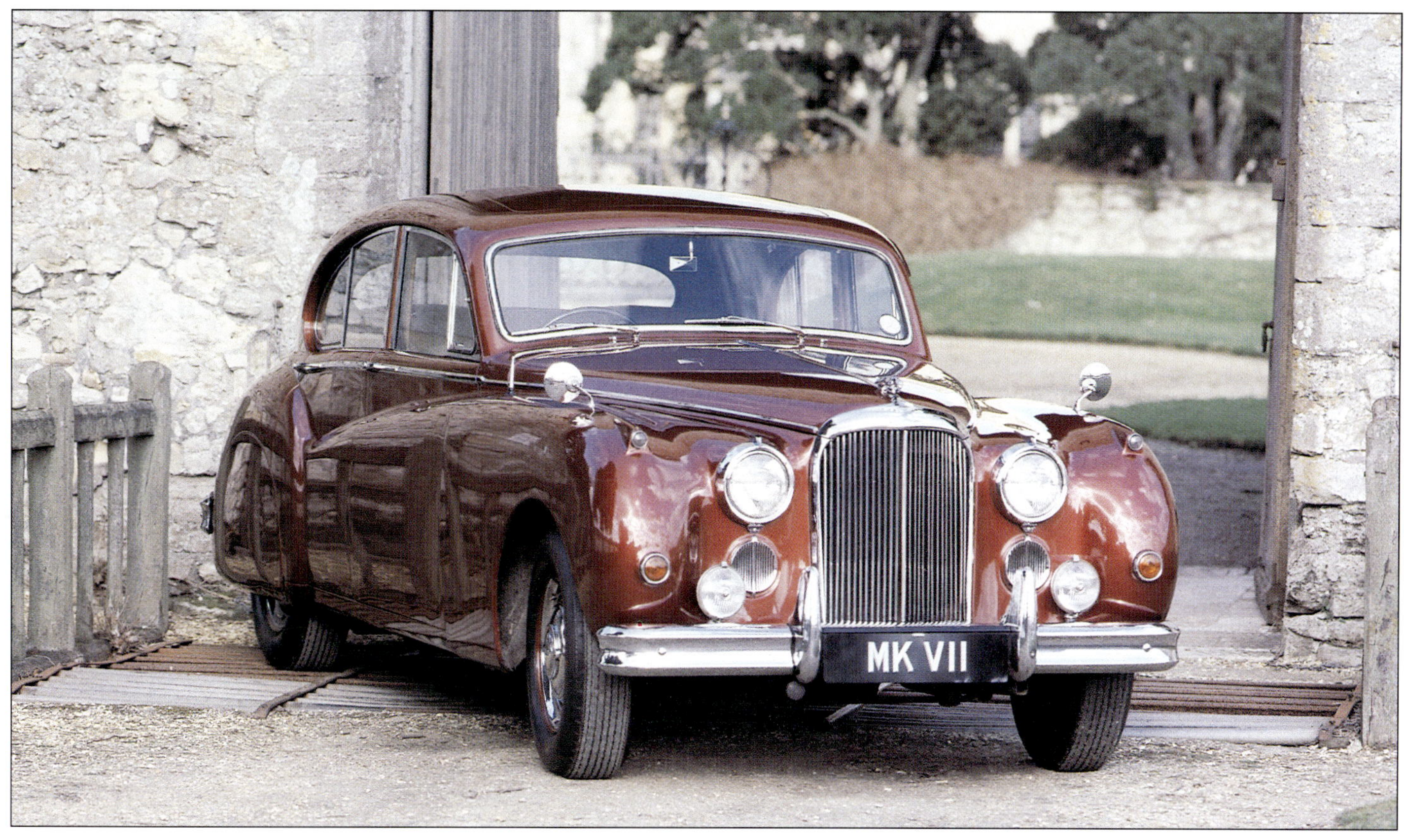

ABOVE: Regal Mk VII that was once owned by the Queen Mother and later converted to a Mk IX, keeping the separate chassis under its fine body.
BELOW: Built in 1954, the last year for the Mk VII, this fine example shows the line and style that set the Jaguar saloon apart from the crowd.

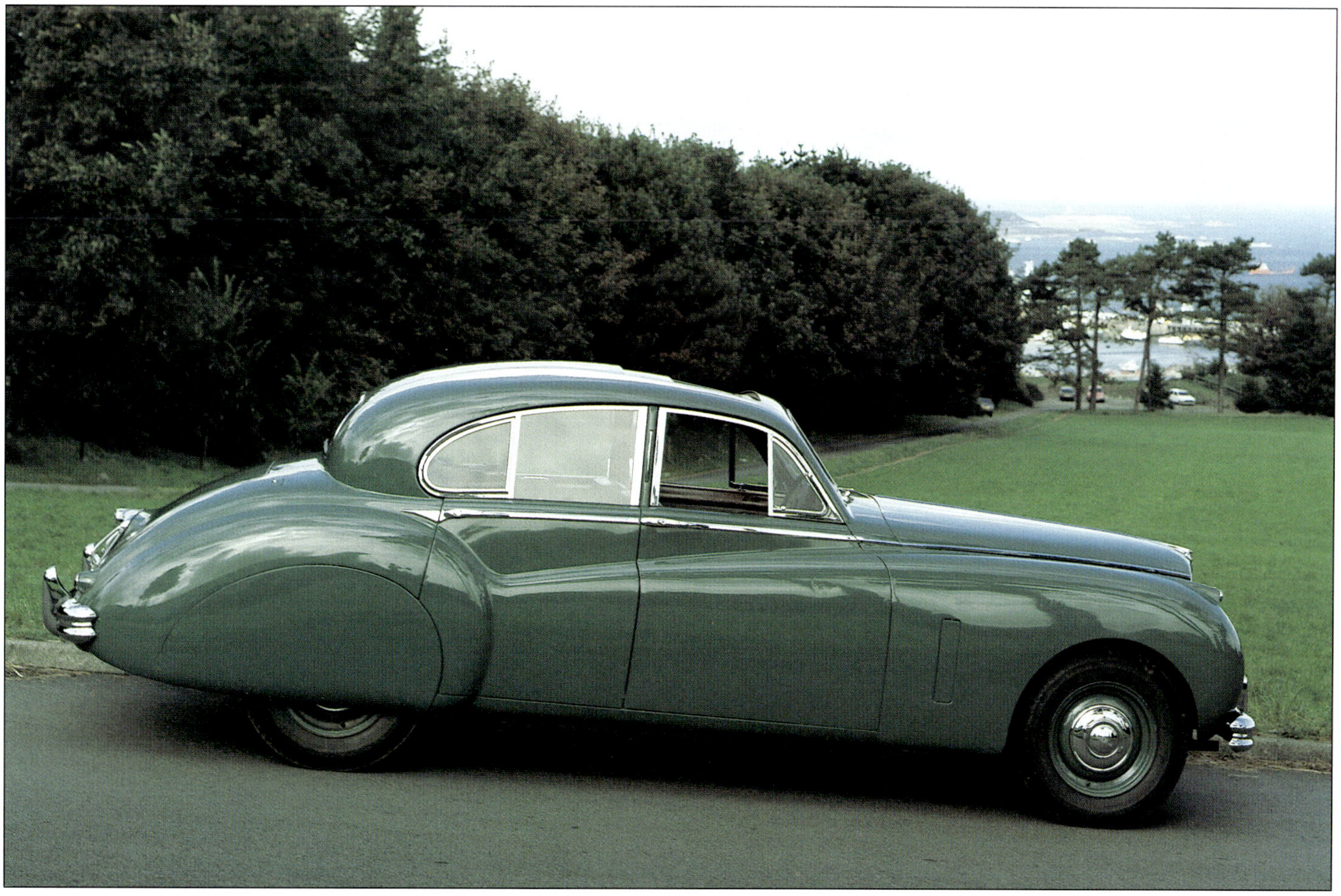

RIGHT: Bonnet mascot on the 1954 Mk VII, typical of the attention paid to the smallest detail of the car.

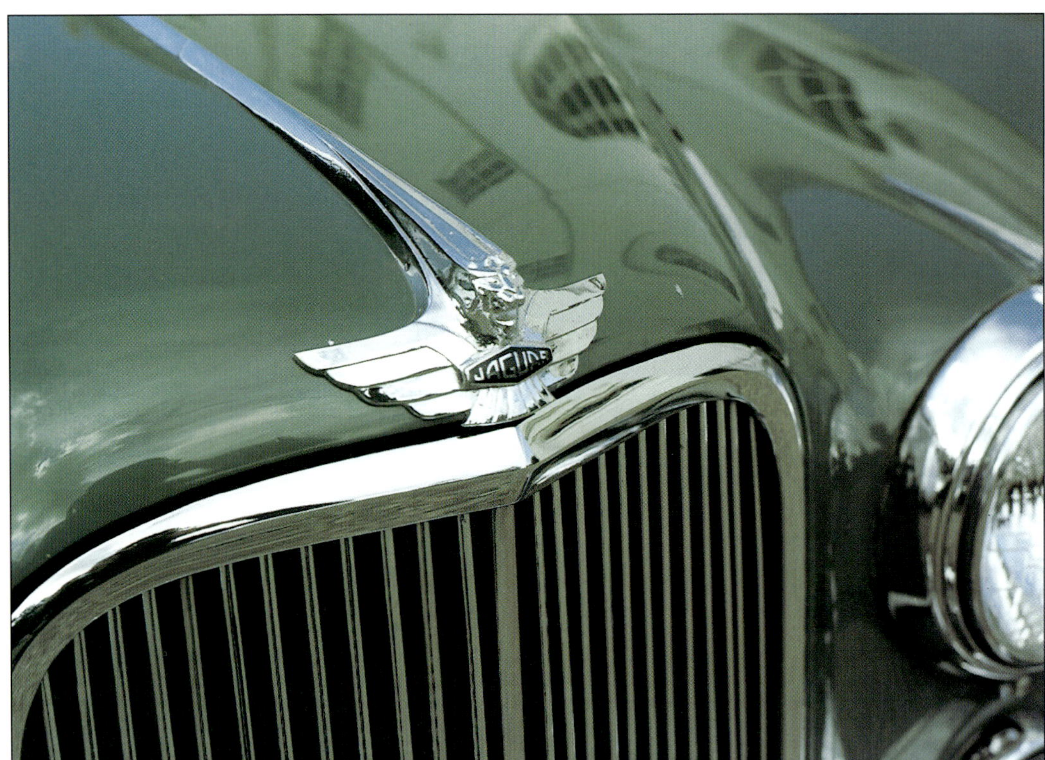

BELOW: From any quarter the big Jaguar saloon kept its line and style, always impressive and dignified.

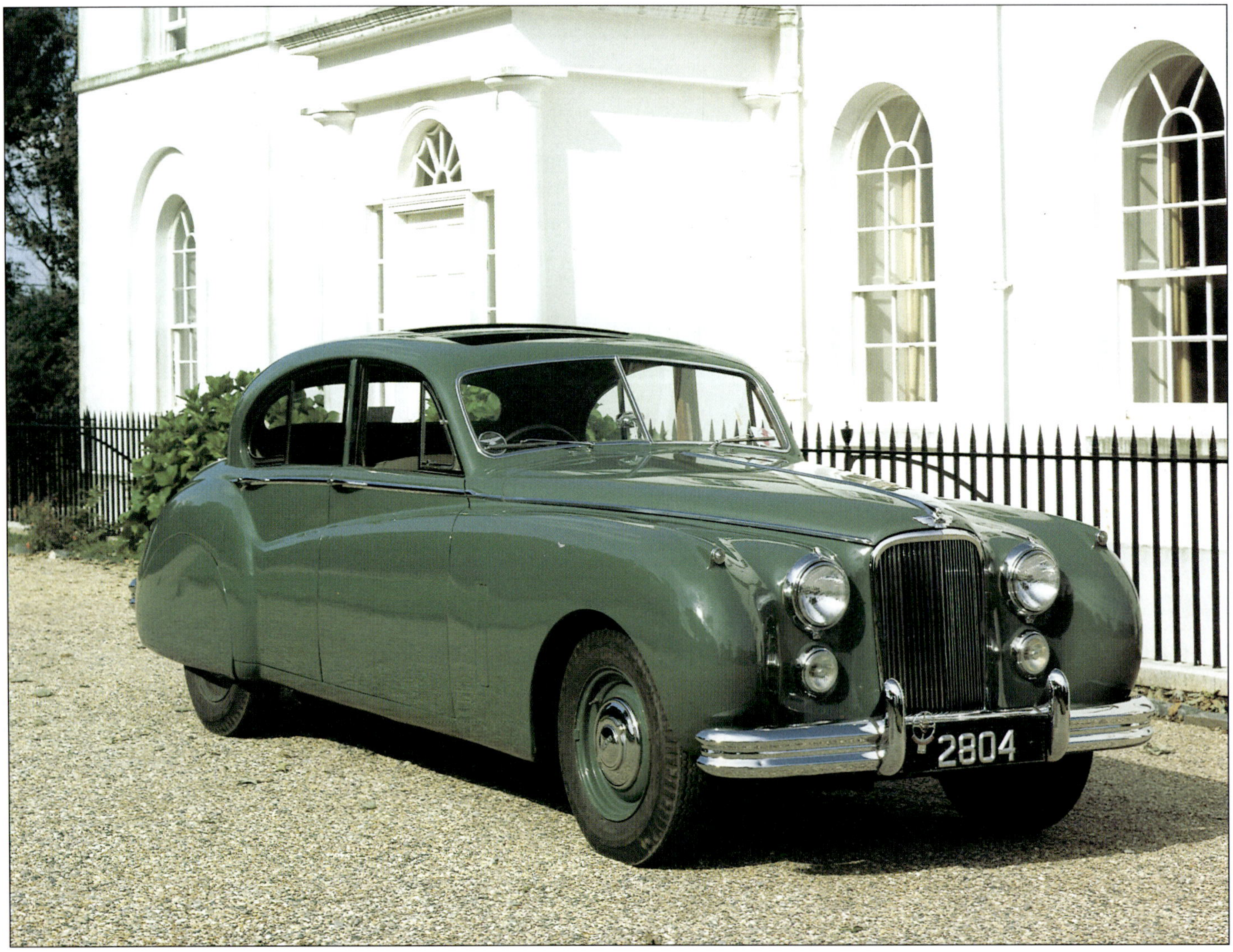

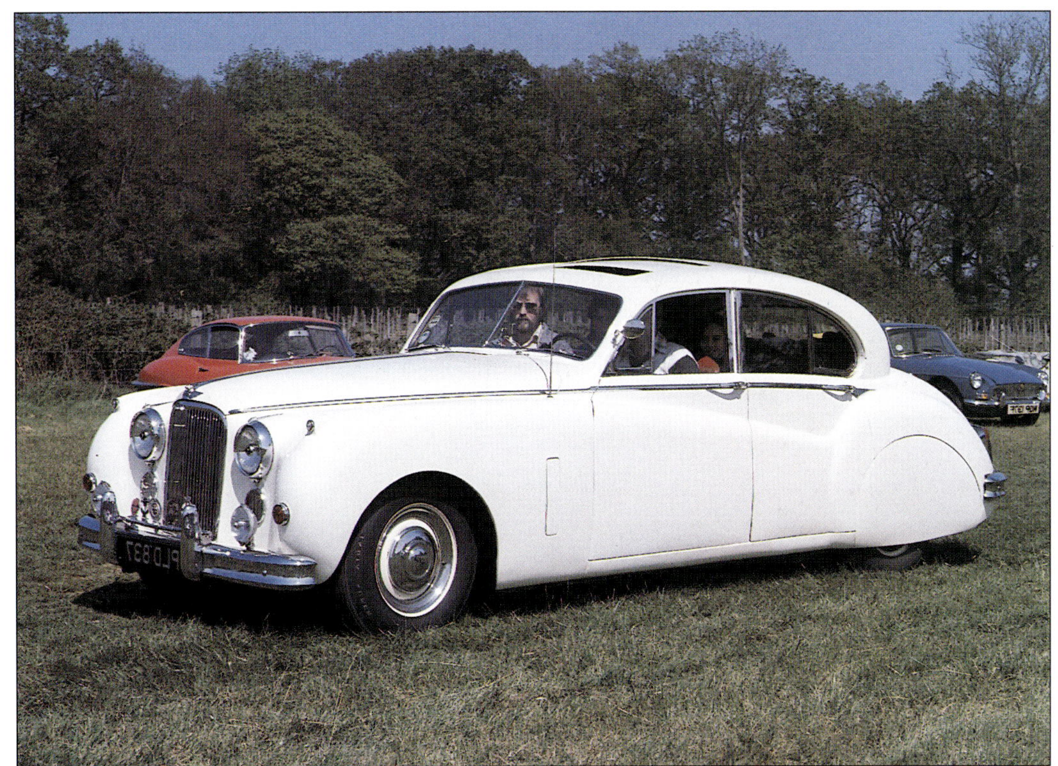

LEFT: The Mk VII became the Mk VIIM as here for 1955 with wrap-around rear bumpers and other changes.

BELOW: The 2.4-litre Mk I saloon was soon joined by a 3.4-litre version, many of them being raced as this one at Silverstone in 1961.

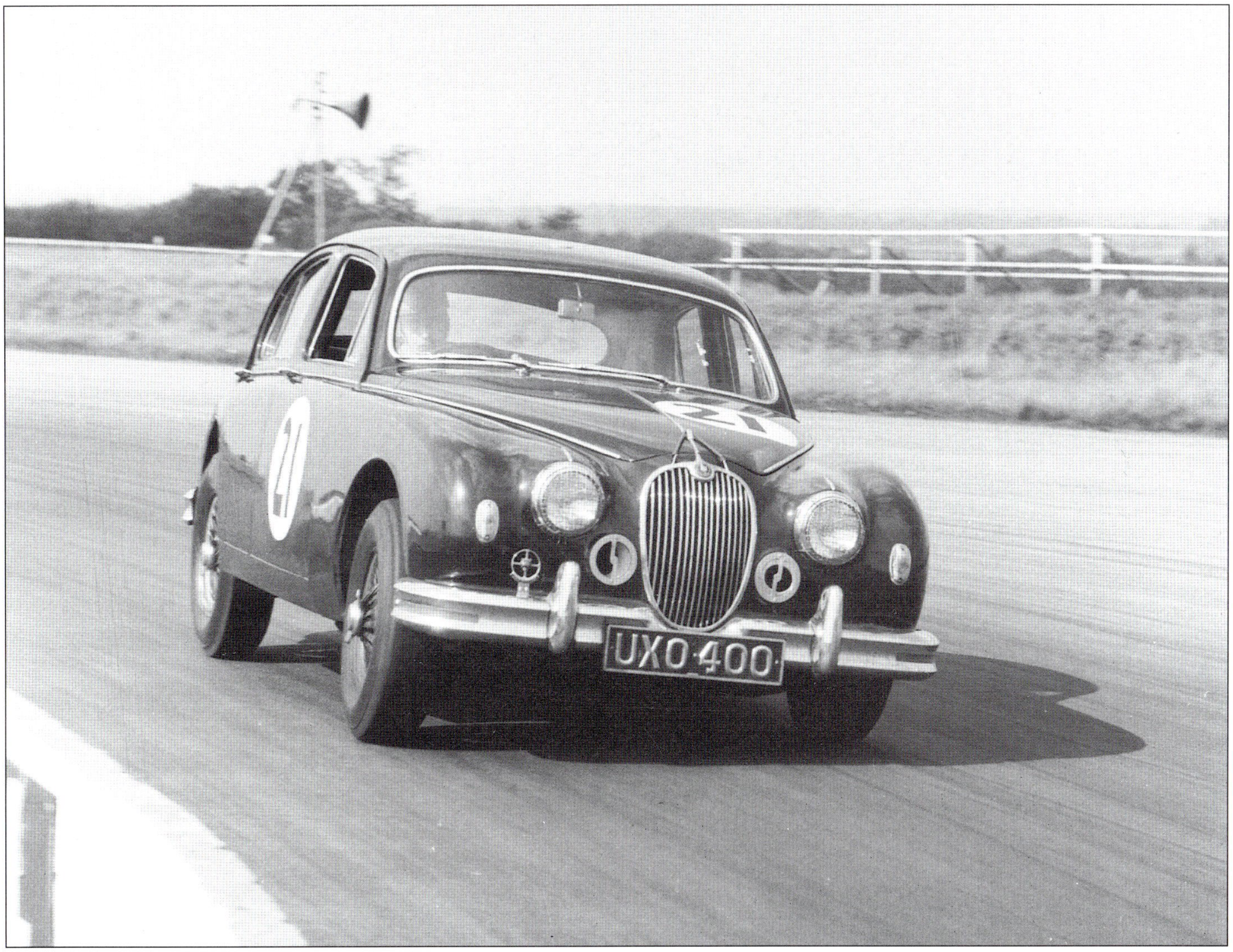

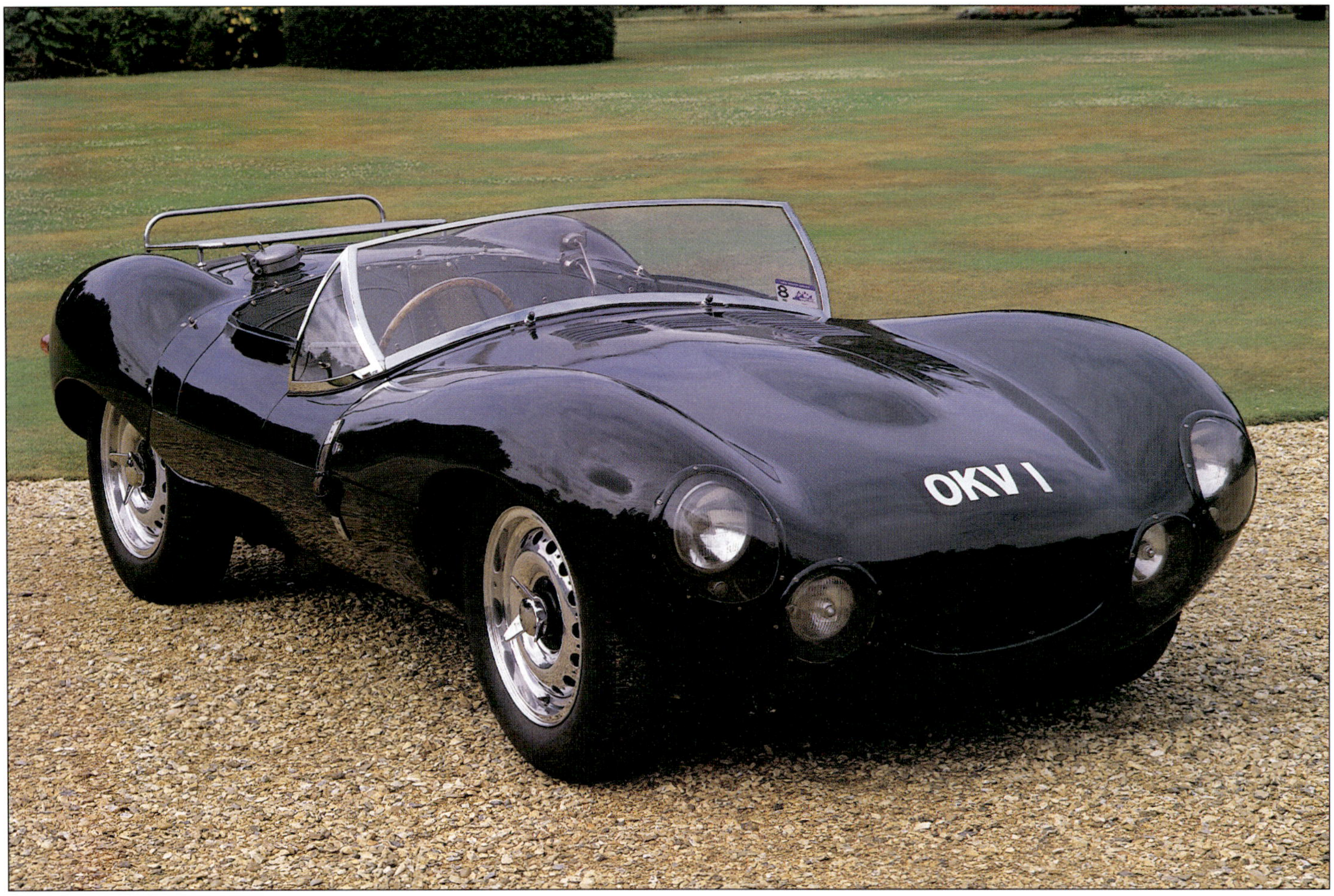

ABOVE: Looking like a rare XK-SS, this car is actually a true D-type, altered for road use with windscreen, luggage rack and open passenger seat area.

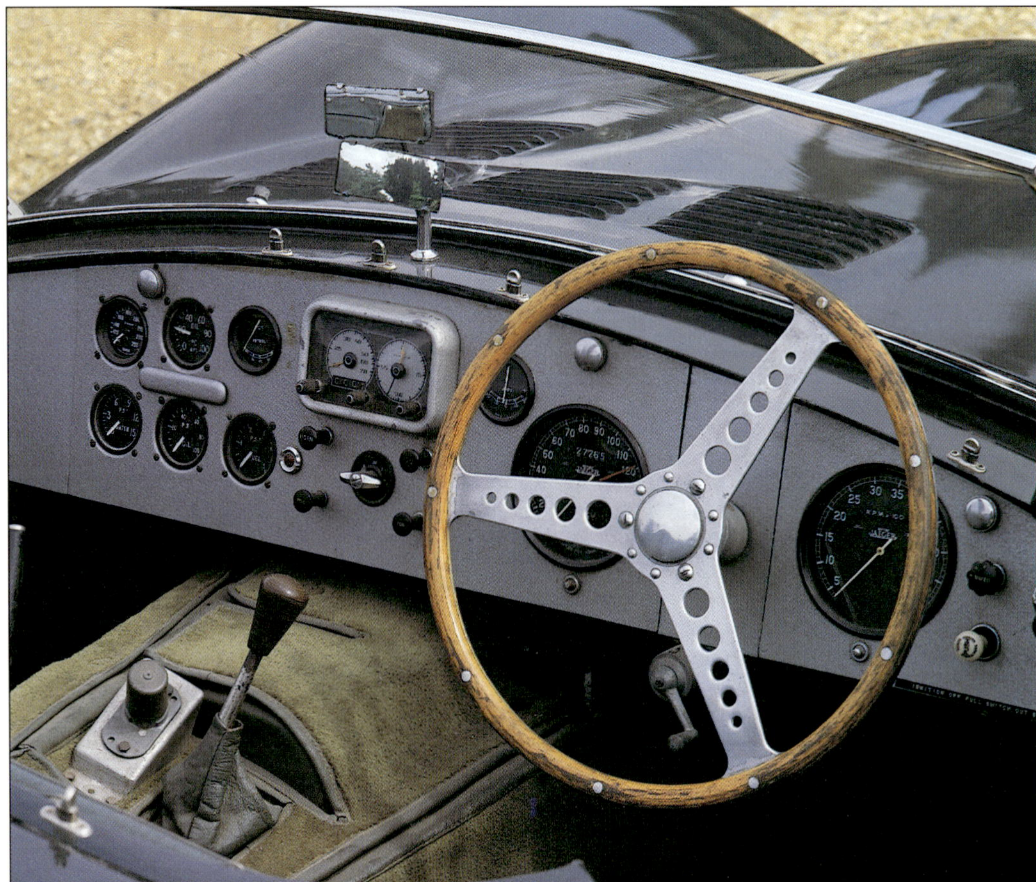

RIGHT: Cockpit of the D-type converted to XK-SS car showing its sparse and functional layout aimed at performance rather than comfort.

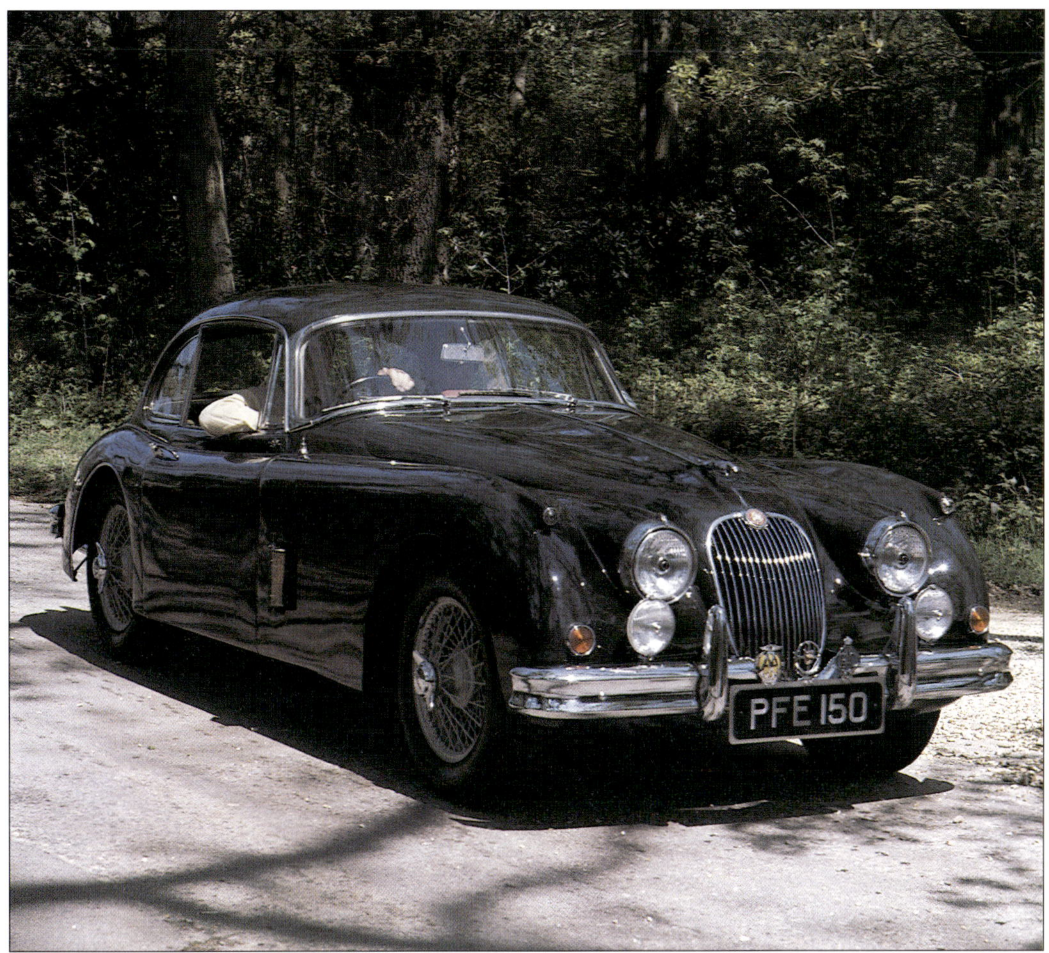

LEFT: During 1957 the XK150 coupé was introduced: this is the fixed-head model, both versions had a higher wing line and disc brakes all round.

BELOW: The XK150 Roadster joined the coupés in 1958, its line its own but clearly derived from the XK120 of a decade before.

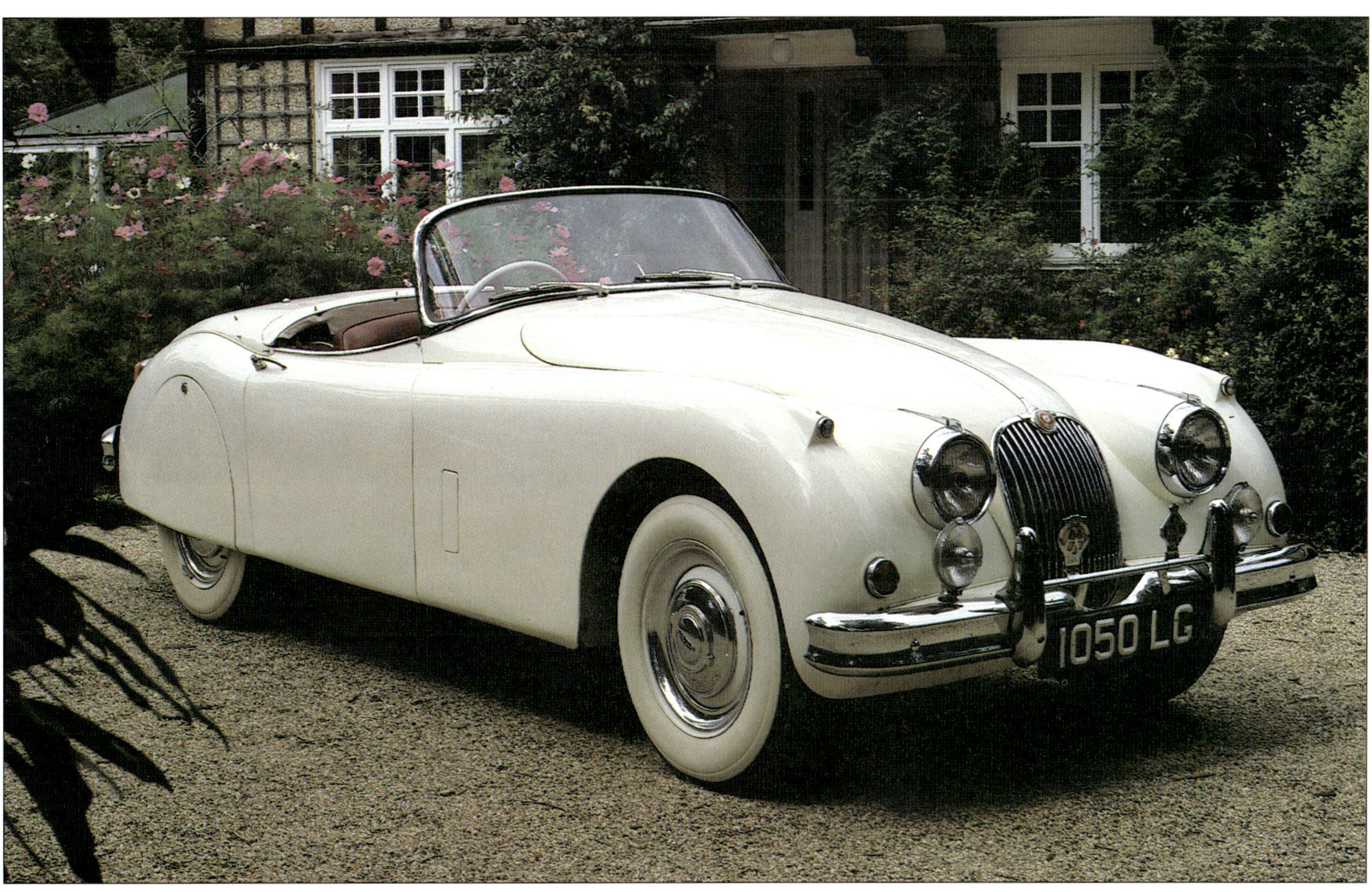

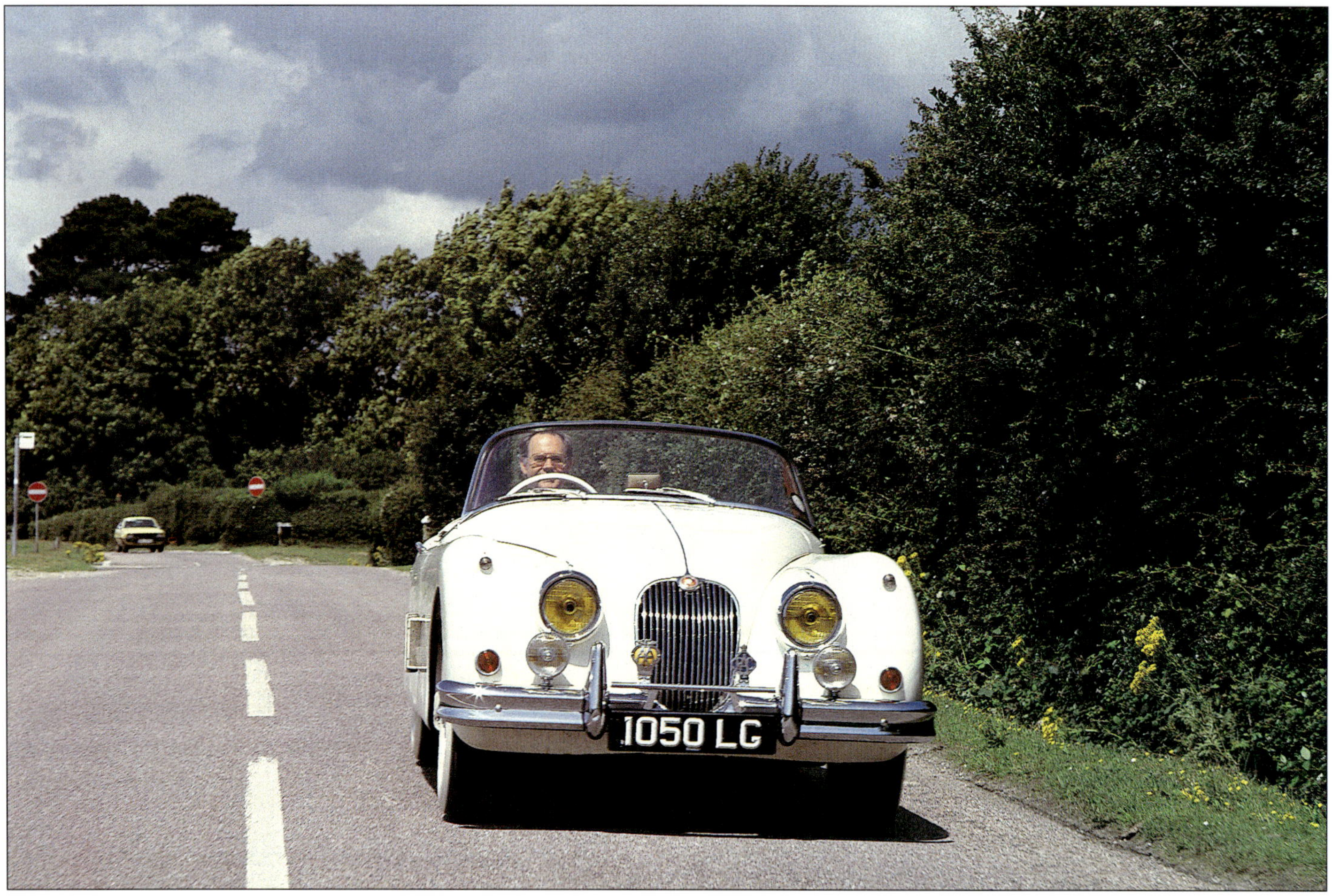

ABOVE: The front aspect of the XK150 Roadster was subtly different from the XK120 but a clear development into a common Jaguar form.

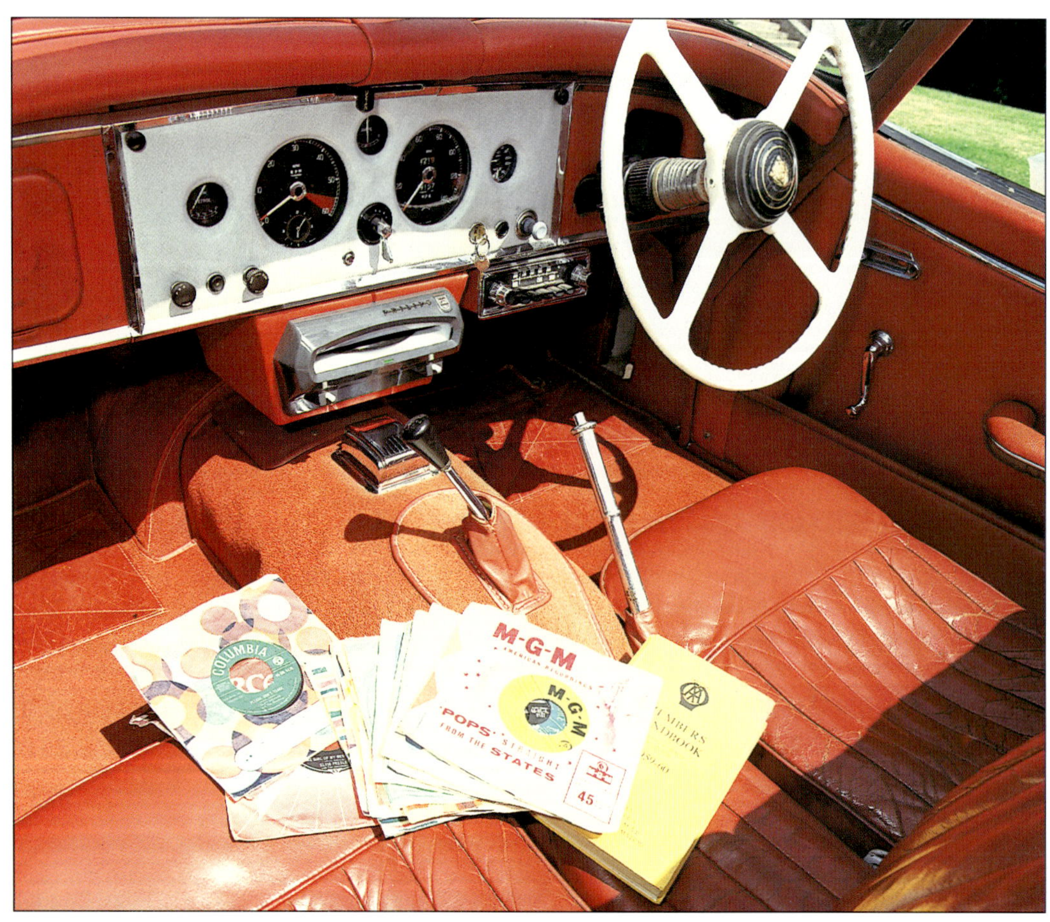

RIGHT: Cockpit of an XK150 with rev-counter in front of passenger, added radio, and a Philips record player in the days before tapes or CDs.

OPPOSITE: Side view of an XK150 that shows the effect on the style of the higher wing line compared to that of the first XK120.

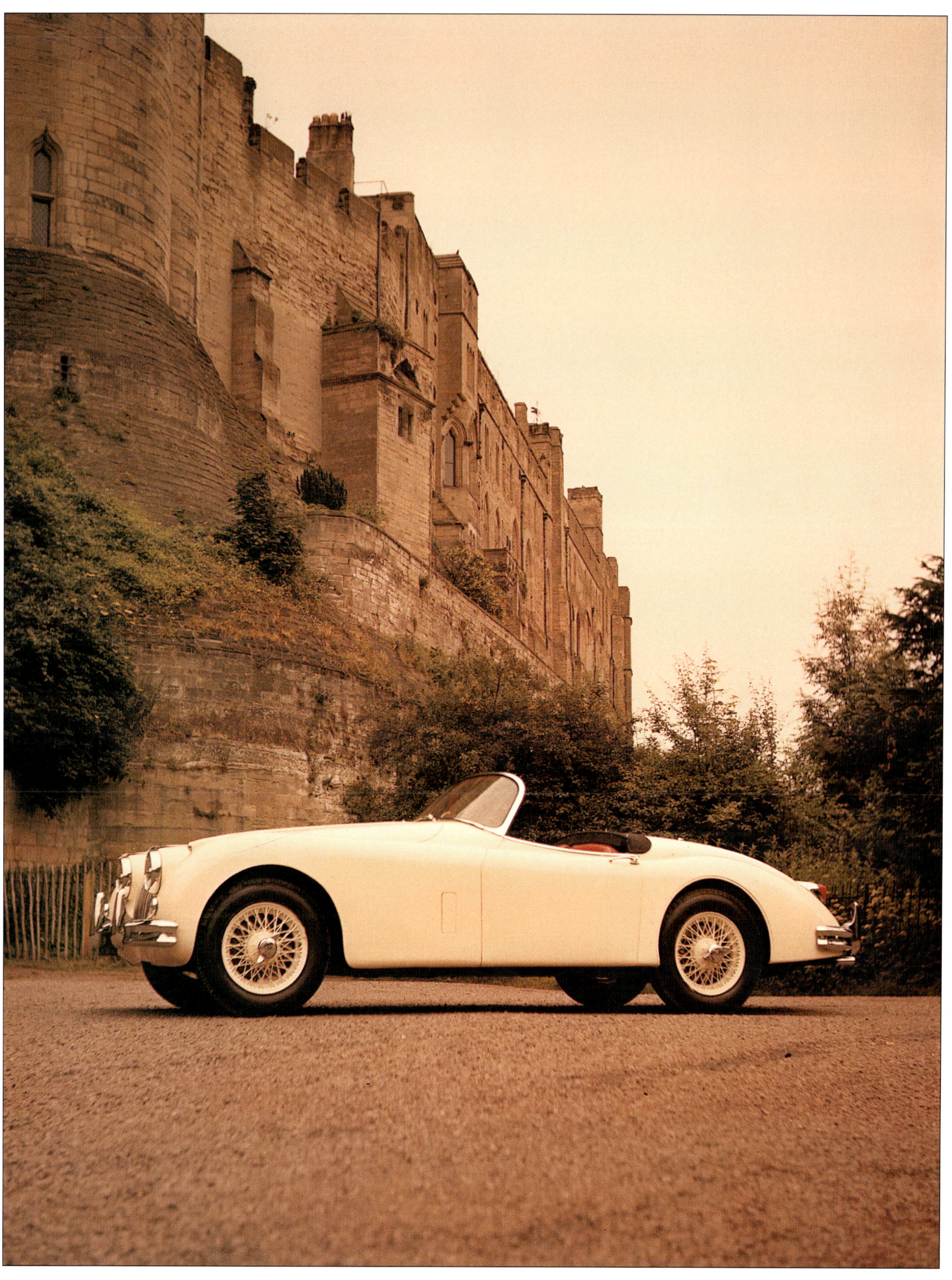

RIGHT: Last big saloon with its own chassis was this Mk IX that had the 3.8-litre engine for pace and, most importantly, disc brakes to stop it.

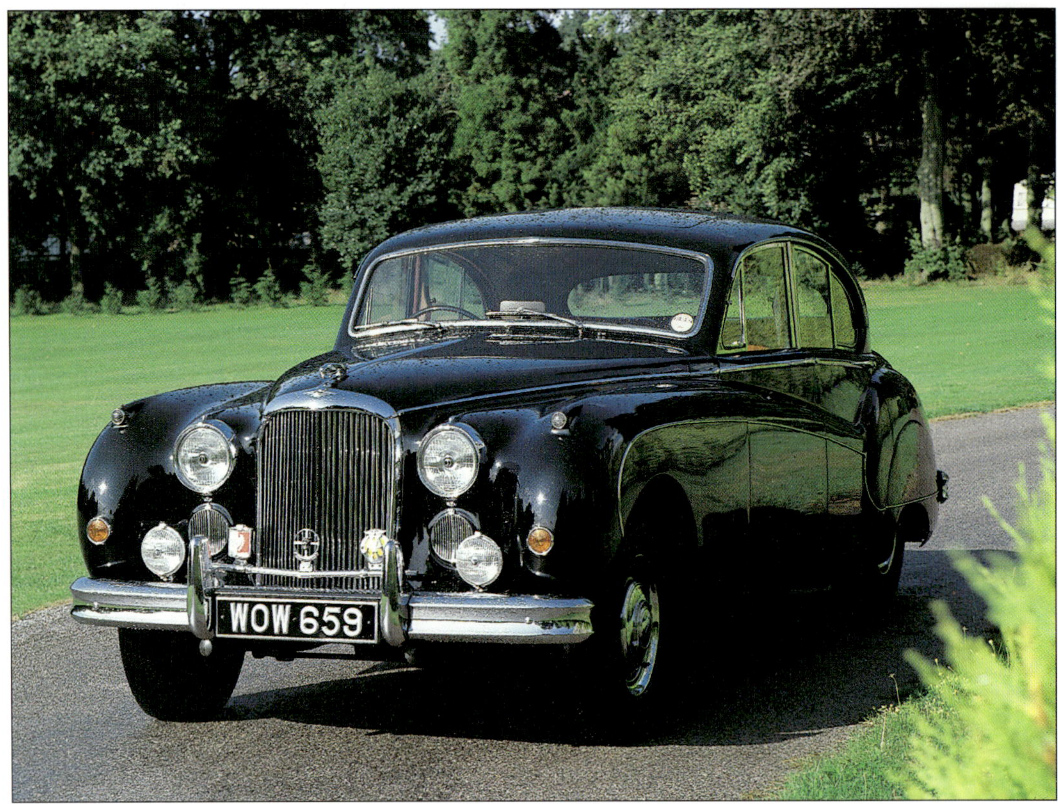

BELOW: Mk II saloon in 3.8-litre form as from 1960, this a 1963 car, and all with disc brakes.

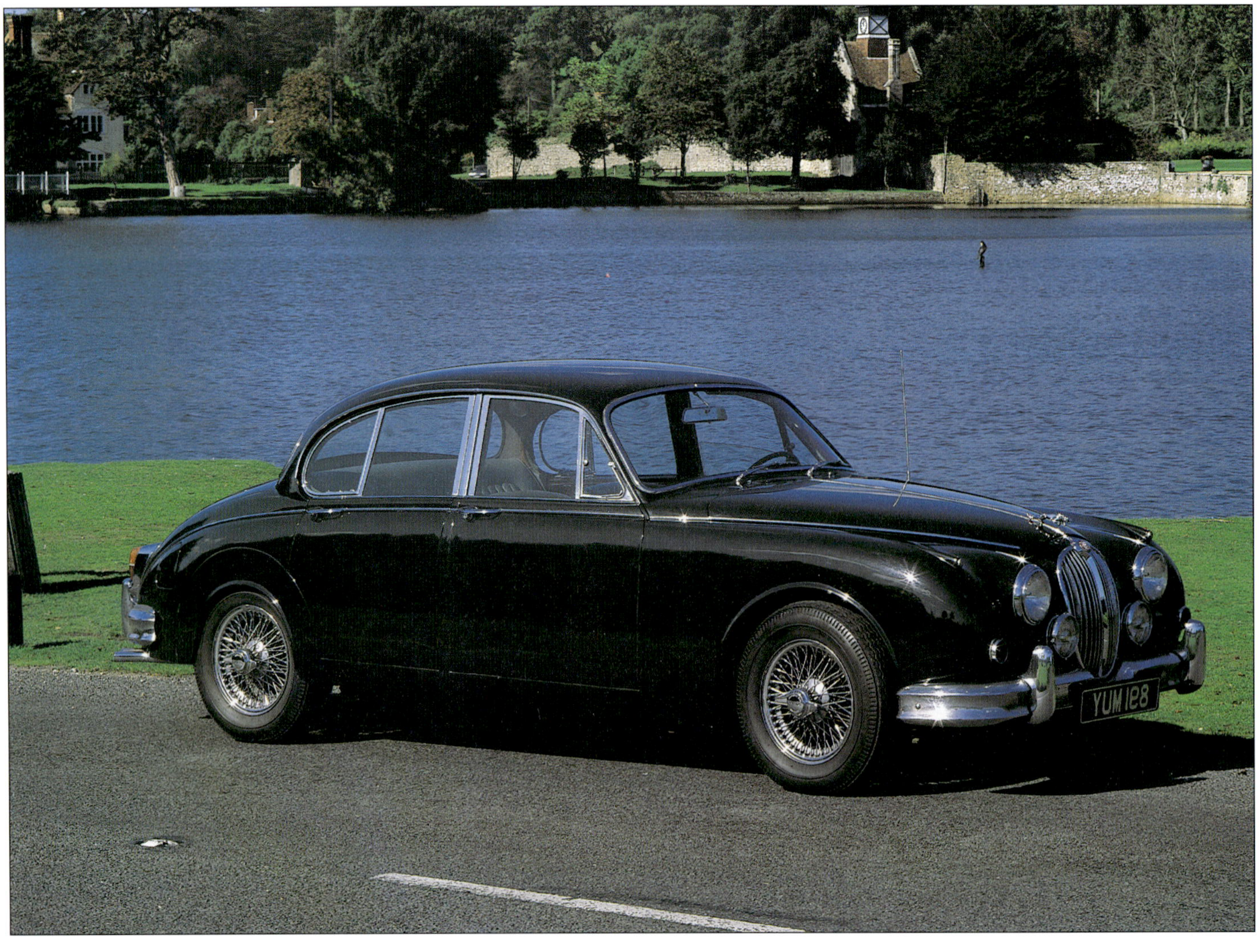

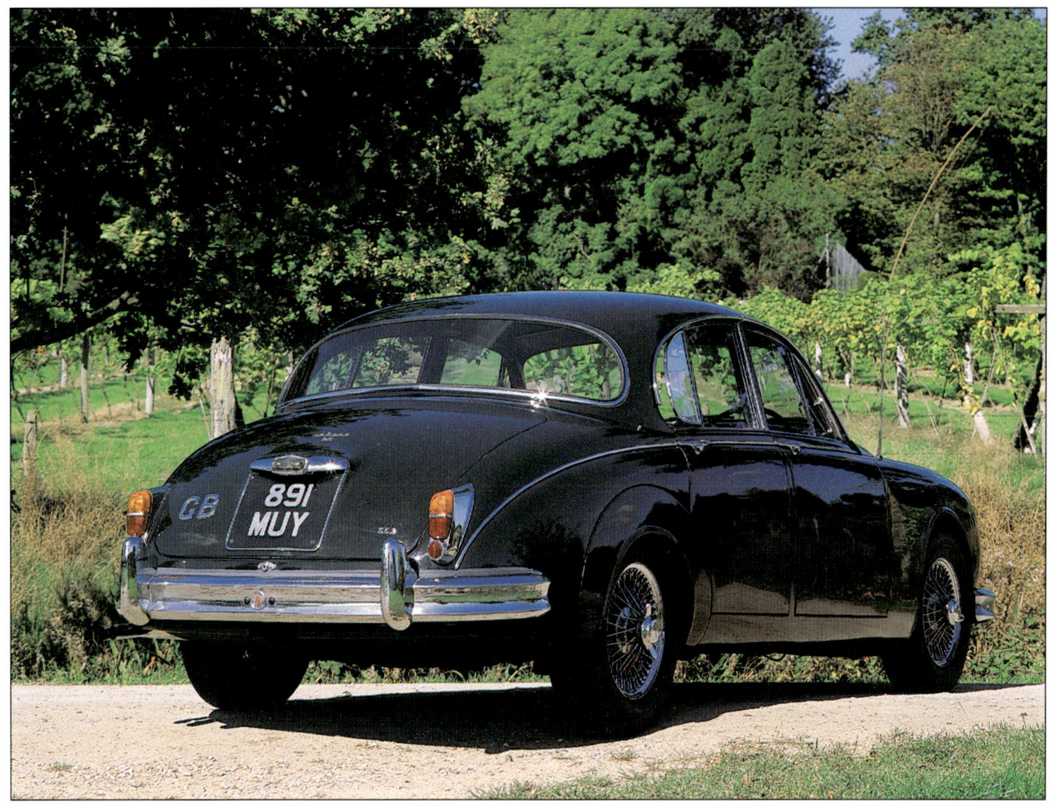

LEFT: The Mk II saloons had a wider rear track and much larger rear window as this view shows.

BELOW: Front quarter view of a 3.4-litre Mk II saloon, its engine far from accessible under that small hatch in the bonnet.

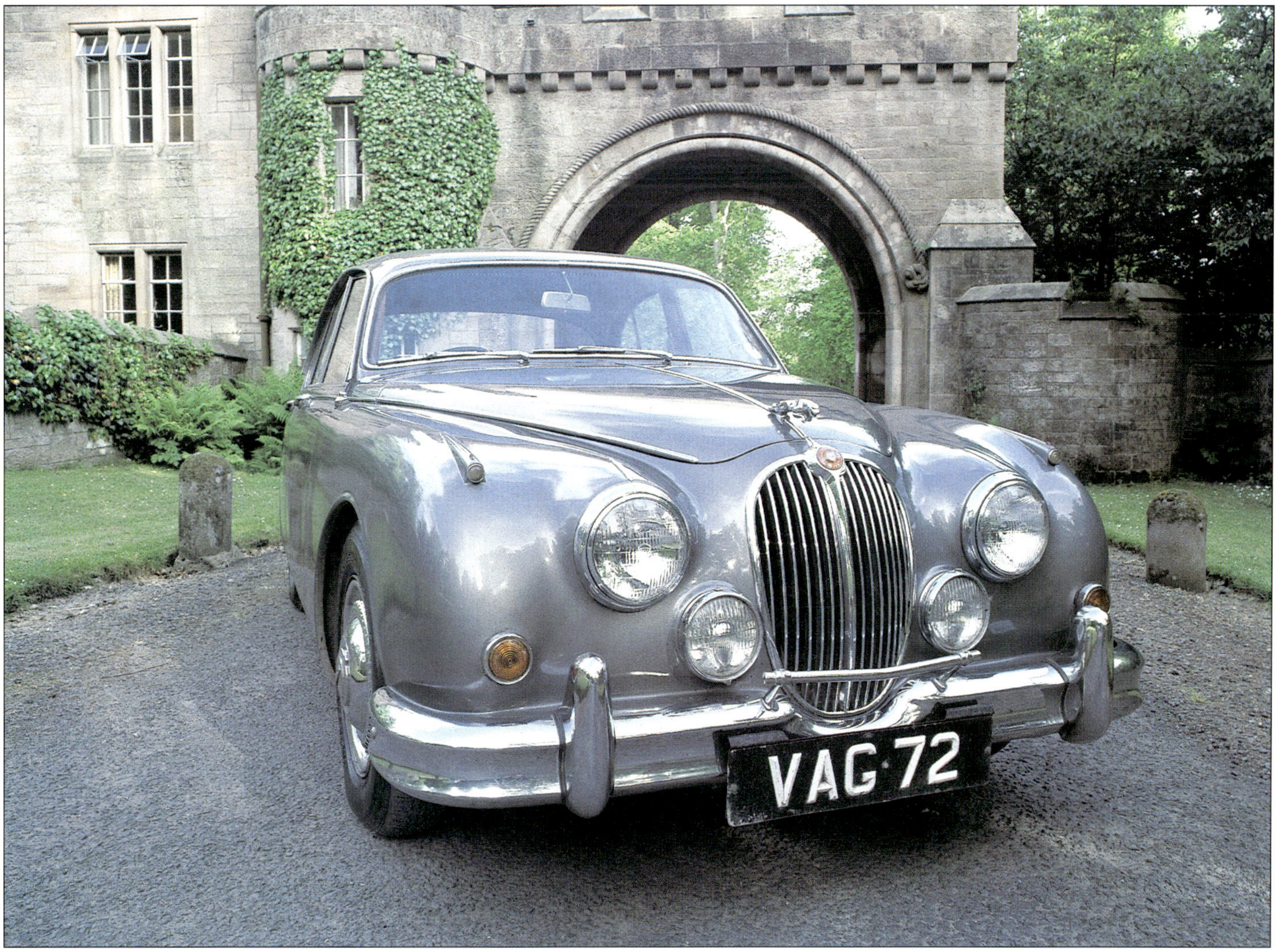

E-TYPE & DAIMLER

1961-1968

PRODUCTION of the XK150 tailed off at the end of 1960, for the magnificent E-type appeared in 1961, as far advanced then as the XK120 had been in 1948. Built in Roadster and coupé forms using the 3.8-litre engine and of unitary construction, its 265bhp could push it over 140mph, one coupé road test reaching 150mph. Naturally there were disc brakes all round but independent rear suspension was new, while the style and shape was a dream. And the basic price was under £1,500, although tax pushed this to over £2,100, but for wonderful looks, tremendous performance and a well tried set of mechanicals in mass production there was really nothing that could begin to touch it.

The advent of the E-type overshadowed the big saloon that became the Mk X 3.8-litre and adopted unitary construction to lose finally its separate chassis. Independent suspension and disc brakes all round, a limited-slip differential and power steering were all features, the new body had a lighter style, but it was still big, heavy and thirsty.

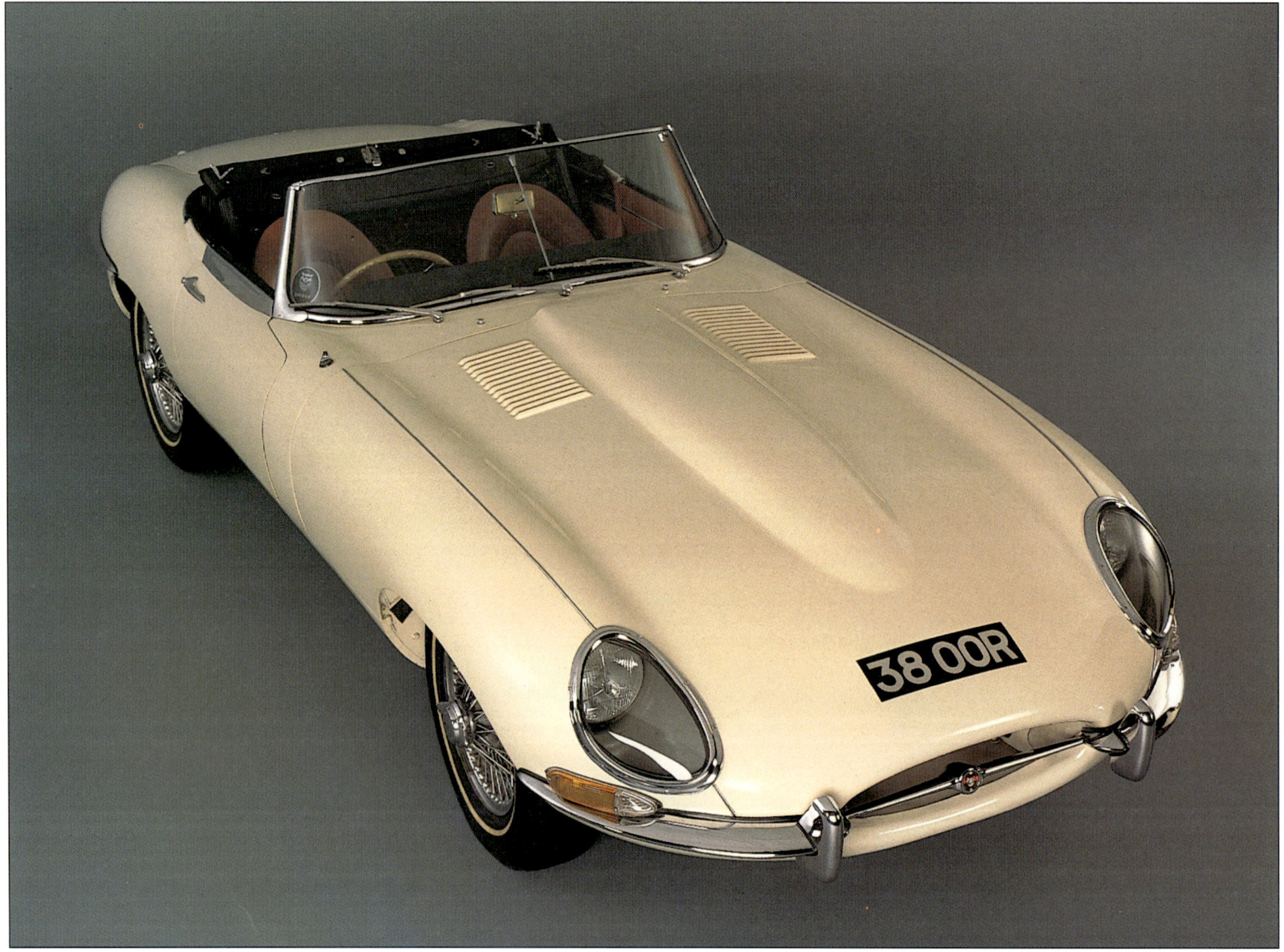

The fabulous E-type in its Roadster form, powered by the well-developed, twin-cam six engine under a striking new body.

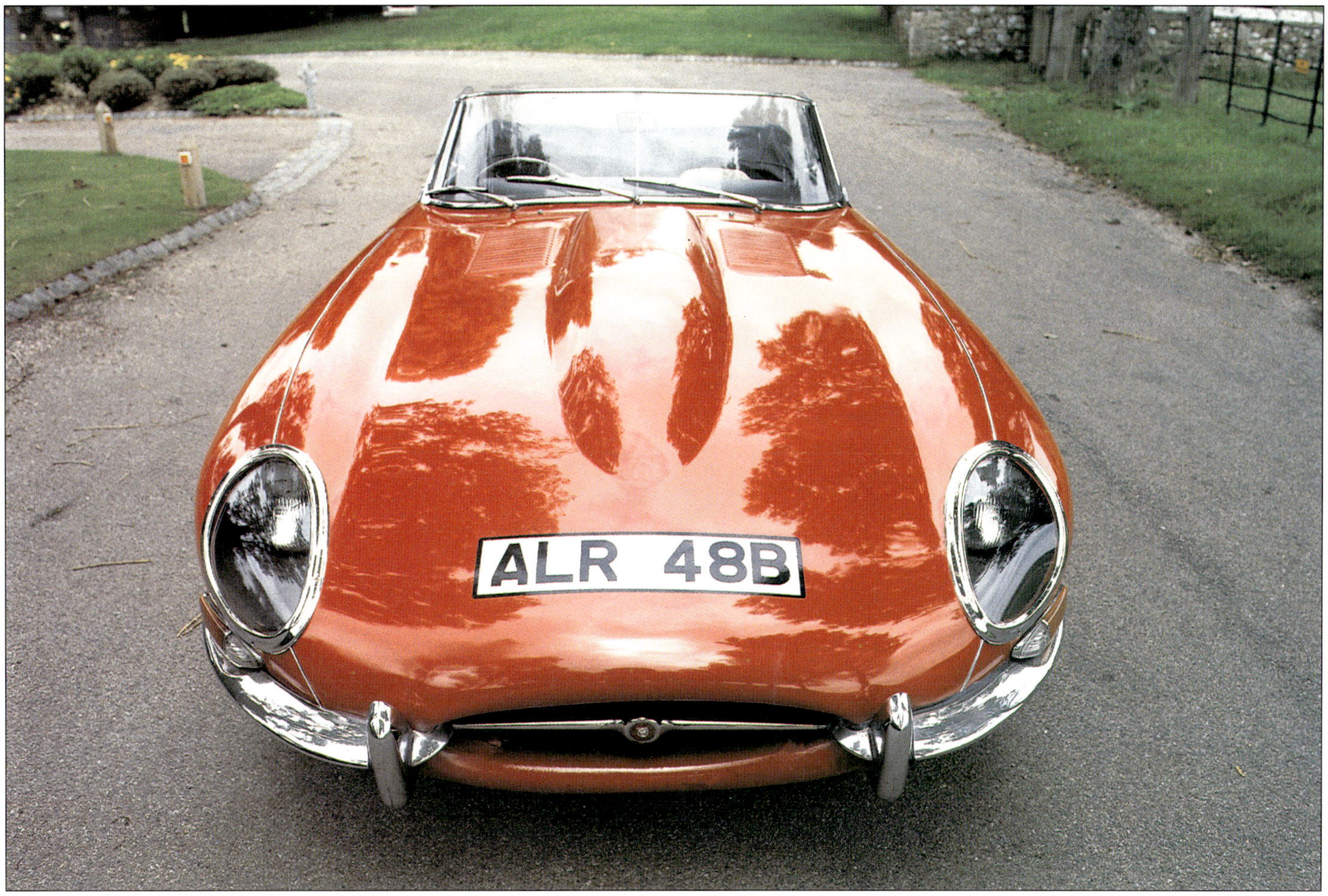

ABOVE: E-type Roadster from 1964 with the 3.8-litre engine under that long, stylish bonnet to give it tremendous performance.

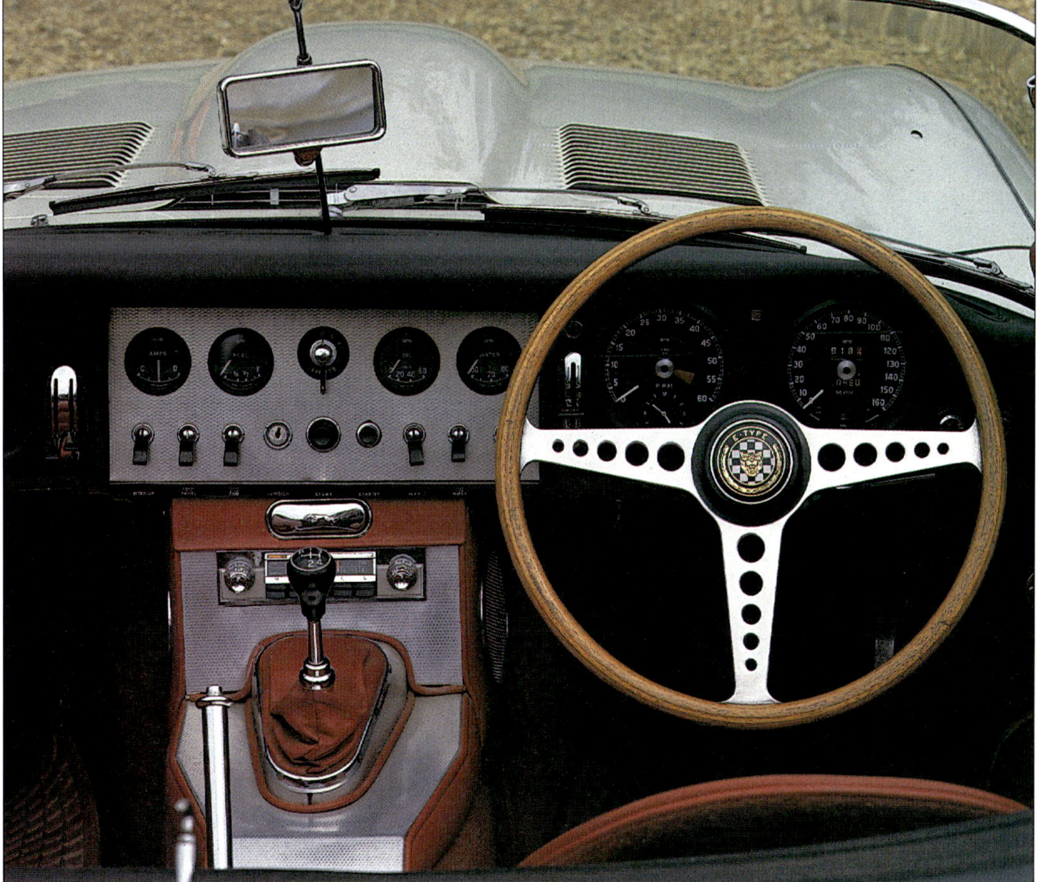

LEFT: Cockpit layout of the E-type with the main instruments now in front of the driver who has to memorise all the minor switches.

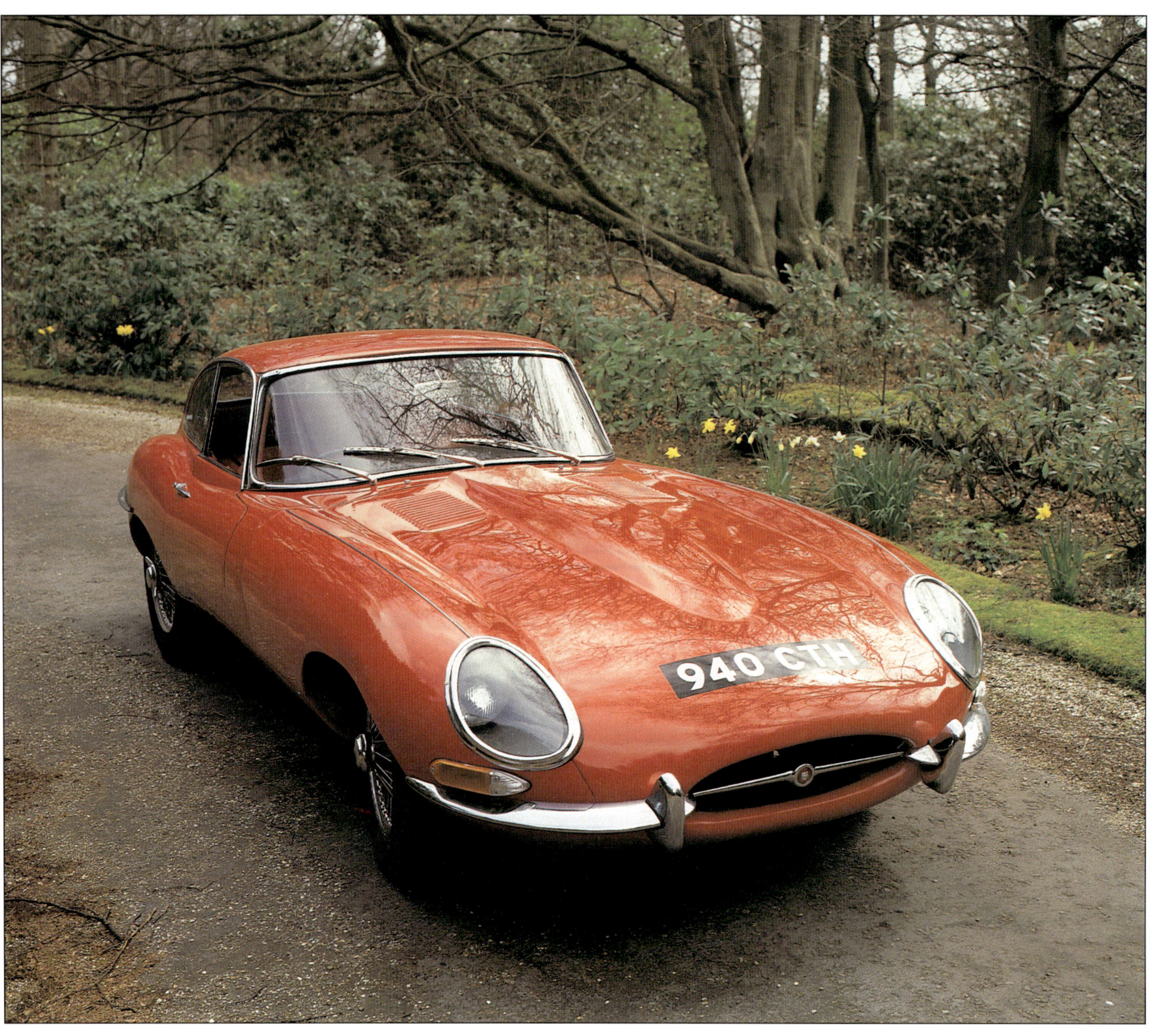

Coupé version of the E-type that retained the elegant line and was good for close to 150mph.

For 1963 the link with Daimler produced the 2½-litre V-8/250. This looked like, and was firmly based on, the Jaguar Mk II body shell and suspension but was fitted with the 2,548cc, overhead-valve, V-8 engine designed by Edward Turner of Triumph motorcycle fame - a design connection due to the Triumph to BSA to Daimler link. It made an excellent package.

The Mk II and Mk X were combined in 1964 to produce the S-type saloon that was intended to slot between the compact and the large. The body line was therefore stretched out, which gave it more internal room and luggage space, there was independent rear suspension and either the 3.4- or 3.8-litre engine was fitted.

The tried and trusted twin-cam engine was stretched some more for 1965, out to 4,235cc, and went into both versions of the E-type and the Mk X to give 4.2-litre models with better low-end and mid-range performance. A year or so later a 2+2 E-type coupé was added to the line but it lacked the grace of the others for it was 9in longer with a higher roof line. It was listed with automatic transmission as well as manual and the extra weight and drag slowed it to a modest 135mph, hardly slow but not to prove a favourite.

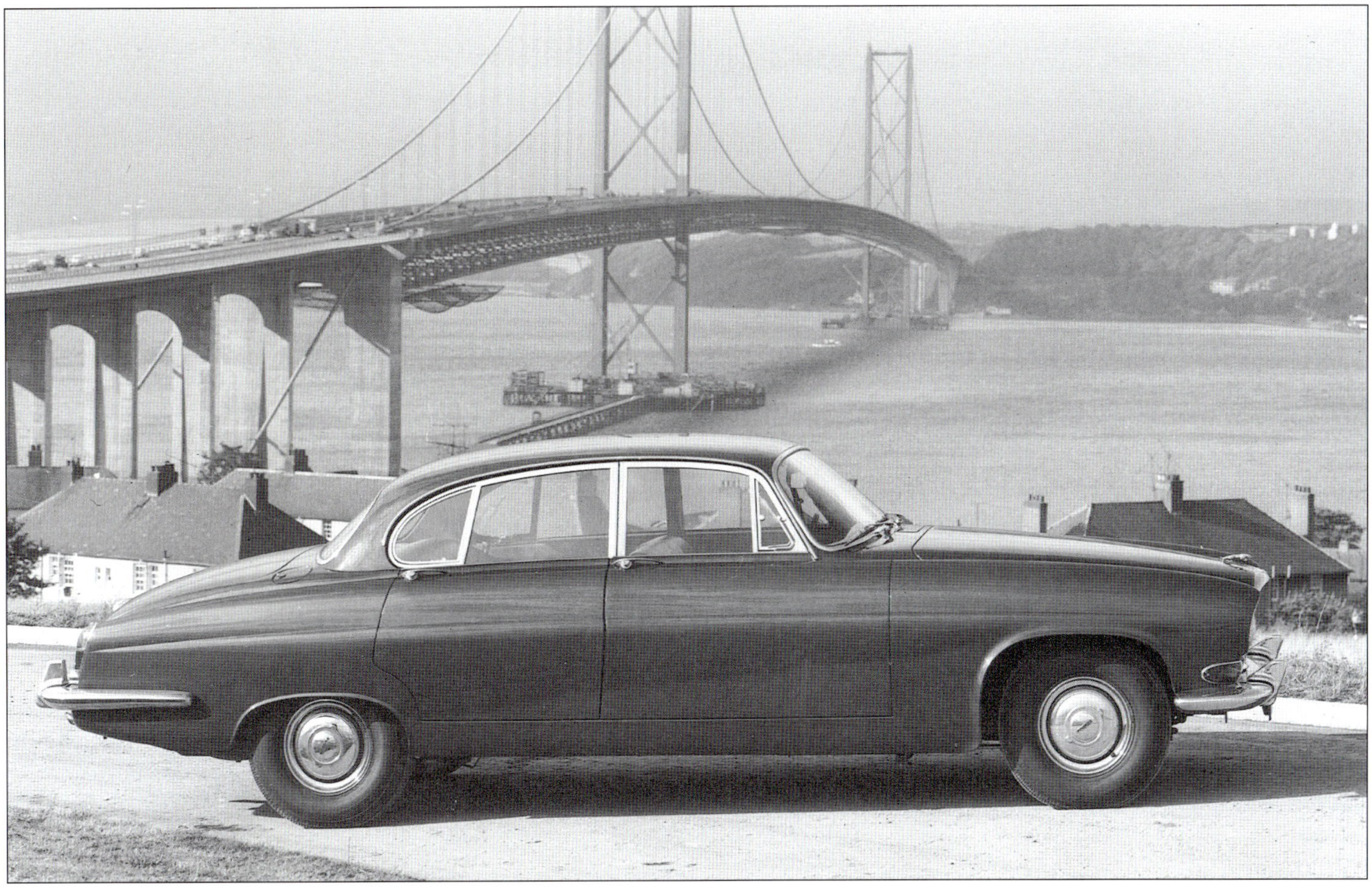

ABOVE: Mk X introduced in 1961 with unitary construction, independent suspension and disc brakes to offer high speed - but thirsty, cruising.
BELOW: The combination of the Jaguar Mk II body and the Daimler V-8 engine resulted in the fine V8/250 saloon in 1963.

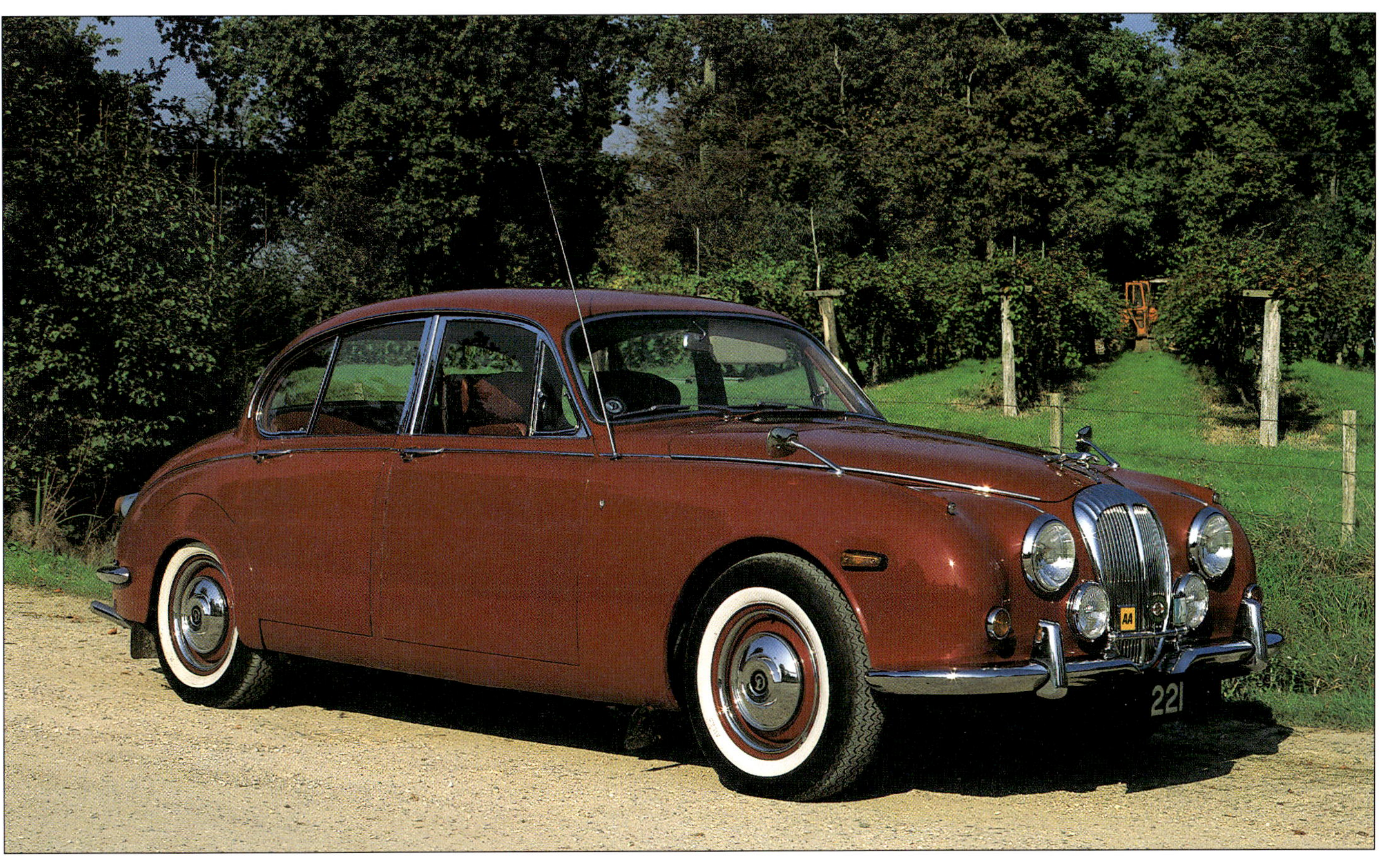

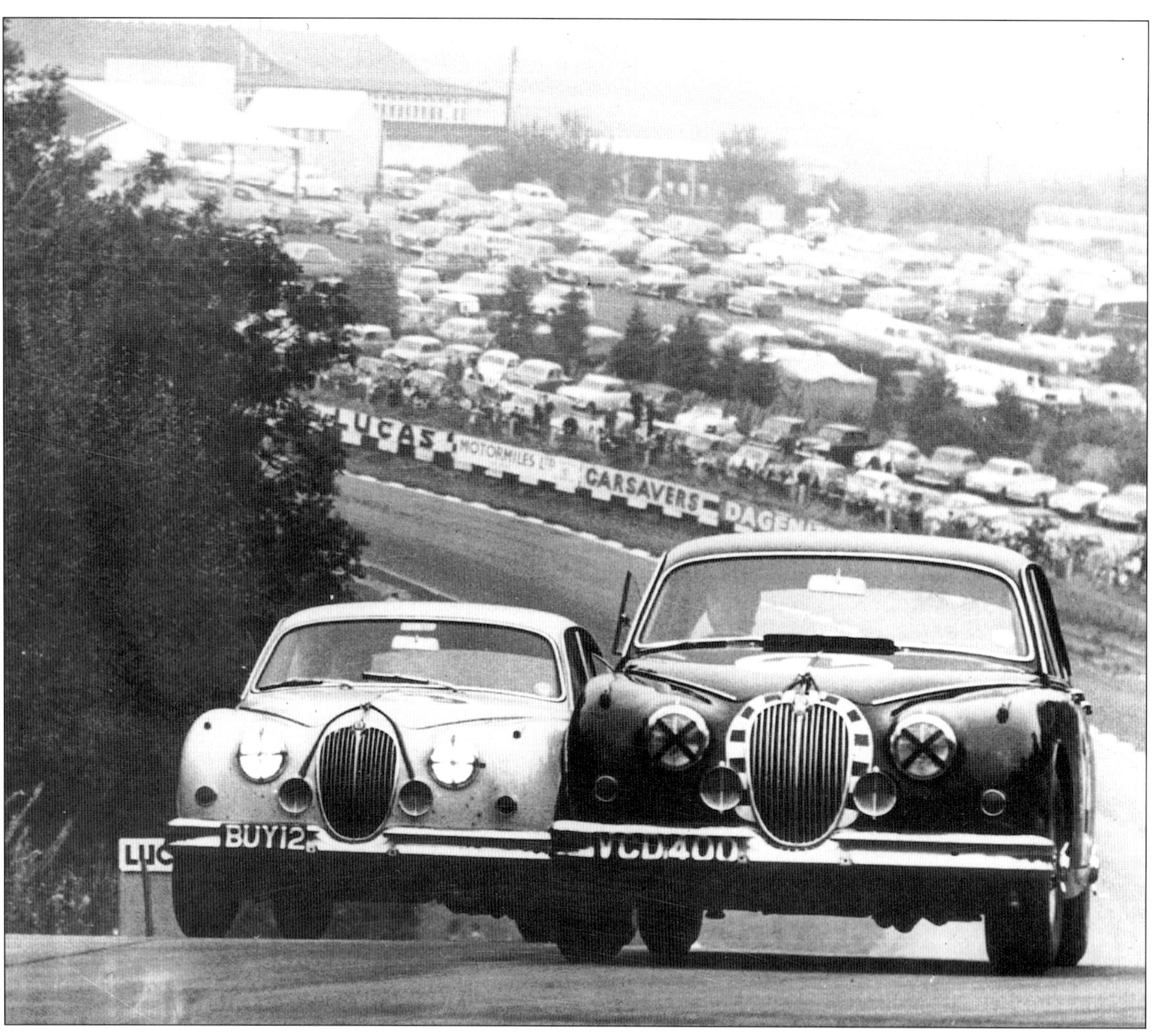

Many Mk II Jaguars were raced in the 1960s and these two 3.8s are at Brands Hatch for a six-hour event in 1962.

The big saloons had changes for 1966 when the Mk X became the 420G with minor alterations - it being perceived more as an executive car, often chauffeur-driven, and a few were built as limousines. There was also a 420 but this was an S-type fitted with the 4.2-litre engine and a new nose to distinguish it. The specification was upgraded and it was also built as the Daimler Sovereign by changing badges, although power steering was then standard.

It was 1966 when the Jaguar-Daimler group sold out to BMC, to become part of British Leyland in 1968; after this Jaguar entered a bad period when quality control and reliability suffered. A revival did come to restore a damaged reputation but it was a dark time for the firm.

Typically, during 1967, the Mk II saloon was replaced by the 240 and 340 which kept the same engines but had the old trim specification cheapened to reduce the price. Better news was the advent of the Series II E-type in 1968 in Roadster, coupé and 2+2 coupé forms. All had lost the sleek headlight enclosure; they may have gained the option of power steering and were fitted with bigger bumpers, but the original clean shape was starting to go.

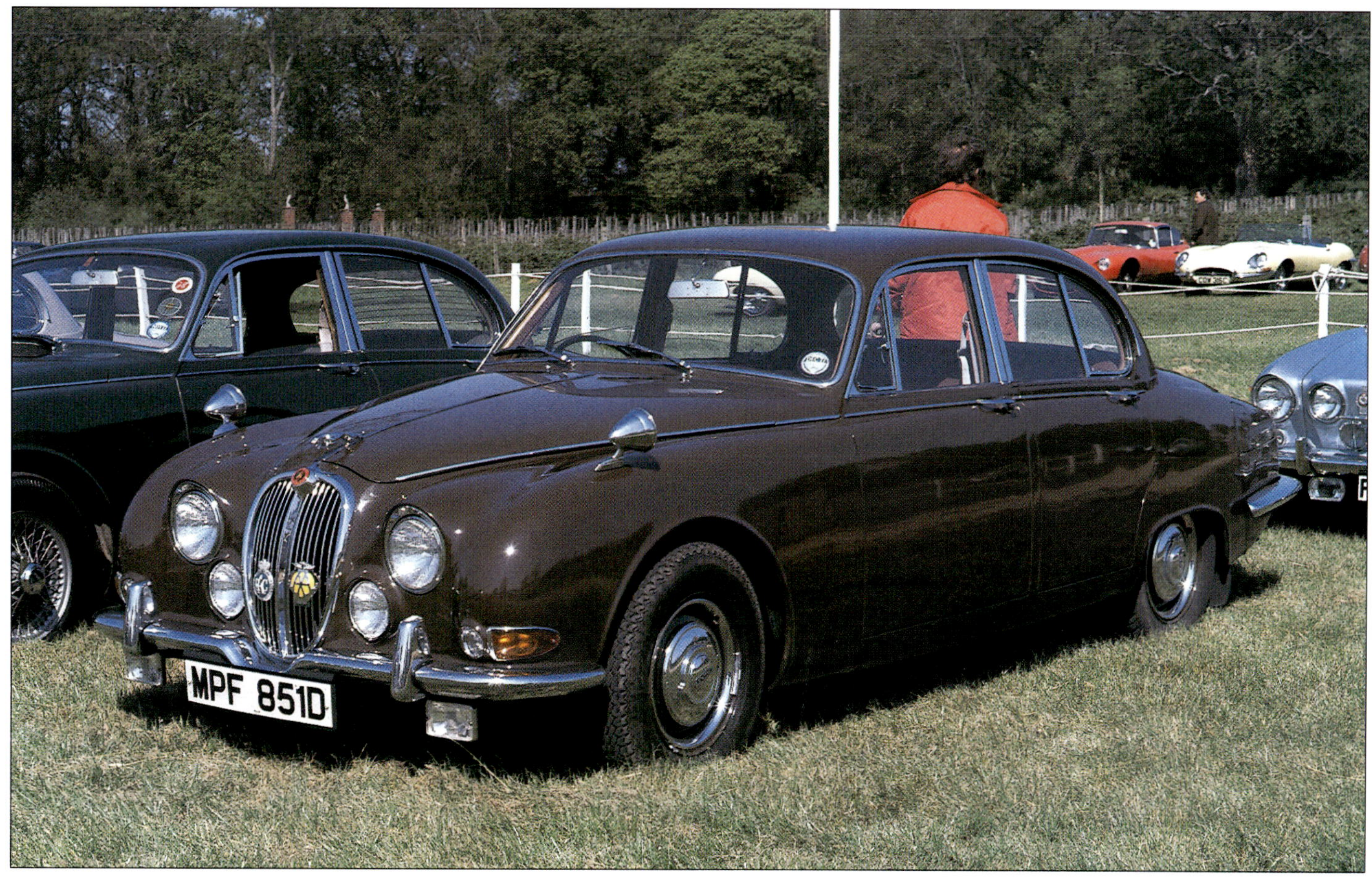

ABOVE: The S-type saloon was created from both the Mk II and Mk X cars to produce a mid-range size to fit between them.
BELOW: Developed from the Mk X, the 420G built from 1966 was an executive saloon, often chauffeur-driven, but also very occasionally built as a limousine.

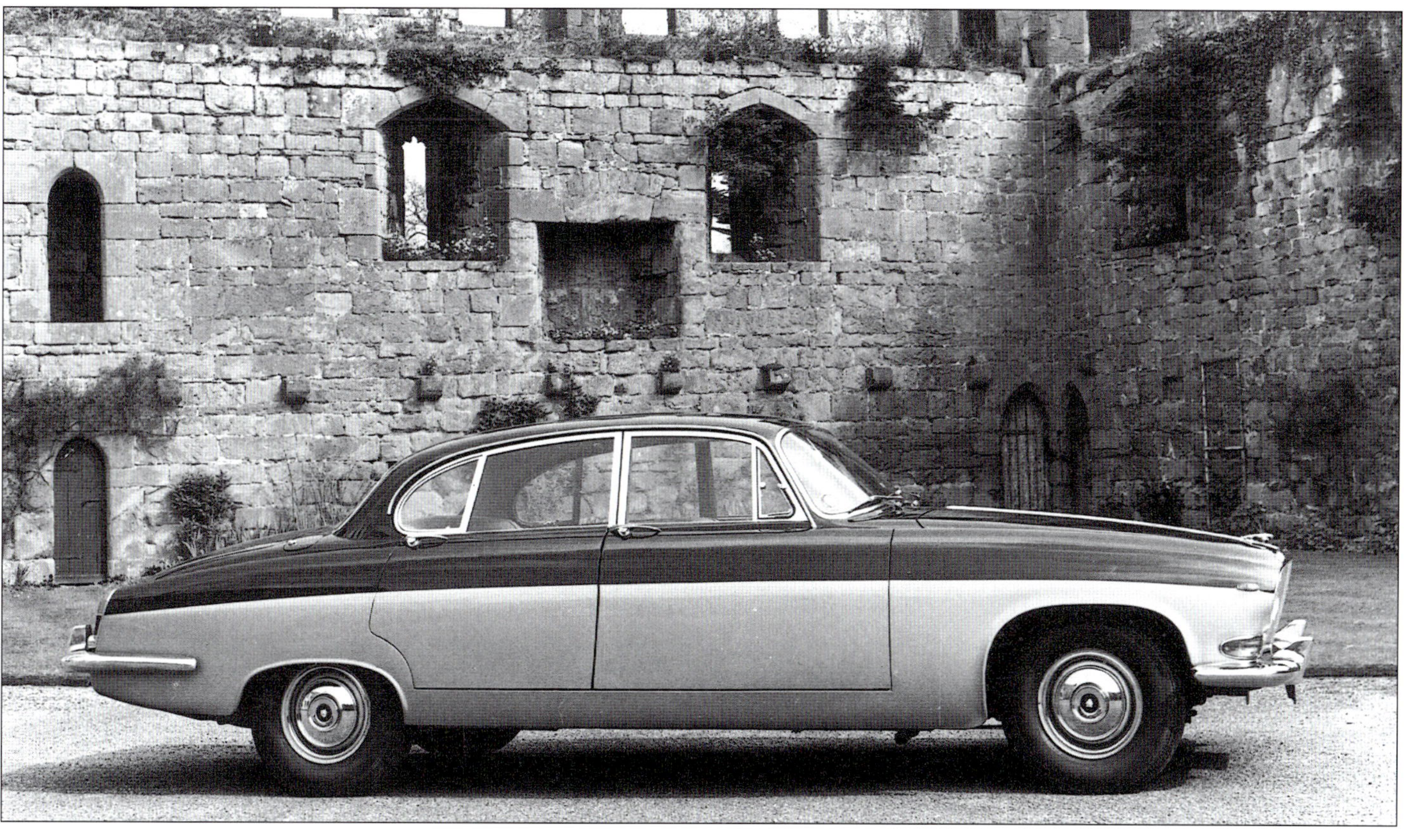

RIGHT: The 420 listed from 1966 was the medium-length S-type car fitted with the 4.2-litre engine, a better specification, and a new nose style.

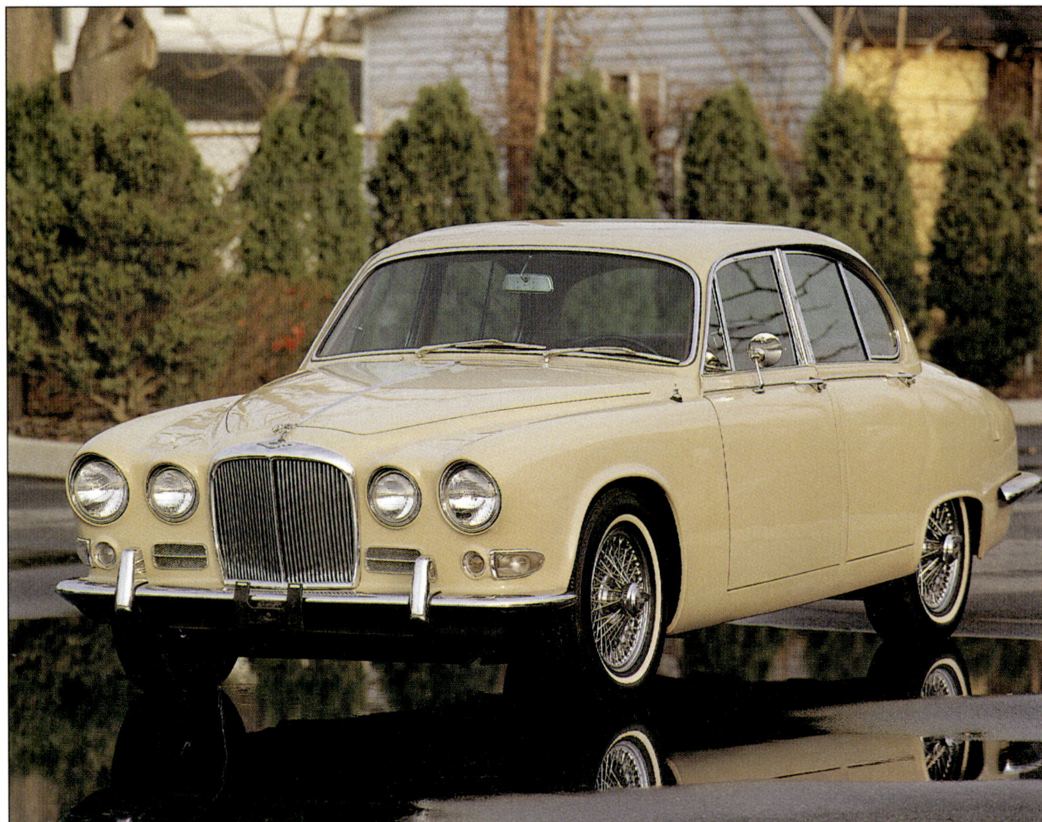

BELOW: The Jaguar 420 became this Daimler Sovereign simply by changing the radiator shell and the badges, and fitting power steering as standard.

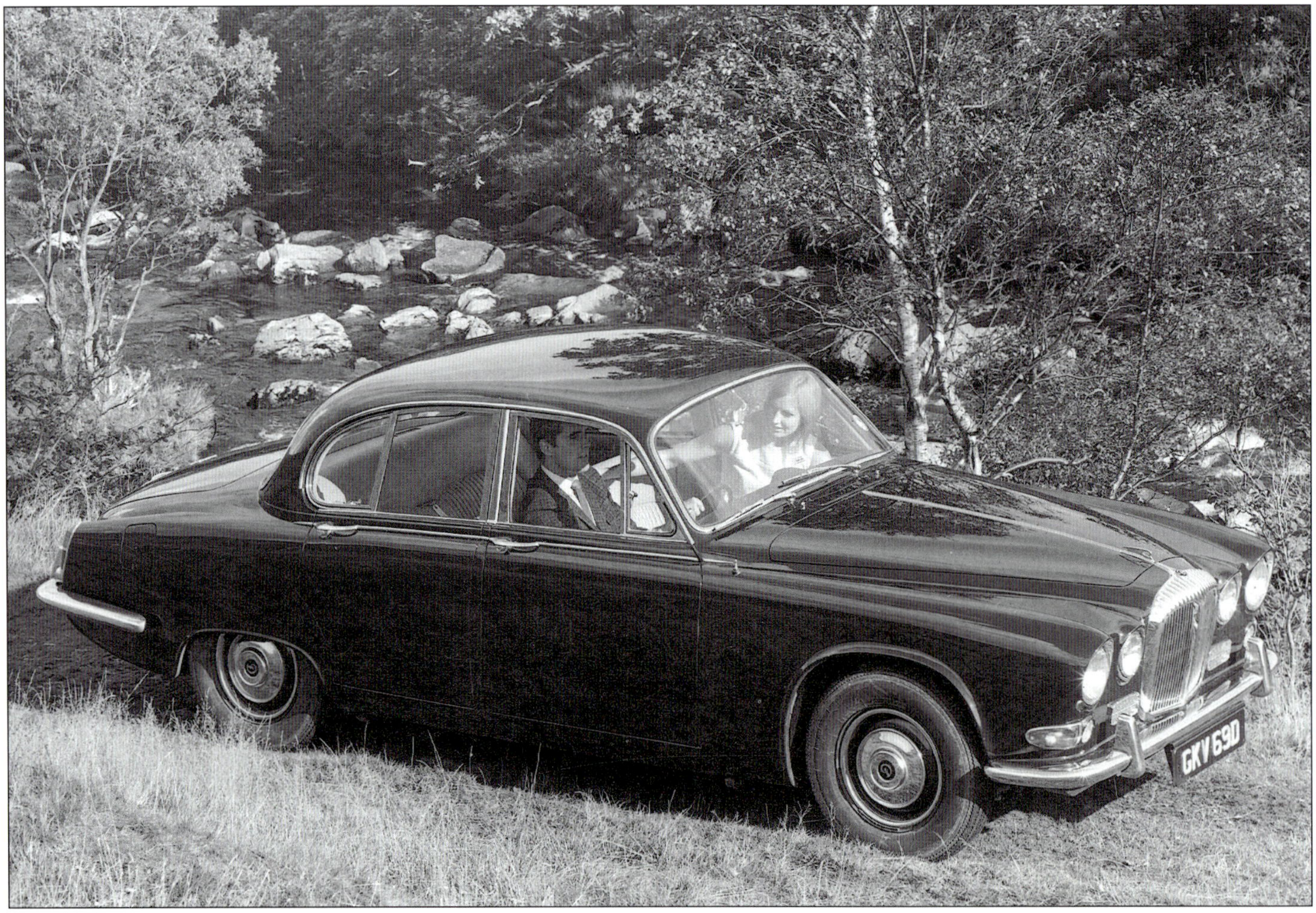

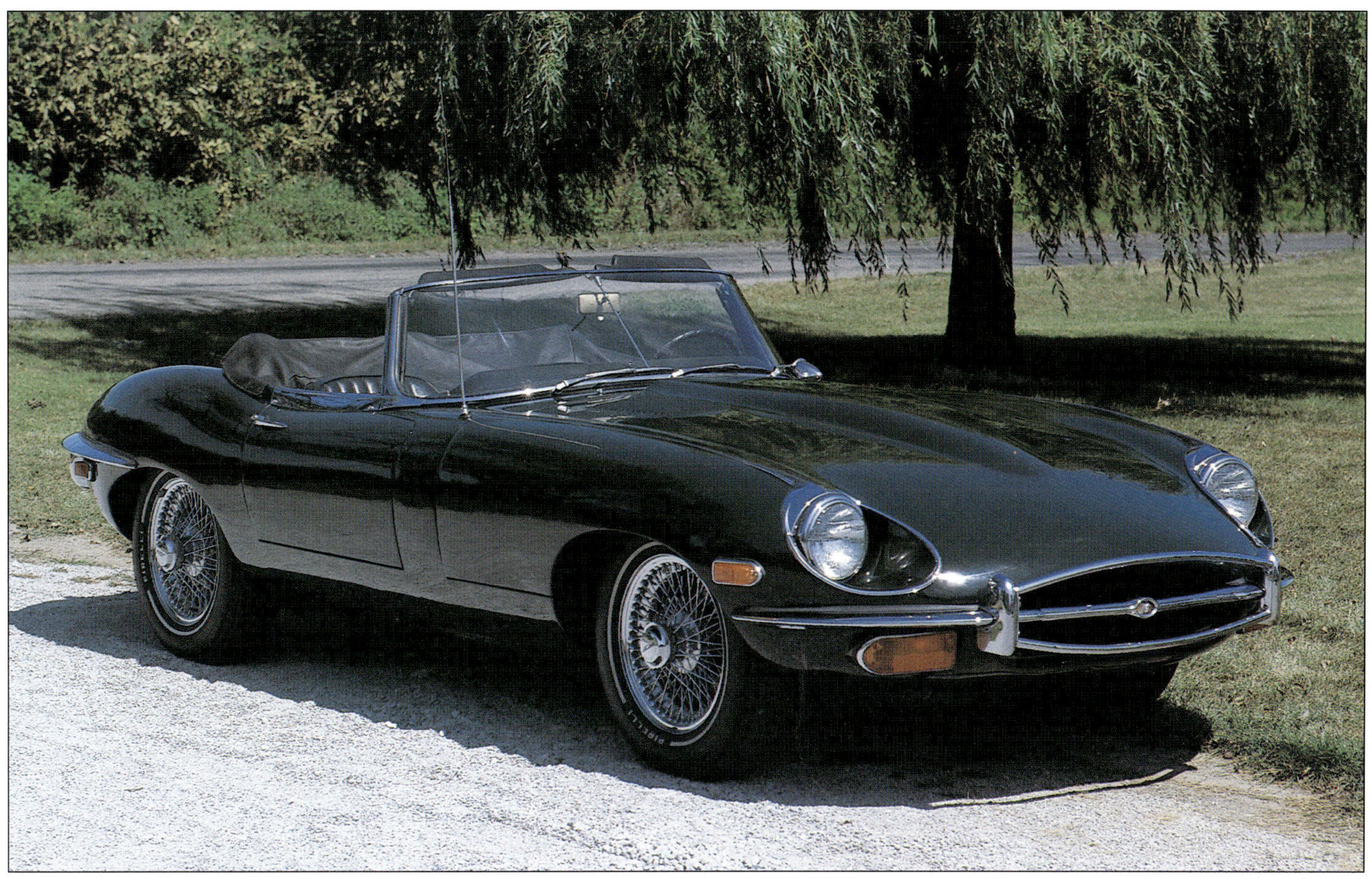

ABOVE: Series II E-type Roadster built from 1968 without the enclosed headlights of the earlier model.
BELOW: Second view of the Series II E-type Roadster, a 1969 car whose clean style was starting to become cluttered.

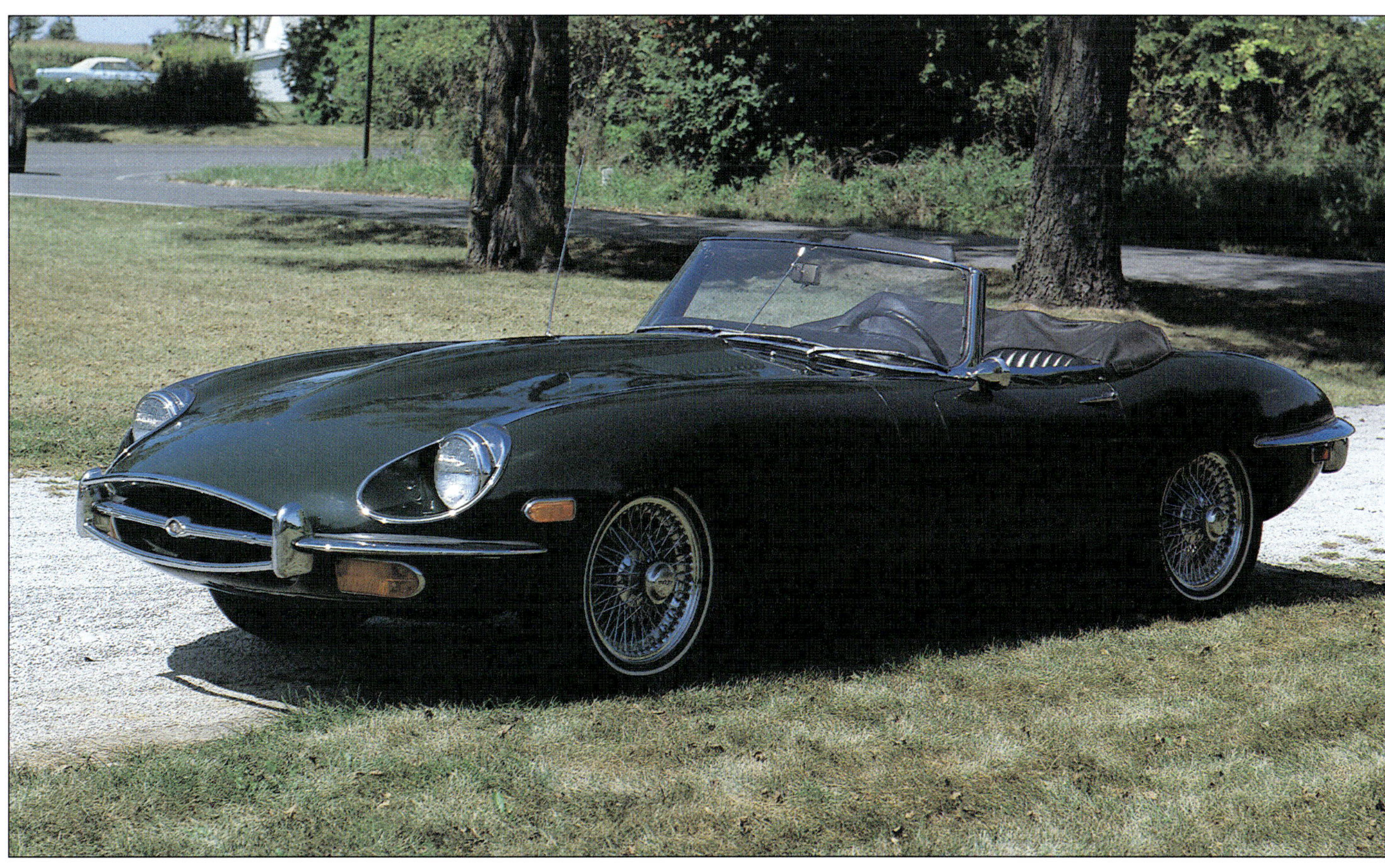

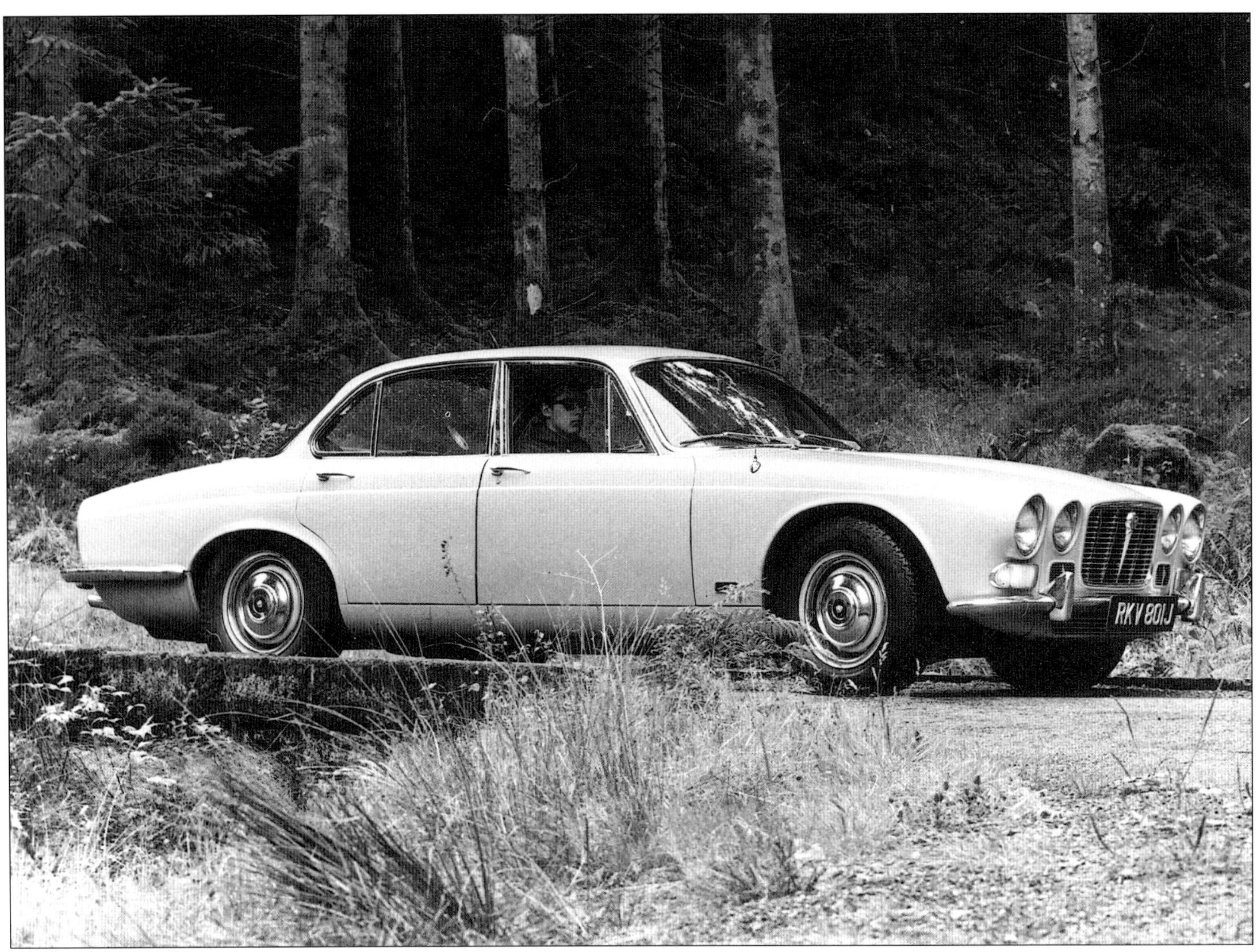

THE XJ LINE
1968-1979

New in 1968, the XJ6 saloon was the first of a series that would run on to modern times, but began with the faithful old twin-cam engine.

THE good news for 1968 was the appearance of the XJ6 saloon that replaced the older cars and was listed as Series I. It was normally fitted with the 4.2-litre engine but could come with the smaller 2,790cc six, this being rare. The XJ6 was a further refinement of the large Jaguar saloon, offering 120mph performance, style, and very full equipment. It was to continue for two decades, as was only fitting for the last of William Lyons's brilliant designs, just as the Swallow, the SS, the XK and the rest had. A Daimler version of the XJ6 appeared in 1969 as the Sovereign Series I, differing only in badges and trim.

Destined to be a larger car and to run even longer was the Daimler DS420. This was based on an extended 420G floorpan and fitted the 4.2-litre engine and Jaguar running gear. On this went an imposing limousine body able to seat seven, built by Motor Panels, and trimmed at first by Vanden Plas, later by Jaguar. A hangover from the days of coachbuilt cars, it was a vehicle for official occasions, dignified and not to be hurried.

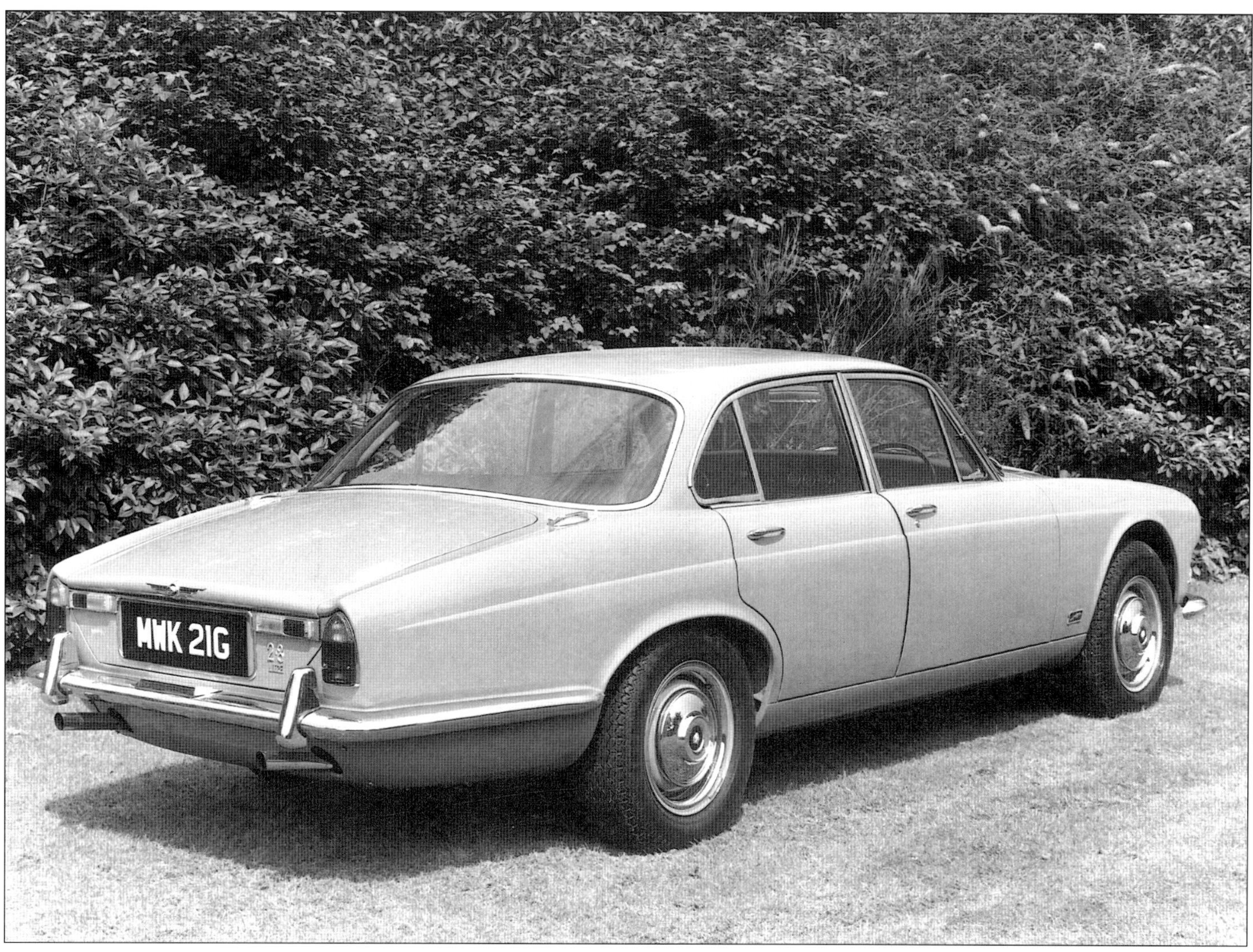

Rear quarter view of the new XJ6 saloon, in this instance fitted with the smaller 2.8-litre engine but just as sleek.

Early in the 1970s the E-type moved on to its final Series III form fitted with a new engine, the magnificent 5,343cc V-12. This had evolved as an addition to the six and, while consideration was given to a V-8, the V-12 gave that extra degree of smoothness and so much more prestige. A single camshaft per bank of cylinders was deemed enough, reducing noise and complexity compared with an experimental twin cam. It proved more than adequate.

The Series III E-type was built in Roadster and 2+2 coupé styles, both on the longer wheelbase floorpan that just allowed the all-alloy engine and its ancillaries to be squeezed in. The extra capacity put the speed back up to the 150mph mark for the last few years of a great car.

Jaguar soon found other uses for its new engine with the XJ12 Series I appearing in 1972 and able to match the E-type in speed and silence but at the cost of a considerable thirst. Other than the engine, the car was the XJ6 and later in the year was joined by a version having a longer wheelbase. Soon afterwards came the Daimler Double Six Series I in both lengths and a simple badge job.

For 1974 the XJ6 in 2.8- and 4.2-litre sizes moved on to the Series II with minor changes and was mirrored by the Sovereign in 4.2-litre guise only. The XJ12 and Daimler Double Six followed suit, always with the longer wheelbase that was to become the norm for the sixes in time.

In 1975 the 3.4-litre engine was added as an alternative for the XJ6 and Sovereign while Jaguar and Daimler coupés extended the model line. For Jaguar

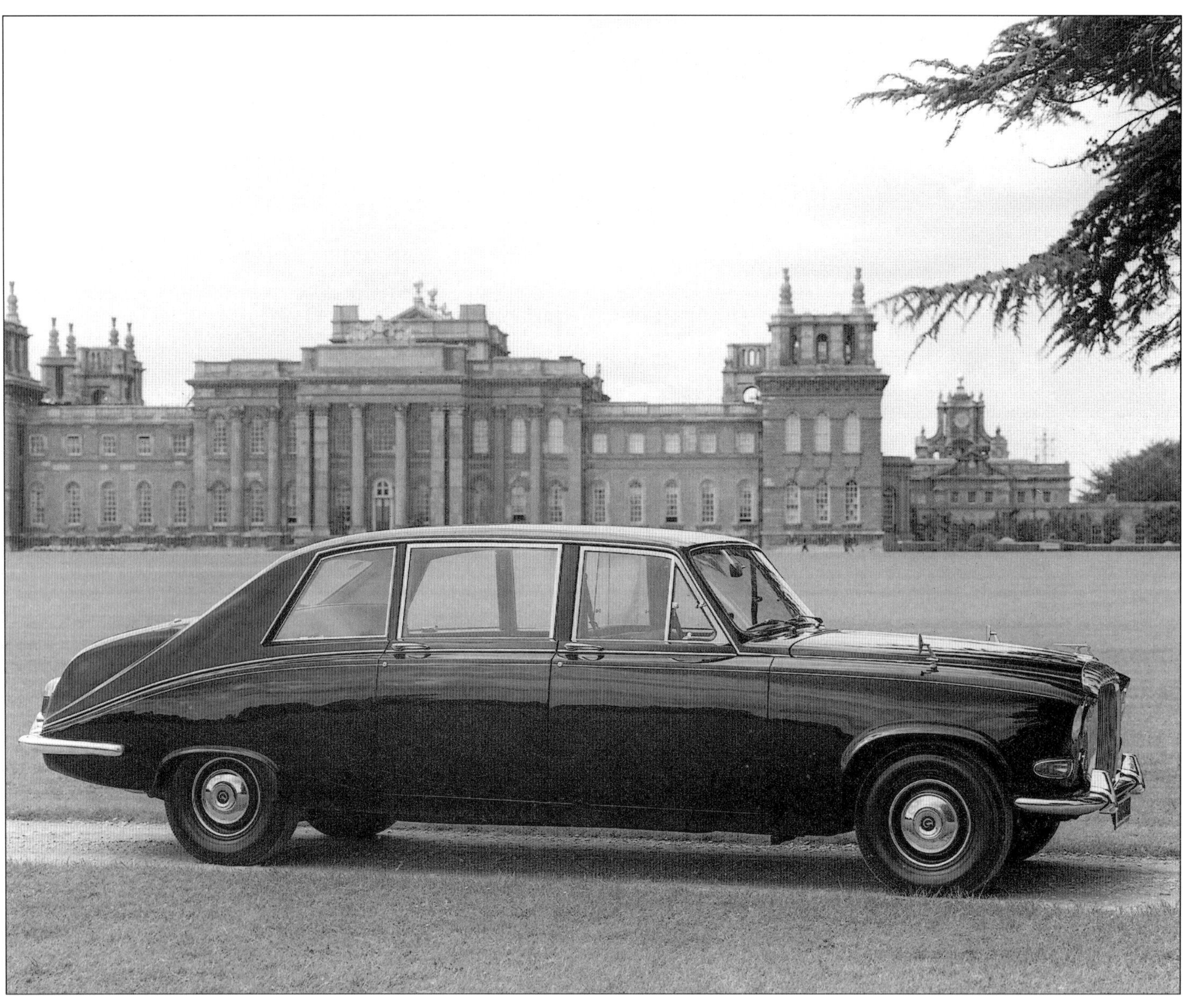

Old fashioned but stately Daimler DS420 in limousine form with coachwork by Vanden Plas. This model was produced for many years, the example illustrated dating from 1976.

there was the XJ6C and XJ5.3C that used the six or V-12 engines in the shorter wheelbase XJ6 chassis under a two-door, pillarless, five-seat coupé body. For Daimler they changed the badges.

There was one further coupé for 1975, intended as a replacement for the E-type, listed as the XJ-S, and only built as a Jaguar with two doors and four seats using the V-12 engine. The wheelbase was further reduced and the body style was not to everyone's taste, being cramped for four, but it slid through the air up to 155mph.

It was 1979 before there were any noticeable changes to the range and then it was to move on to Series III models. The sixes became the XJ 3.4 and XJ 4.2 with the upper part of the saloon body mildly restyled and with a sleeker front end. The manual gearbox had five speeds and the Daimler version was only built with the larger engine, still as the Sovereign but much later simply as the '4.2'. The XJ12 and Double Six had the same changes but not the manual transmission while the XJ-S simply ran on.

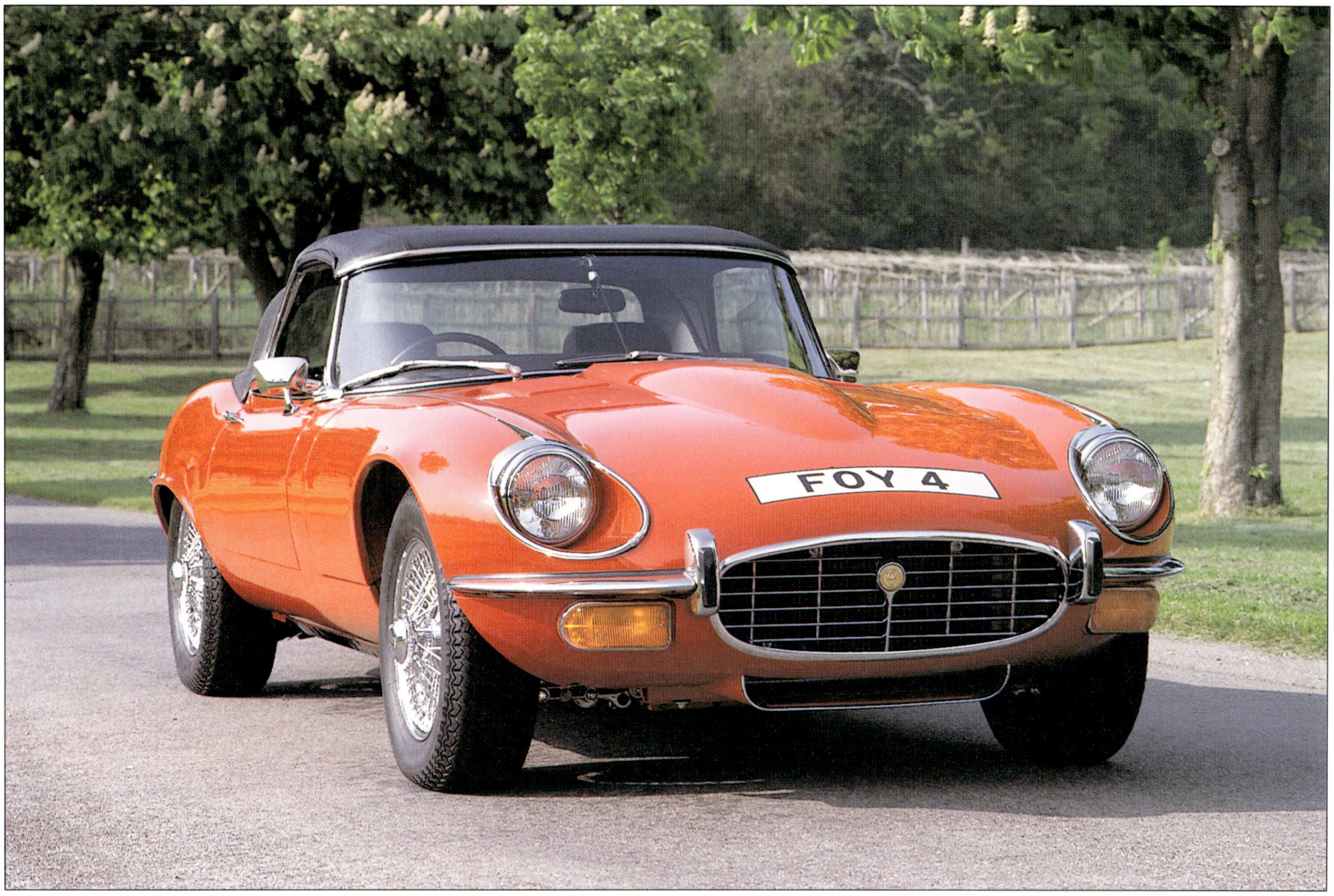

ABOVE: Final Series III style of the E-type built from 1971 when it was fitted with the magnificent V-12 engine.
BELOW: The longer wheelbase of the Series III E-type went some way to restoring the fine line as this rebuilt car, seen in 1990, shows.

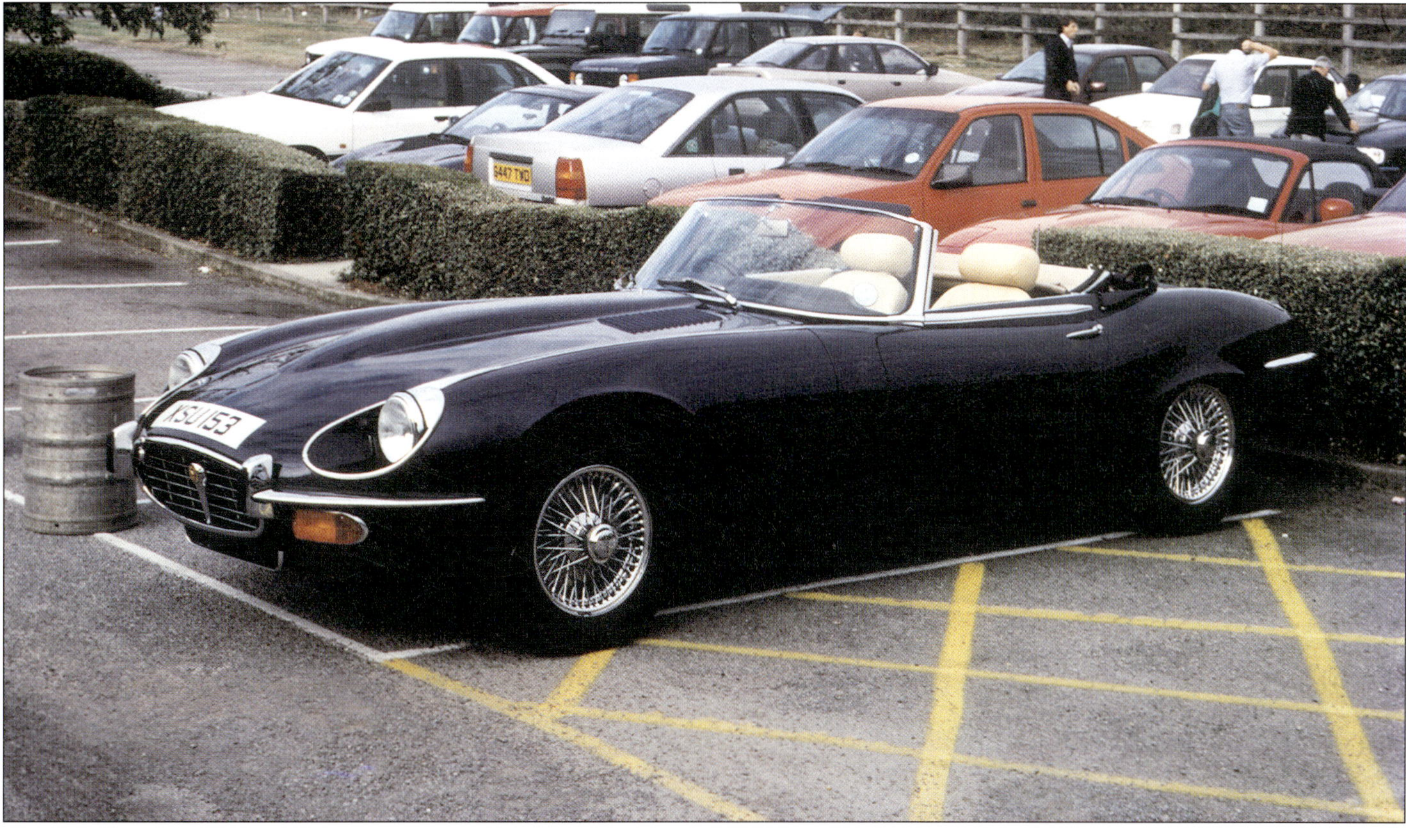

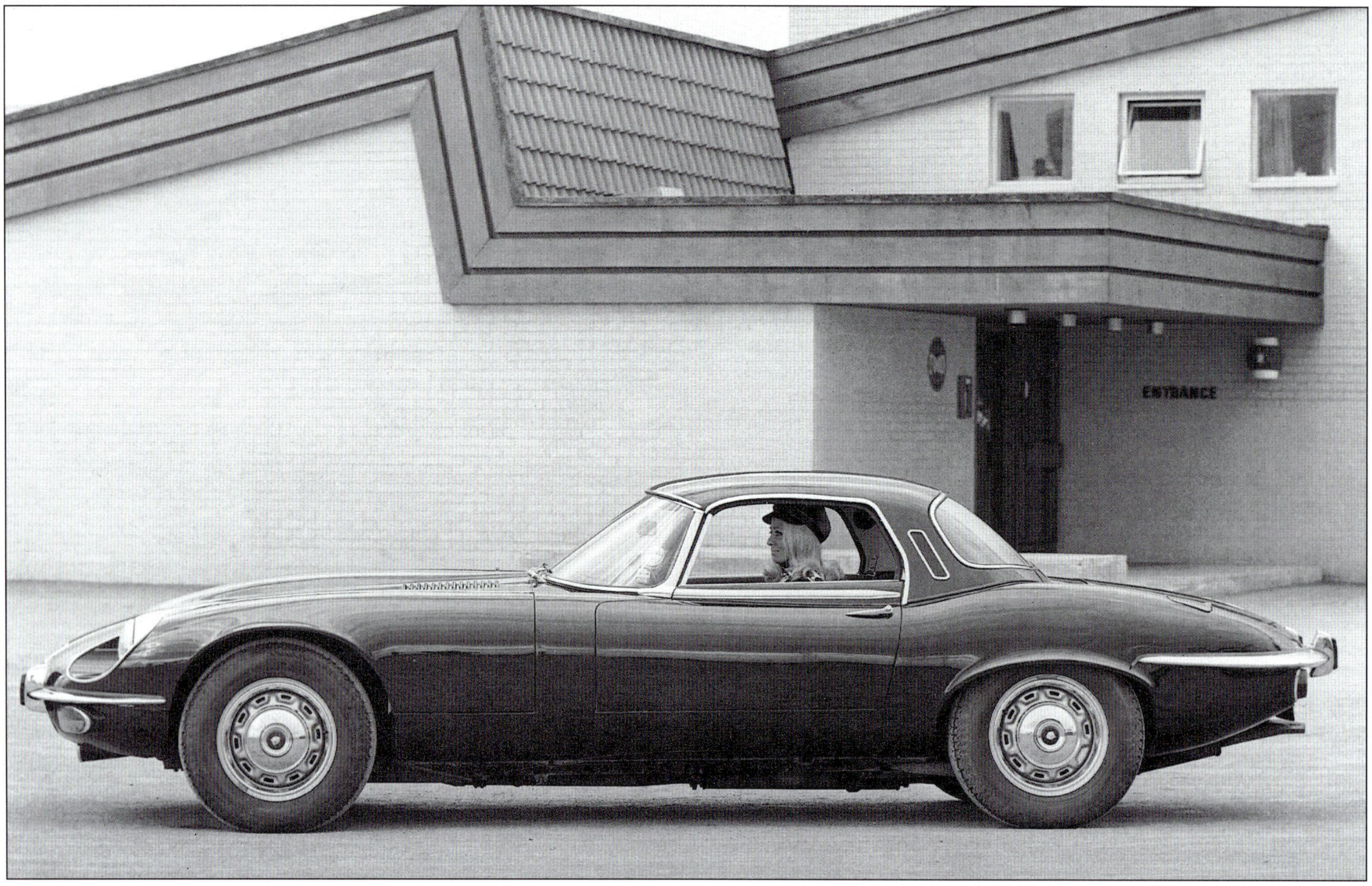

ABOVE: The 2+2 coupé version of the Series III E-type showing off its fine sweeping lines in 1971.
BELOW: Still able to run close to 150mph after 20 years thanks to its great V-12 engine and smooth shape, the Series III E-type.

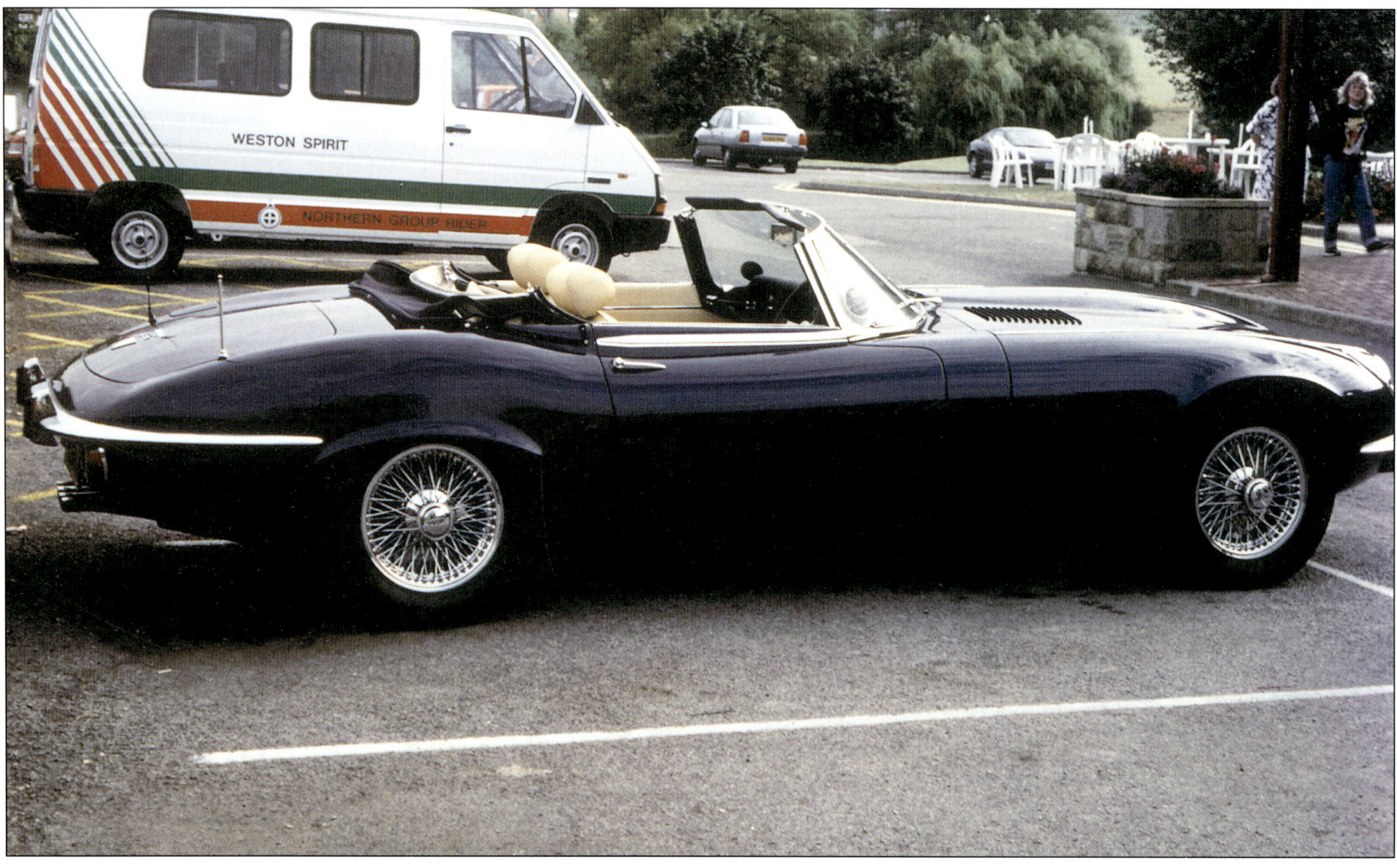

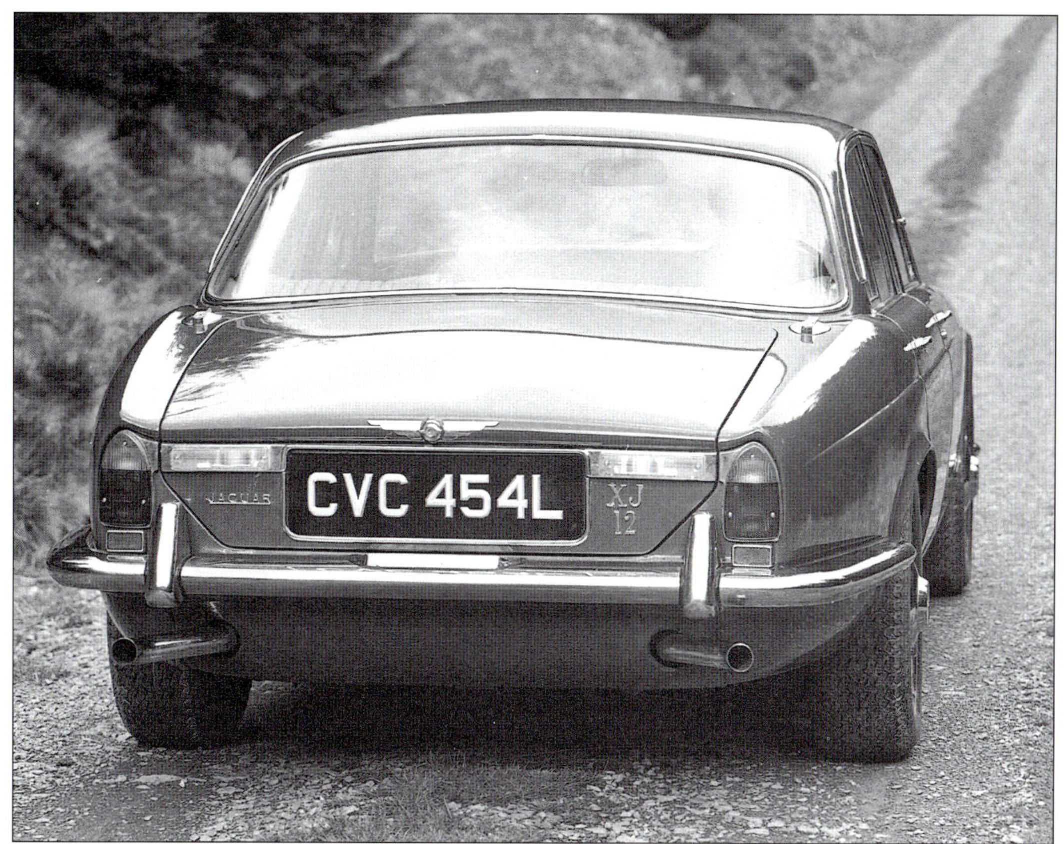

LEFT: The new V-12 engine was soon fitted into the saloon body to create the XJ12 that carried a discreet badge to tell other drivers.

BELOW: Daimler Double Six with the V-12 engine and, aside from the radiator, a Jaguar XJ12 with the same flowing lines and performance.

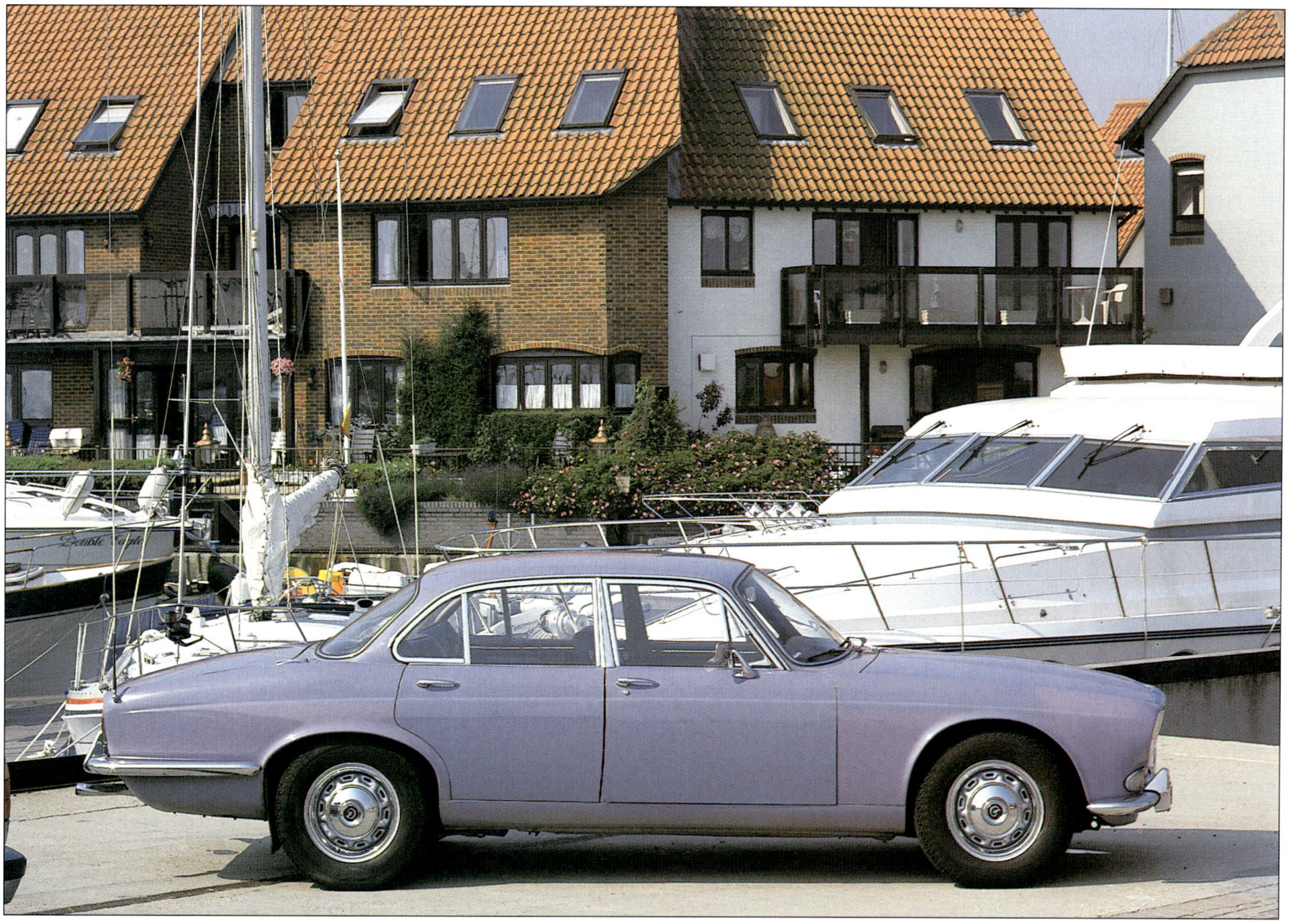

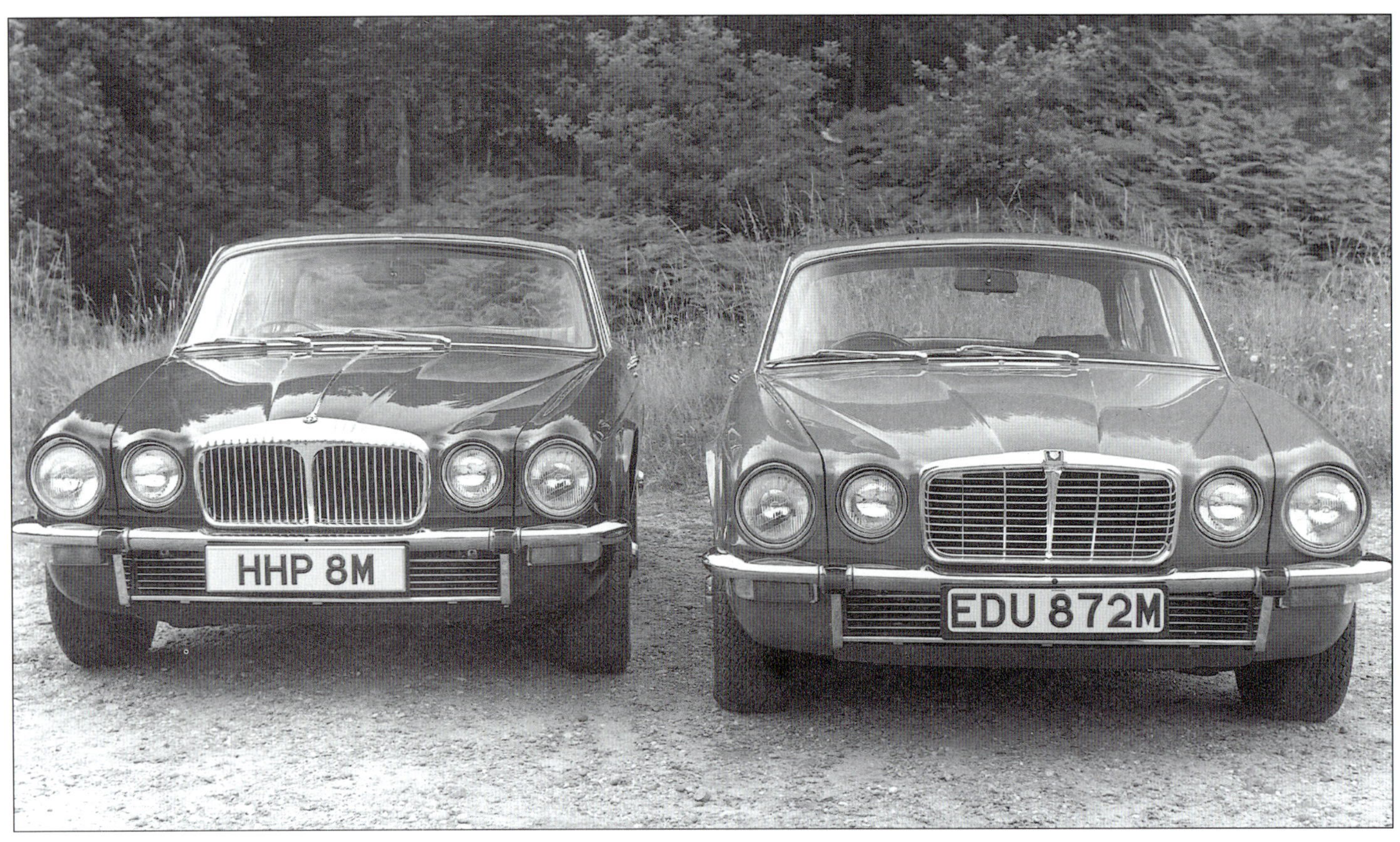

ABOVE: Series II models appeared in 1974 as the long-wheelbase XJ6 on the right and matching Daimler Sovereign to the left.
BELOW: The XJ12 saloon became a Series II model in 1974, this fine example from four years later and with a 'V' incorporated in its badge.

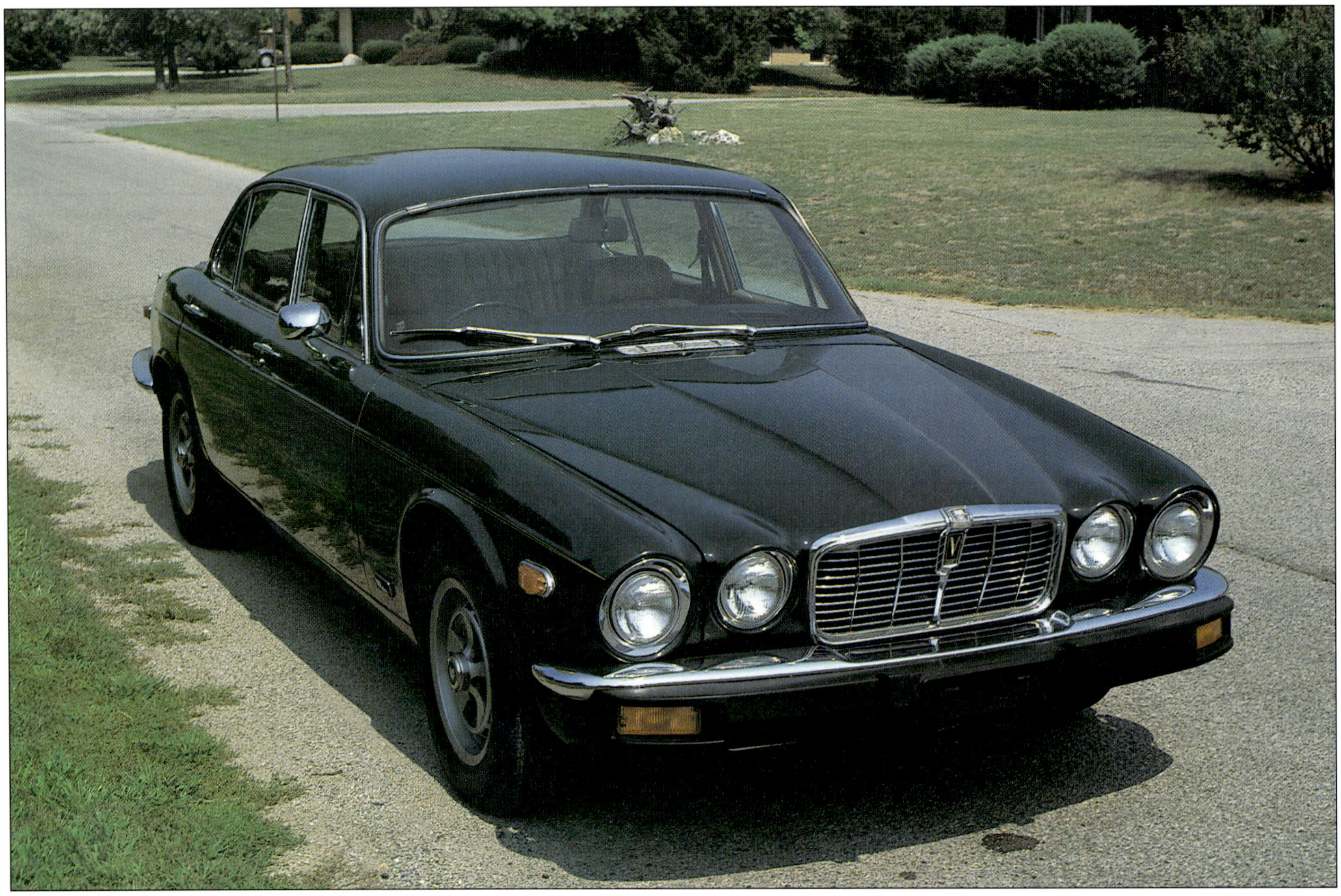

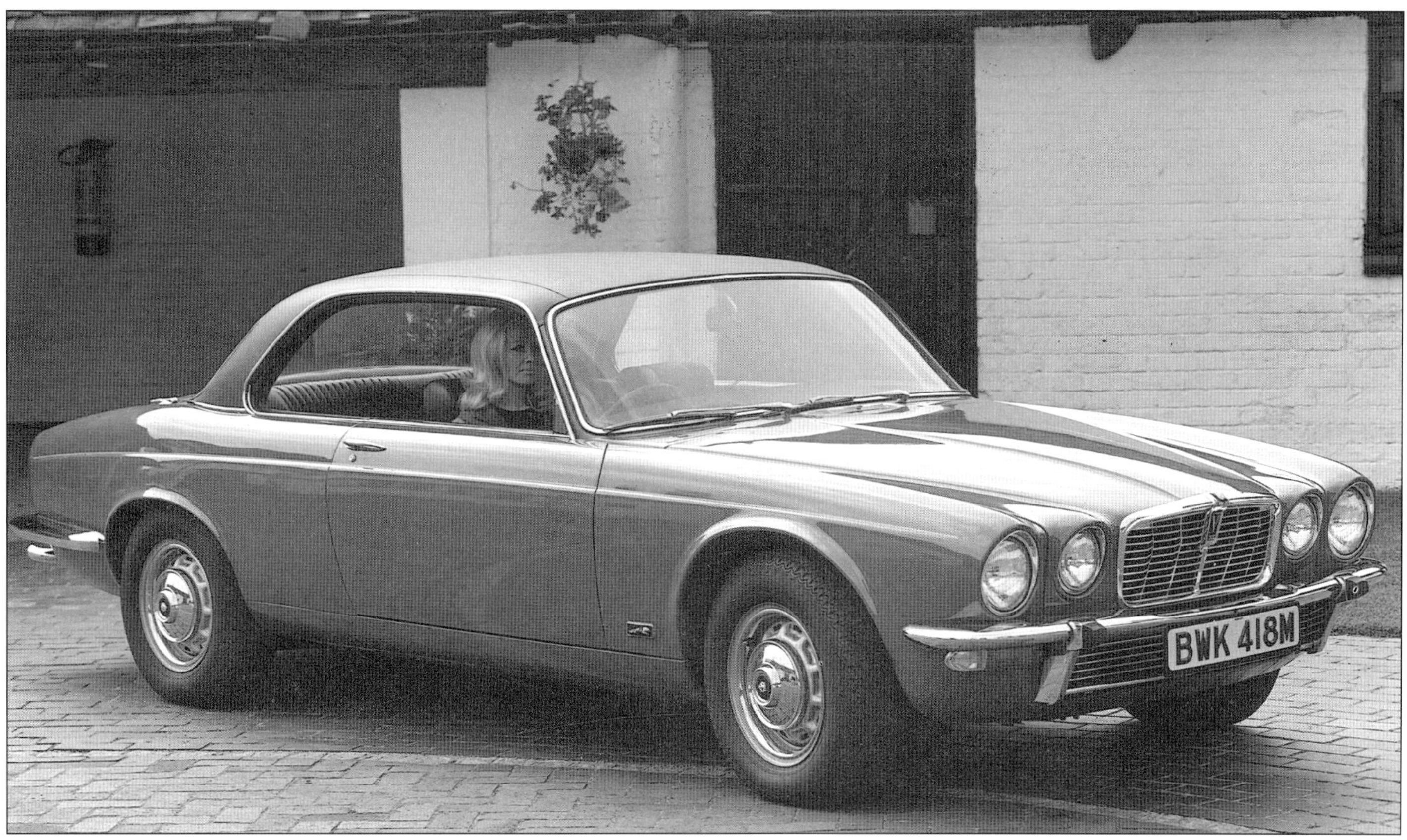

ABOVE: This two-door coupé took over from the E-type in 1975, and was announced as the XJ12C but listed as the XJ5.3C in the salesroom.
BELOW: The smaller XJ6C coupé that shared the body style and most of the mechanics of the V-12 car.

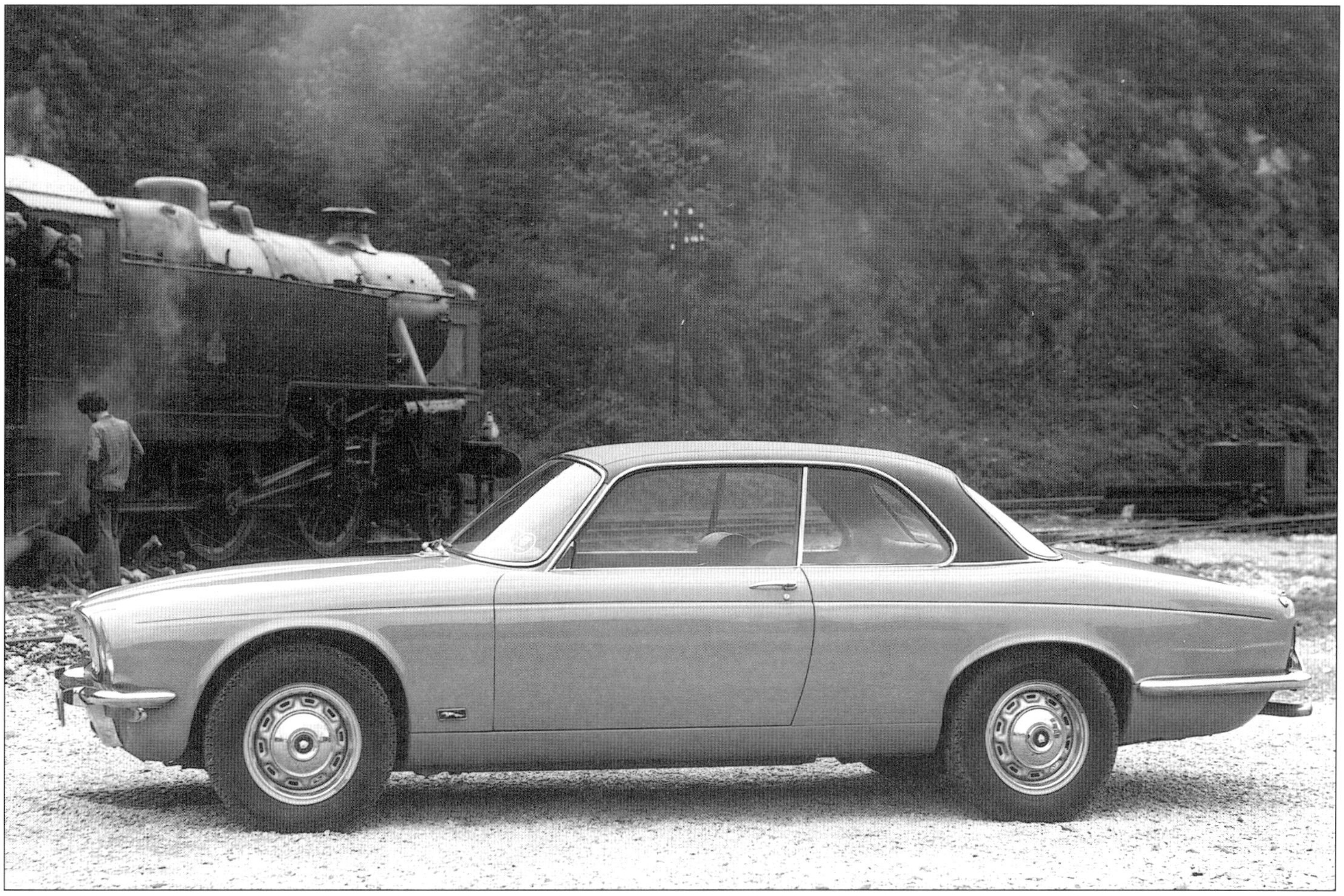

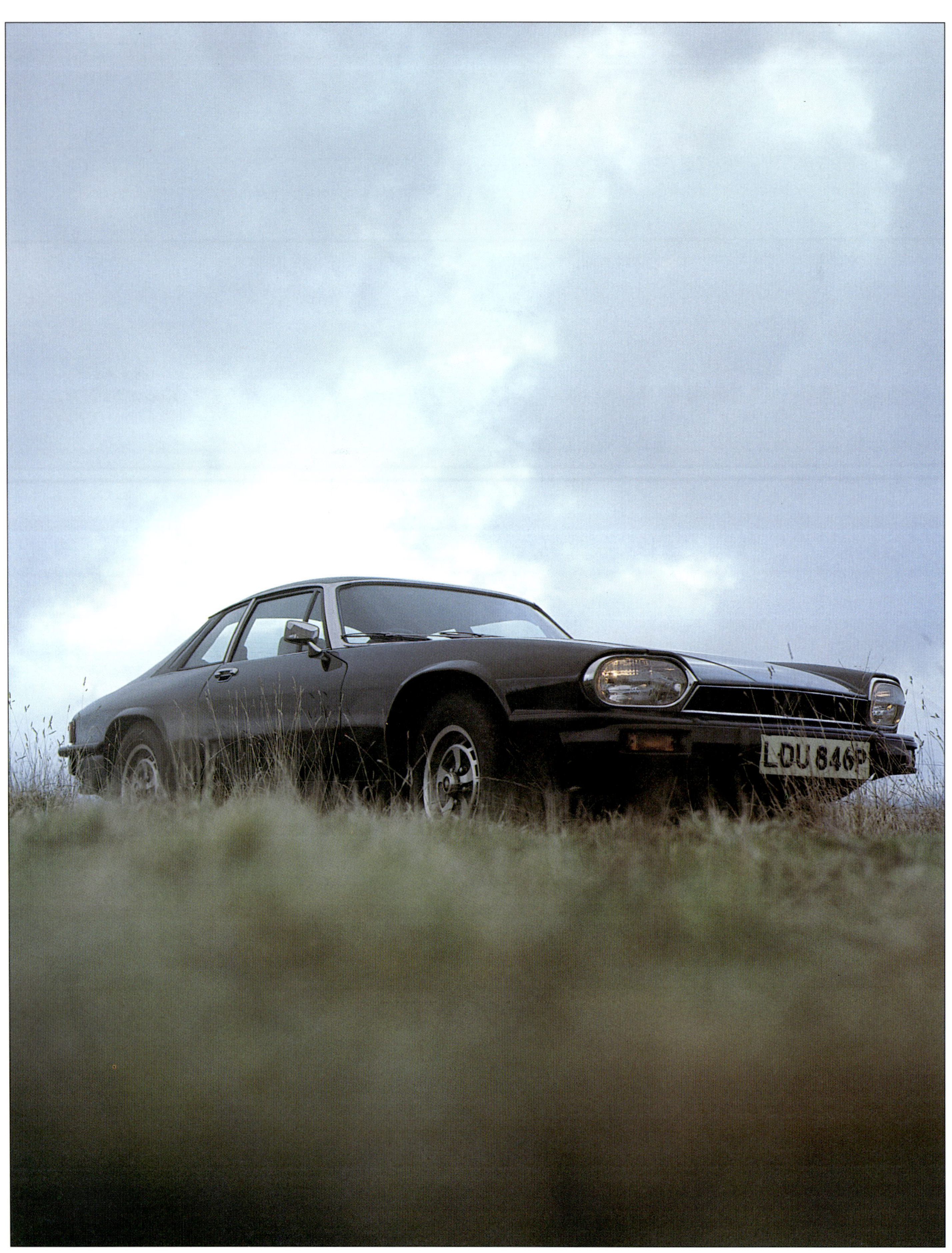

Built as a two-door coupé for four, the XJ-S fitted the V-12 engine, could run to 155mph and remained in production to 1993.

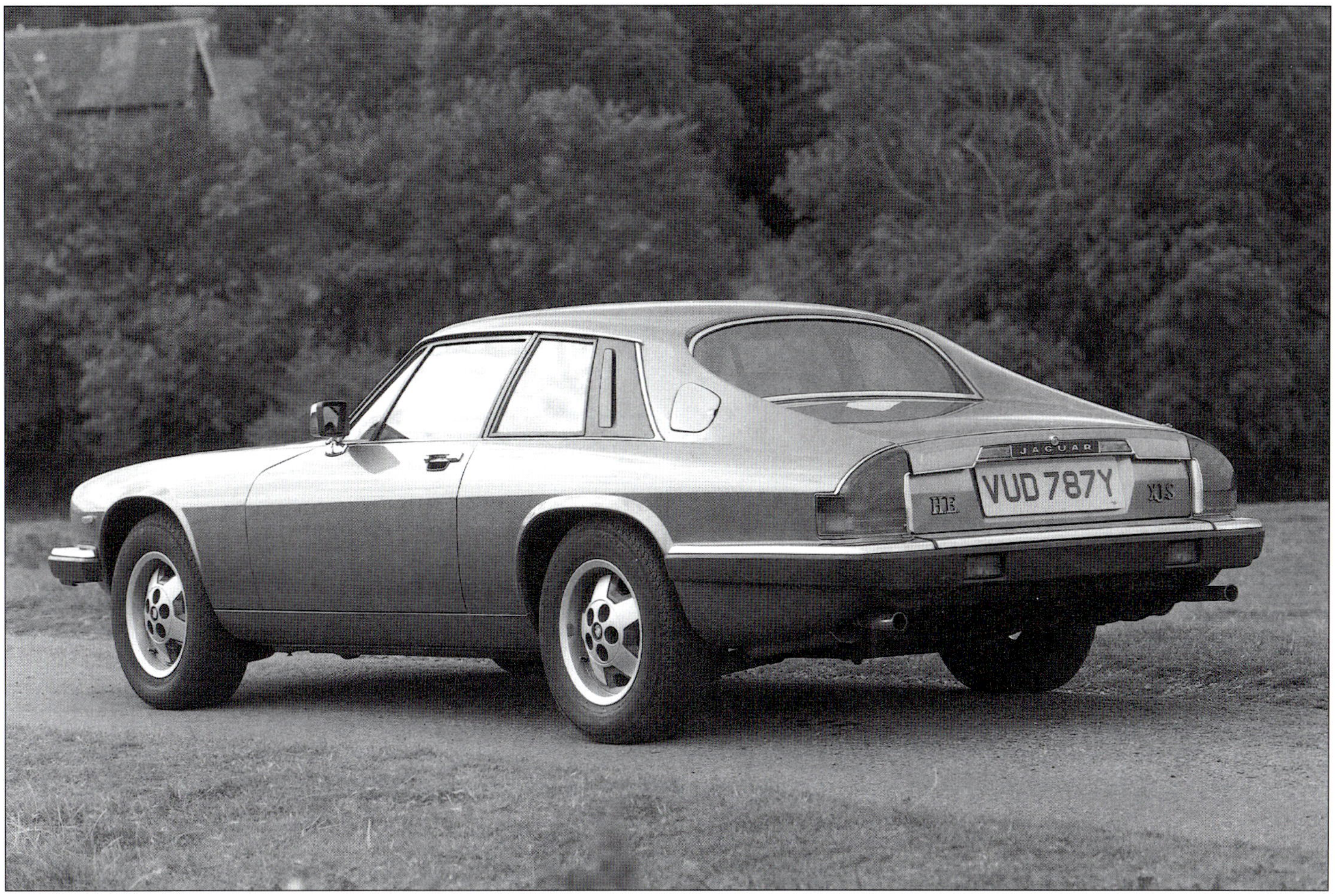

ABOVE: Rear quarter view of the XJ-S showing the fine lines that allowed it to slide through the air so easily.
BELOW: The XJ6 saloons took Series III form from 1979, this the better equipped Sovereign build as for 1984.

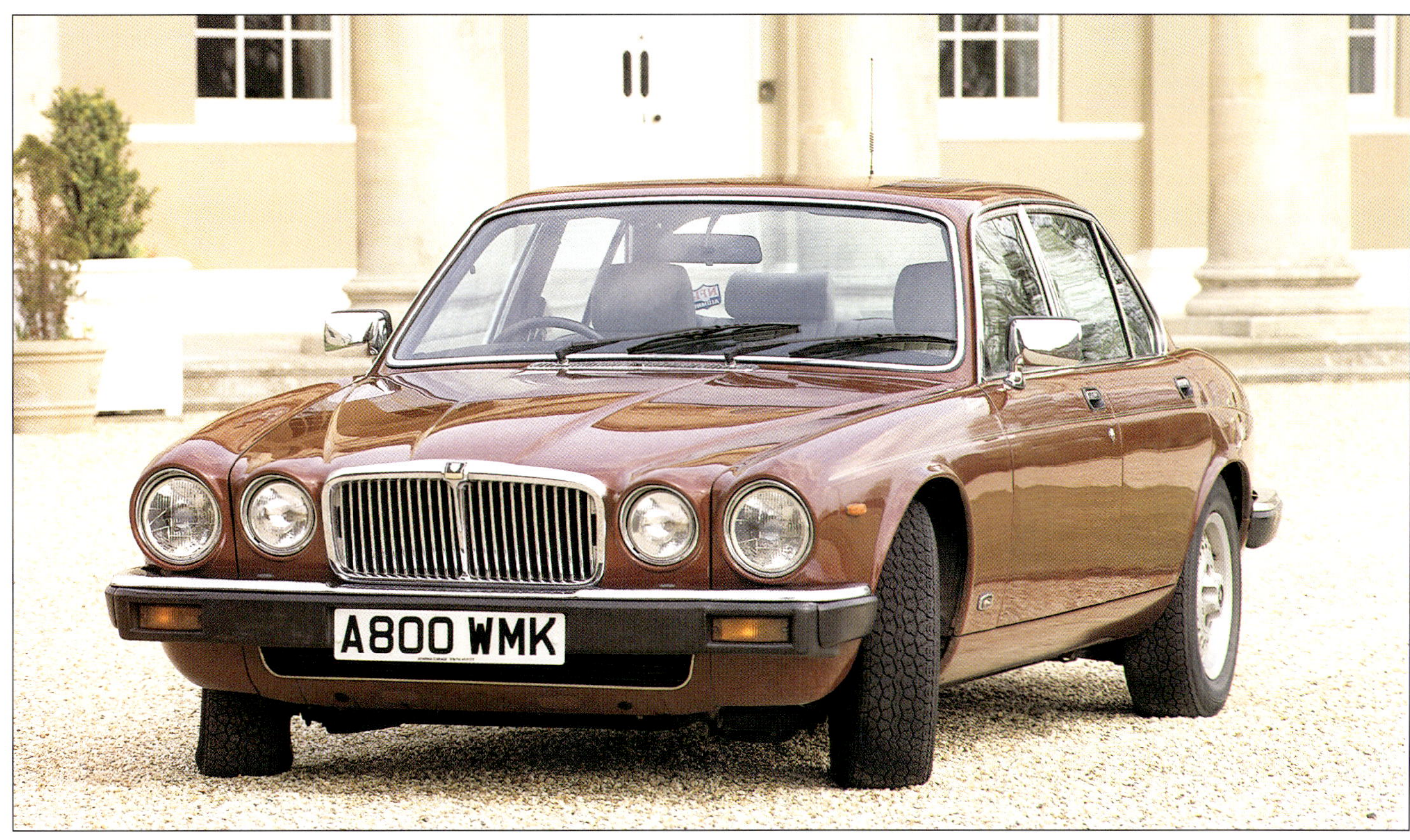

JAGUAR ALONE AGAIN

1980-1989

IN 1980 the name of Jaguar Cars returned to the Browns Lane factory in Coventry, away from the British Leyland conglomerate, and in 1984 it went public, the share floatation being well over-subscribed. From the start of the decade major steps were taken to boost the quality and reliability of the cars and the efficiency of all aspects of the business. It took time but it did happen, productivity boomed and build standards rose dramatically.

Sadly, Sir William Lyons died early in 1985, but not before he had seen the renaissance of the firm he had founded so long ago.

Prior to then, in 1983, the sports line was extended to add the XJ-S 3.6 in coupé and cabriolet forms. As well as bringing back an open model, the first since the end of the E-type in the mid-1970s, the company introduced a new 3.6-litre engine as the start of the process of replacing the aged XK-six. The engine remained a twin-cam six but had four valves per cylinder, was of all-alloy construction and much more fuel-efficient thanks to its more modern and compact combustion chambers.

The coupé was as for the XJ-S but to create the cabriolet Jaguar had to add an amount of bracing to restore the hull rigidity. The final design had roof panels that lifted off, a style known as Targa in Europe, and a folding rear screen. Two years later the XJ-S 5.3 Cabriolet was added using the same body but both versions were dropped late in 1987.

Before then the XJ12 became listed as the Sovereign in 1983 and in 1986 this name began to be applied to better equipped versions of a new range of XJ6 models. These used a new body known as the XJ40 and were fitted with either the

Side view of the 1984 XJ6 4.2 Sovereign that shows the fine lines of the mildly restyled body.

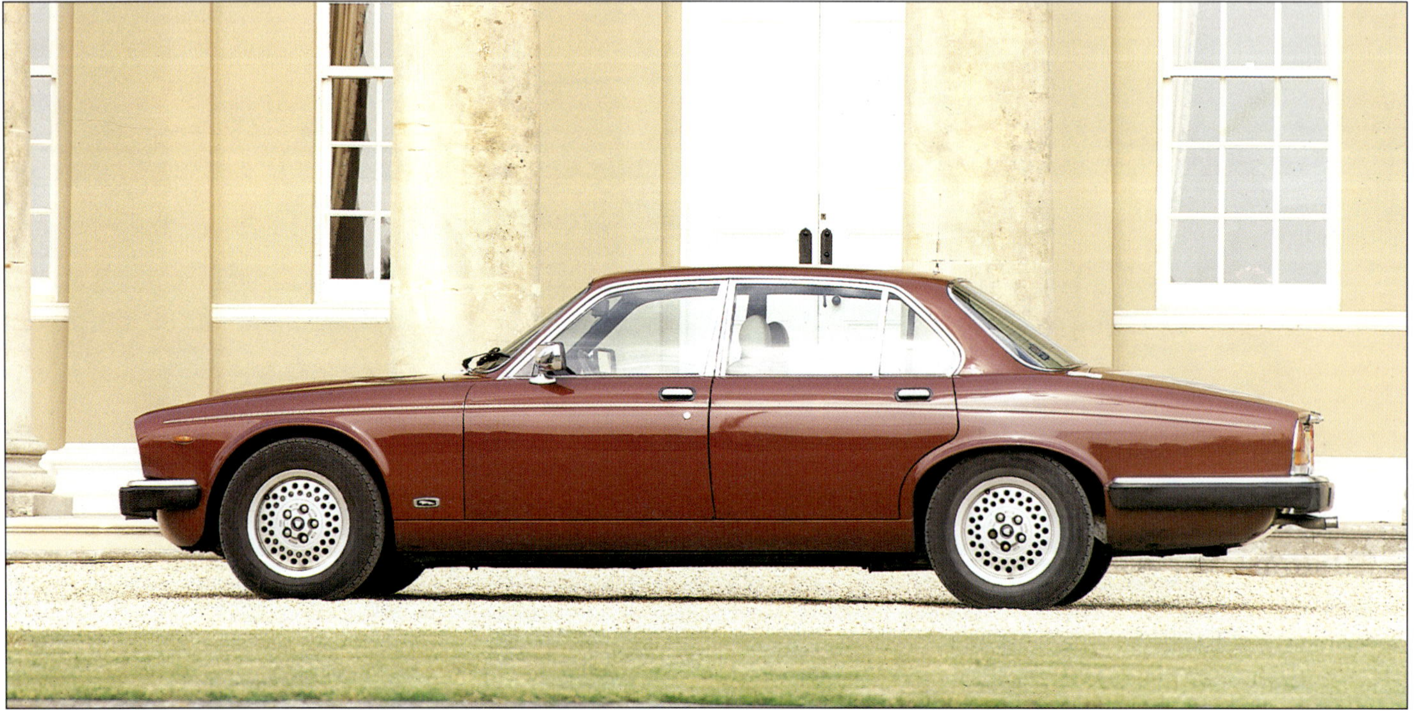

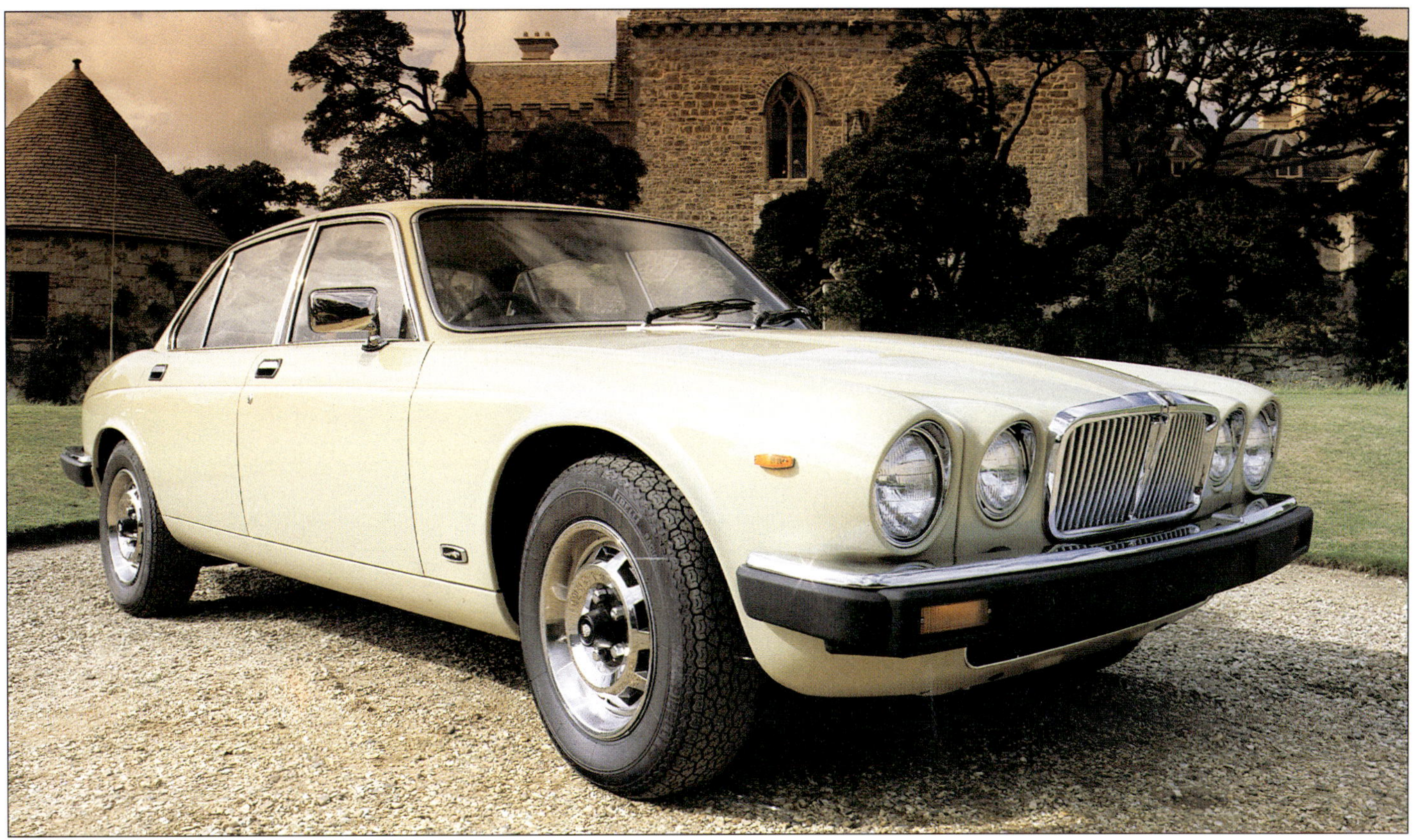

ABOVE: Series III XJ6 fitted with the 3.4-litre engine but otherwise as the other models, in this case a 1982 car.
BELOW: To celebrate 50 years of Jaguar, dealer Guy Salmon produced this Golden Jubilee XJ-S model with discreet gold plating touches.

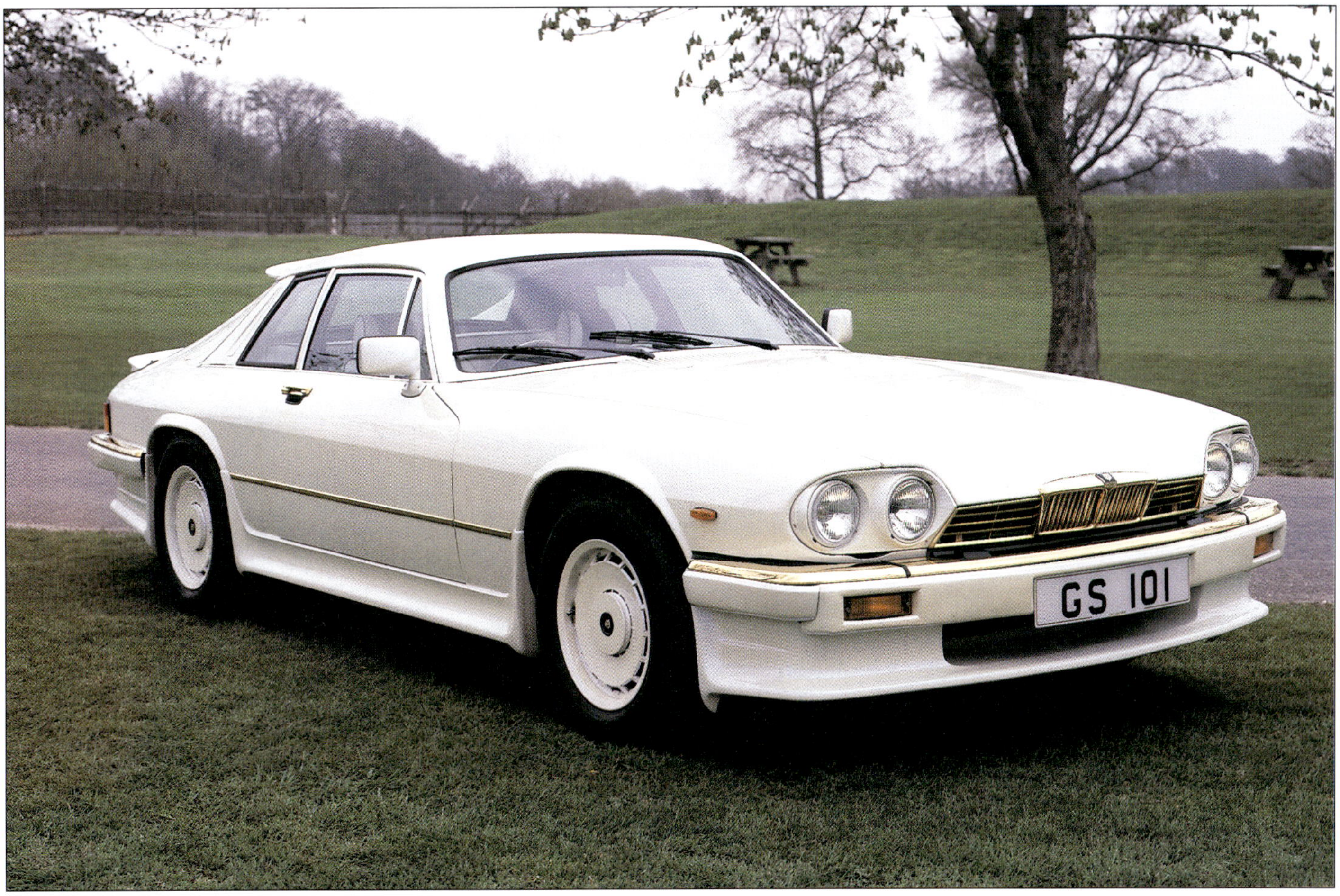

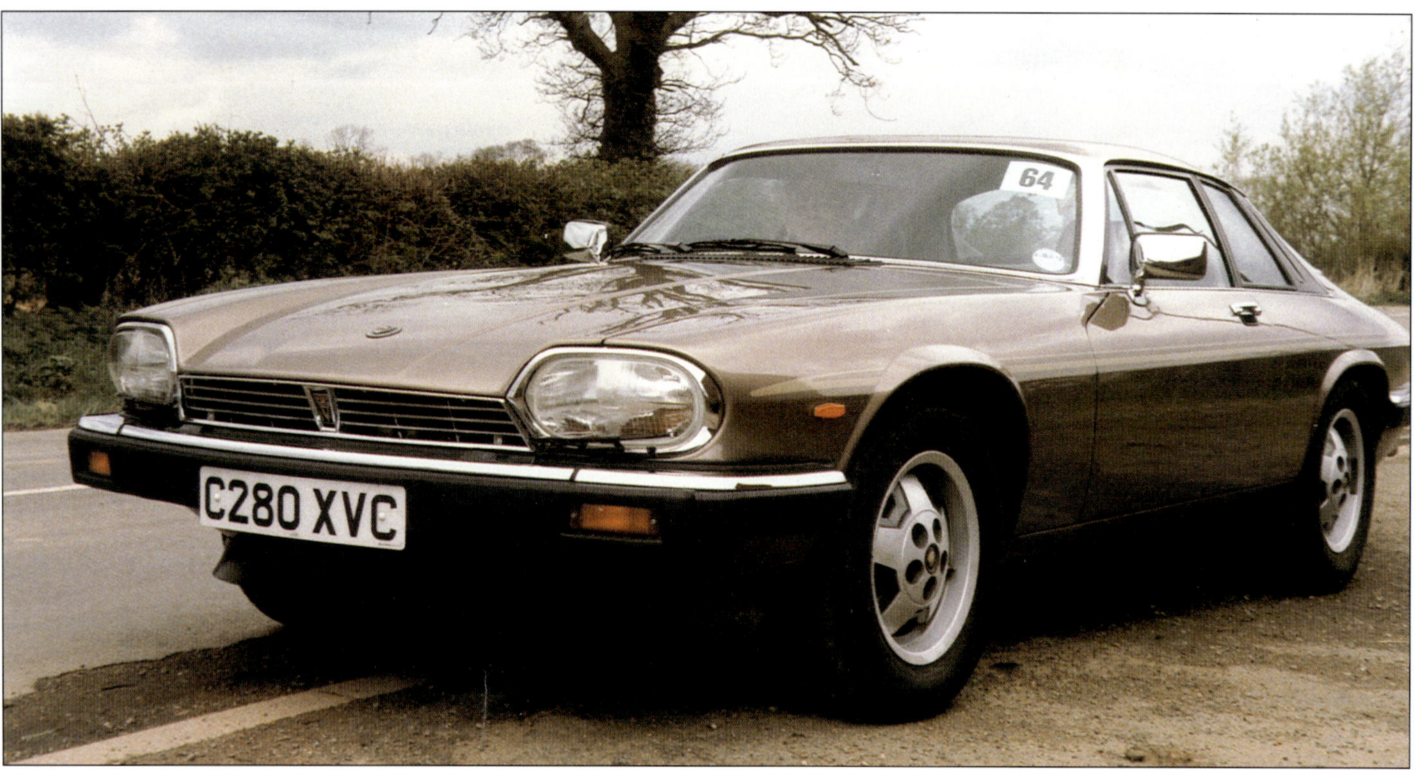

Standard 1985 XJ-S 5.3 Coupé, with the V-12 engine, being enjoyed by the author who found it most pleasing to drive.

new 3.6-litre engine from the XJ-S or a 2.9-litre version that had just two valves per cylinder and a single overhead camshaft.

Transmission for all was a five-speed manual or four-speed automatic, the latter having a J-gate selection lever. This gave the driver the option of choosing drive on one side to let the car do the work, the other allowing the choice of three manual positions to gear for road conditions. The Sovereign versions had different headlight styling and came with options such as ABS brakes and air conditioning as standard. The Daimler version was, if anything, better equipped and only built with the 3.6-litre engine.

For 1988 the cabriolet body was further strengthened to produce the open XJ-S 5.3 Convertible with an electric folding hood, the V-12 engine still able to push it up to the 150mph mark. The year also brought Jaguar Sport versions of the XJ saloons listed as the XJR 3.6 and the XJR-S 5.3, these based on the coupé body with sports suspension plus a small rear spoiler.

Late in 1988 Jaguar unveiled its XJ220 concept car at the British Motor Show, utilising the V-12 engine mounted aft of the cockpit in a very low and sleek package. Some of this came from the XJR-9 that had taken the firm to its sixth Le Mans victory, the first since 1957, and the XJR-8 of 1987 that had taken the world sports car title, winning eight of the ten events.

The XJ6 3.6 was replaced by the larger XJ6 4.0 for 1989 along with the Sovereign 4.0 and later the Daimler 4.0. The XJ12, having been the Sovereign for some years, became simply the V12. The next year saw the smaller XJ6 grow to be the XJ6 3.2 and Sovereign 3.2 while the V-12 sports model was stretched to 5,993cc to become the XJR-S 6.0. At the same time the smaller XJR became the XJR 4.0 to follow the trend of the saloon. From a year or two earlier the sports cars were handled by JaguarSport and offered improvements in handling as well as the extra urge. This led to a Sports Handling Pack for 1991 that was generally available for most of the range as the car and means of controlling it became ever more sophisticated.

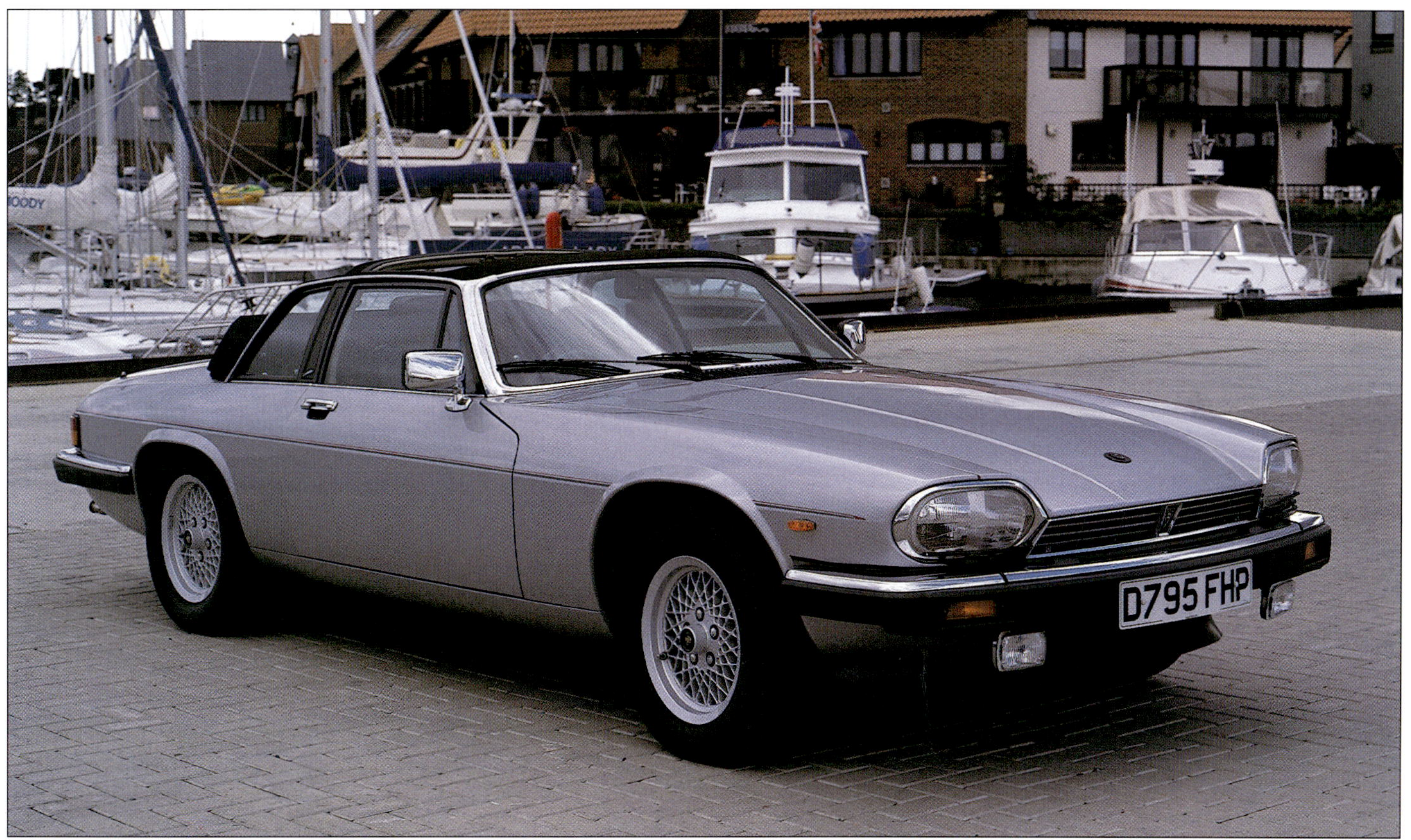

ABOVE: Cabriolet version of the XJ-S 5.3 built from 1985 with braced hull to restore the strength lost in the removal of the saloon top and needed to cope with V-12 power.
BELOW: This view of the XJ-S 5.3 Cabriolet shows the Targa-type roof with its detachable panels removed and rear screen furled.

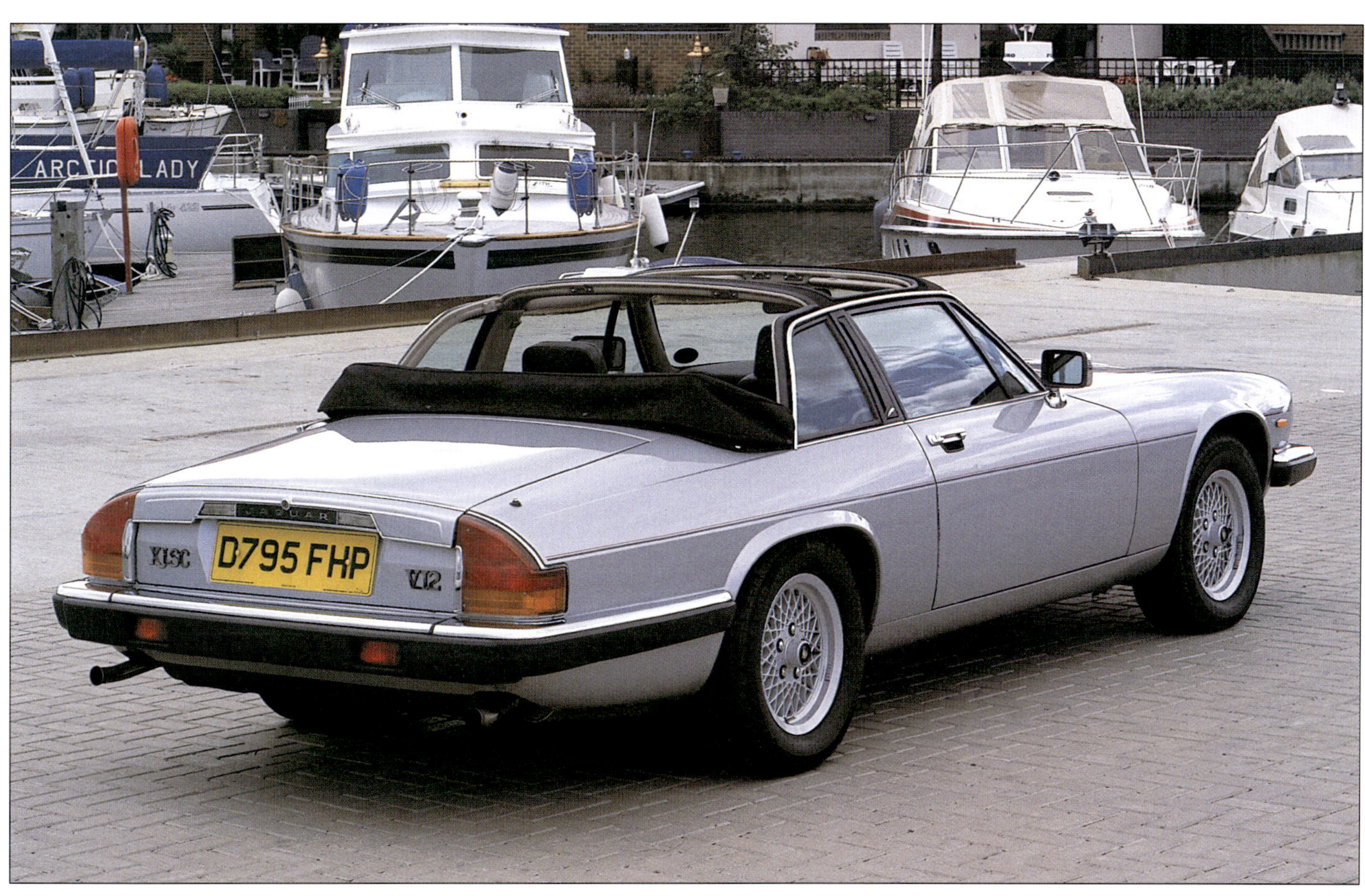

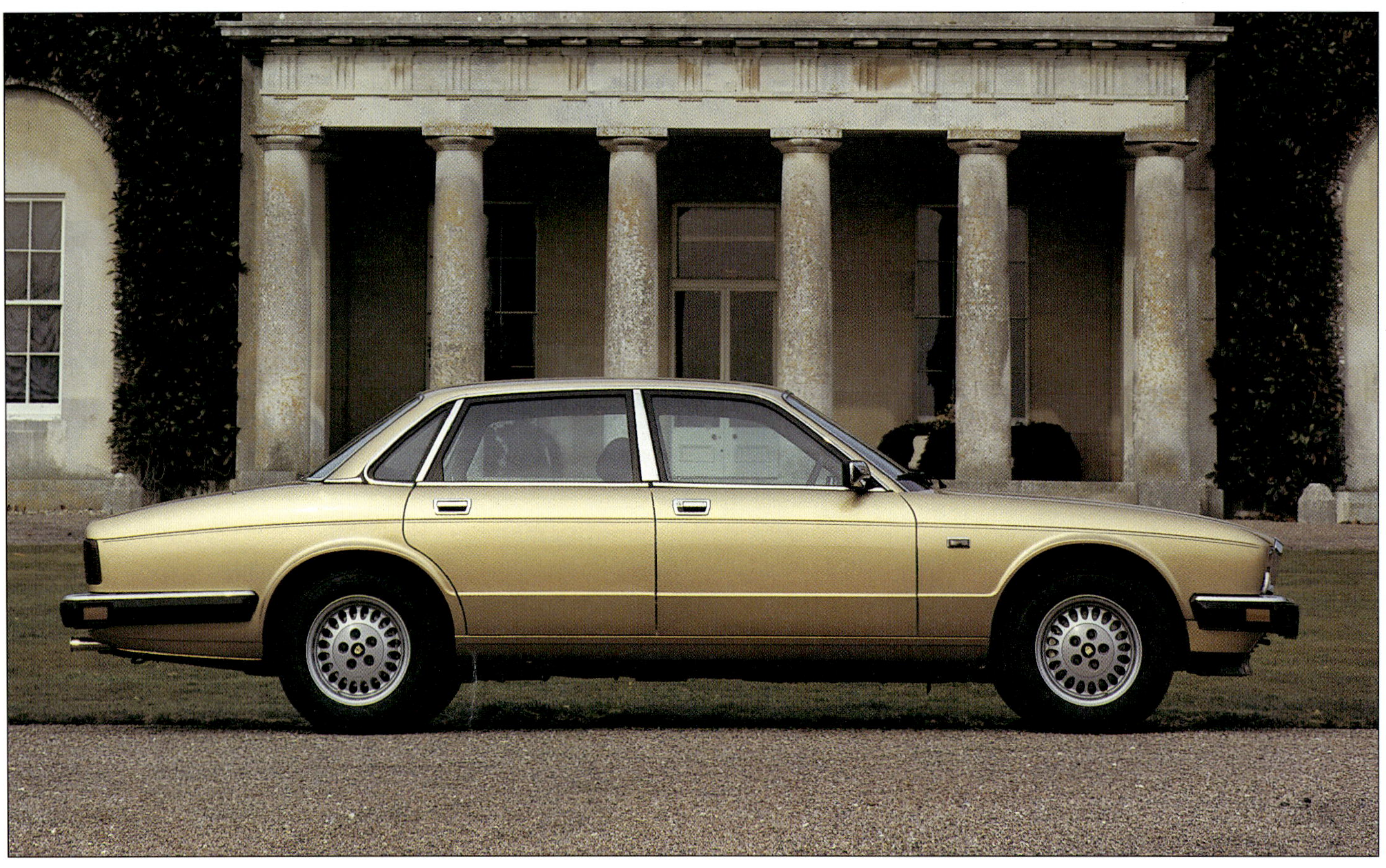

ABOVE: From 1986 the saloons used the lighter and sleeker XJ40 body, here shown as a 1987 XJ6.
BELOW: Coupé XJ-S 3.6 as for 1988 during its eight-year production run, the two-door body having its own distinctive line and style.

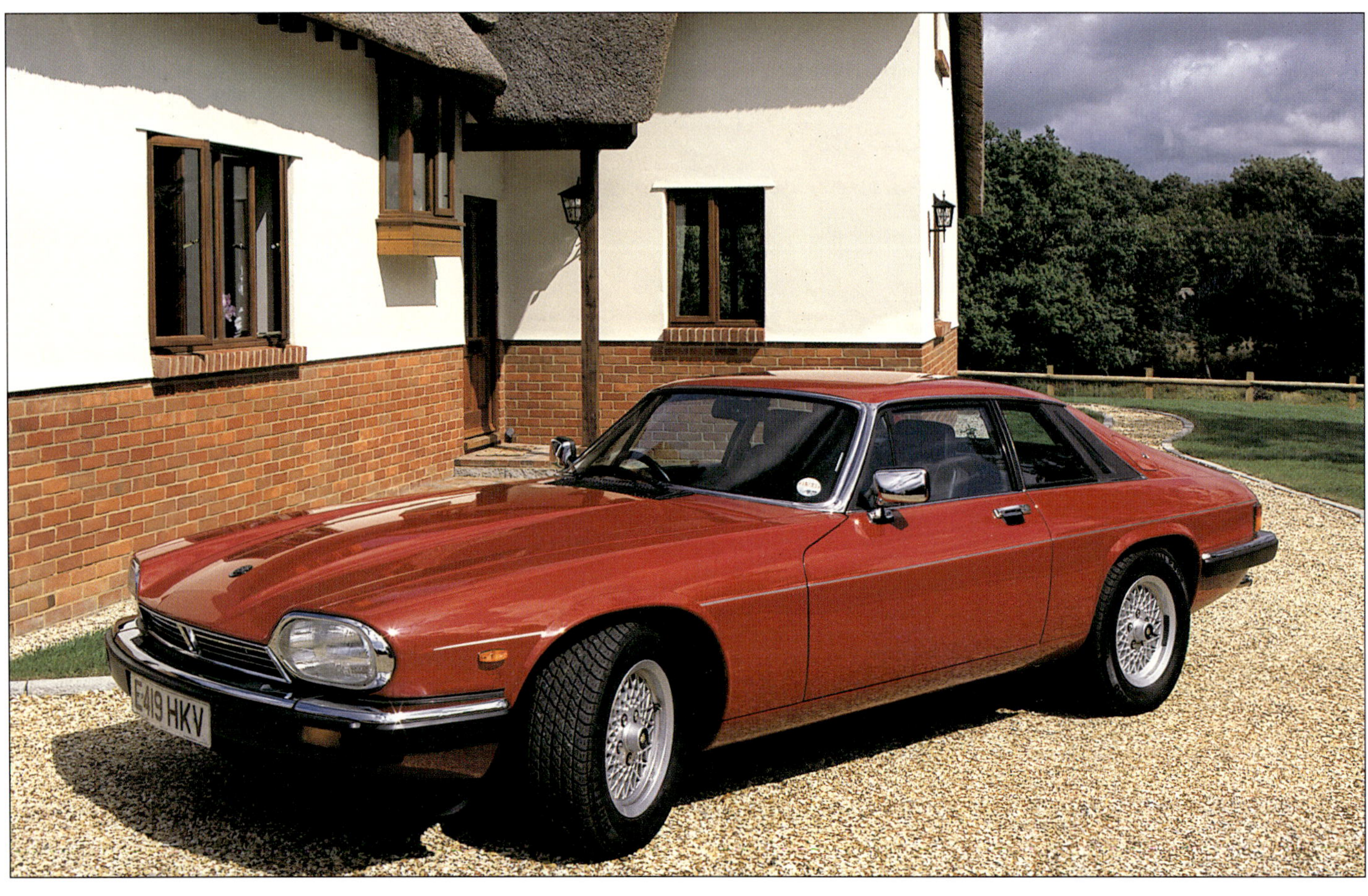

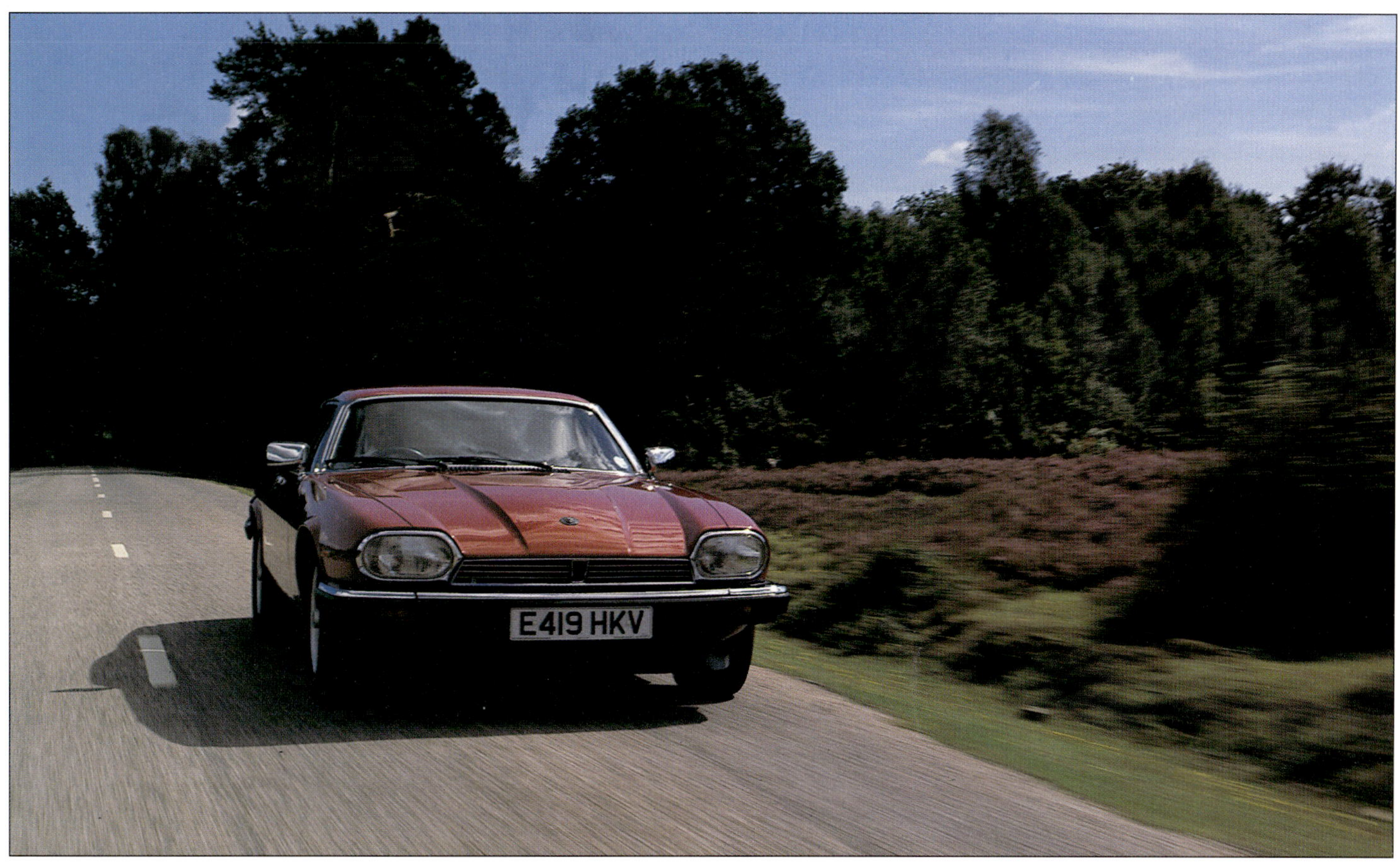

ABOVE: The 1988 XJ-S 3.6 coupé out on the road and performing in the expected manner without the thirst of the V-12 engine.
BELOW: Sovereign version of the 1988 XJ6 3.6 saloon was better equipped than standard and also built as a Daimler.

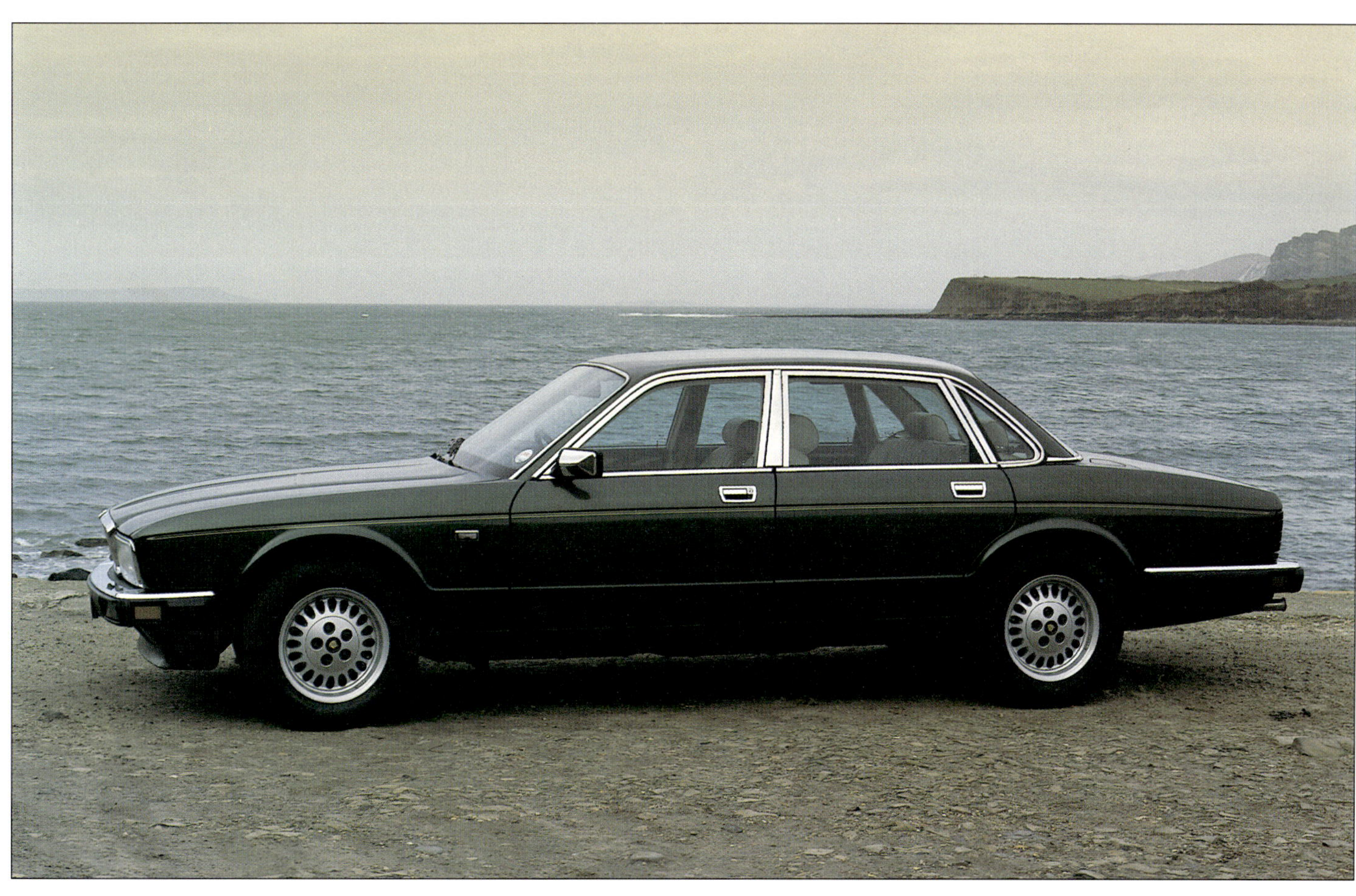

RIGHT: This rear quarter view shows the discreet badges of the XJ6 Sovereign, but not its engine type or size.

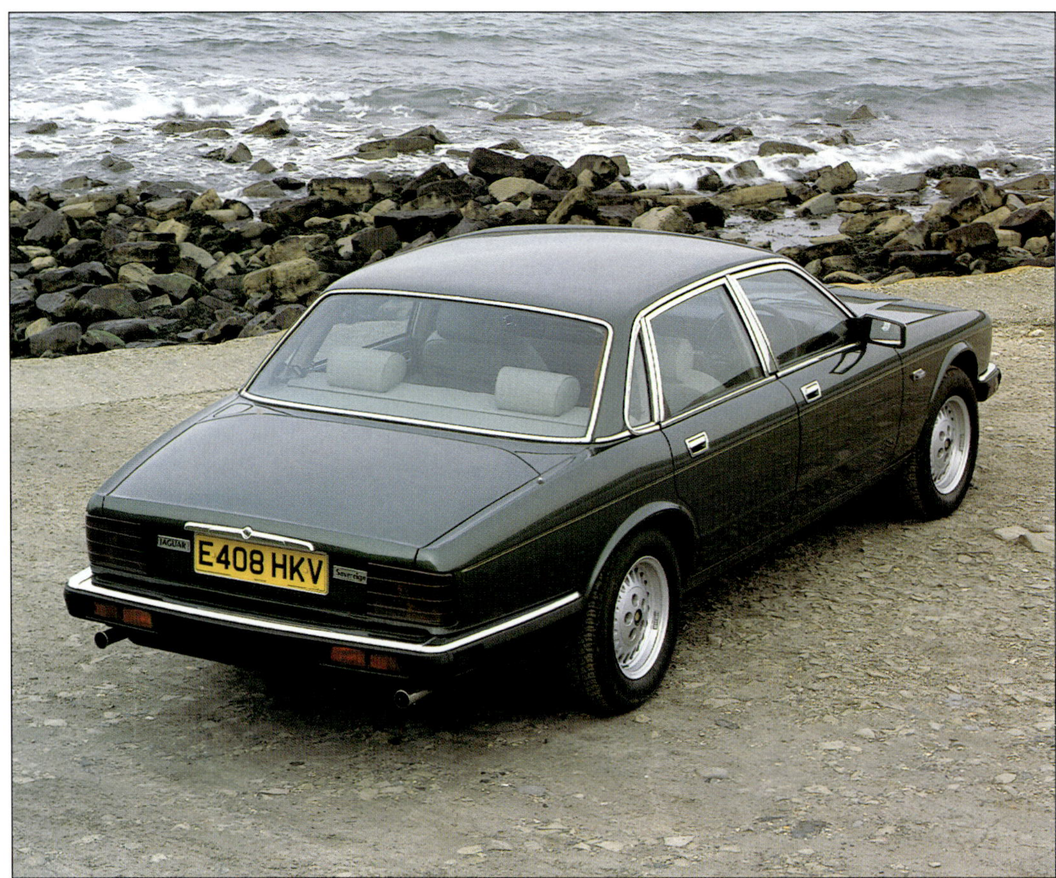

BELOW: With the top up, the XJ-S 5.3 Convertible could run up to 150mph, the whole package making a most desirable car.

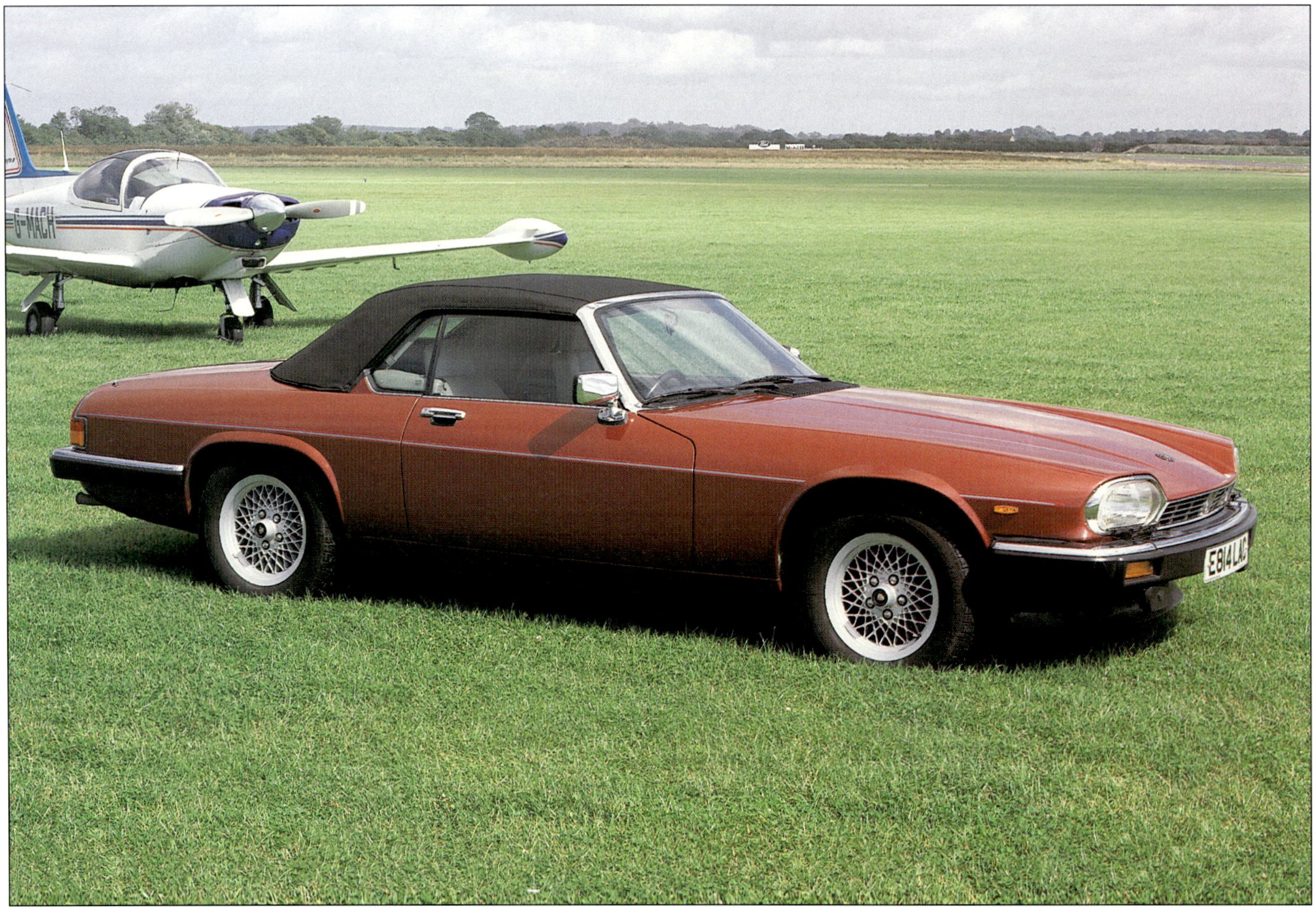

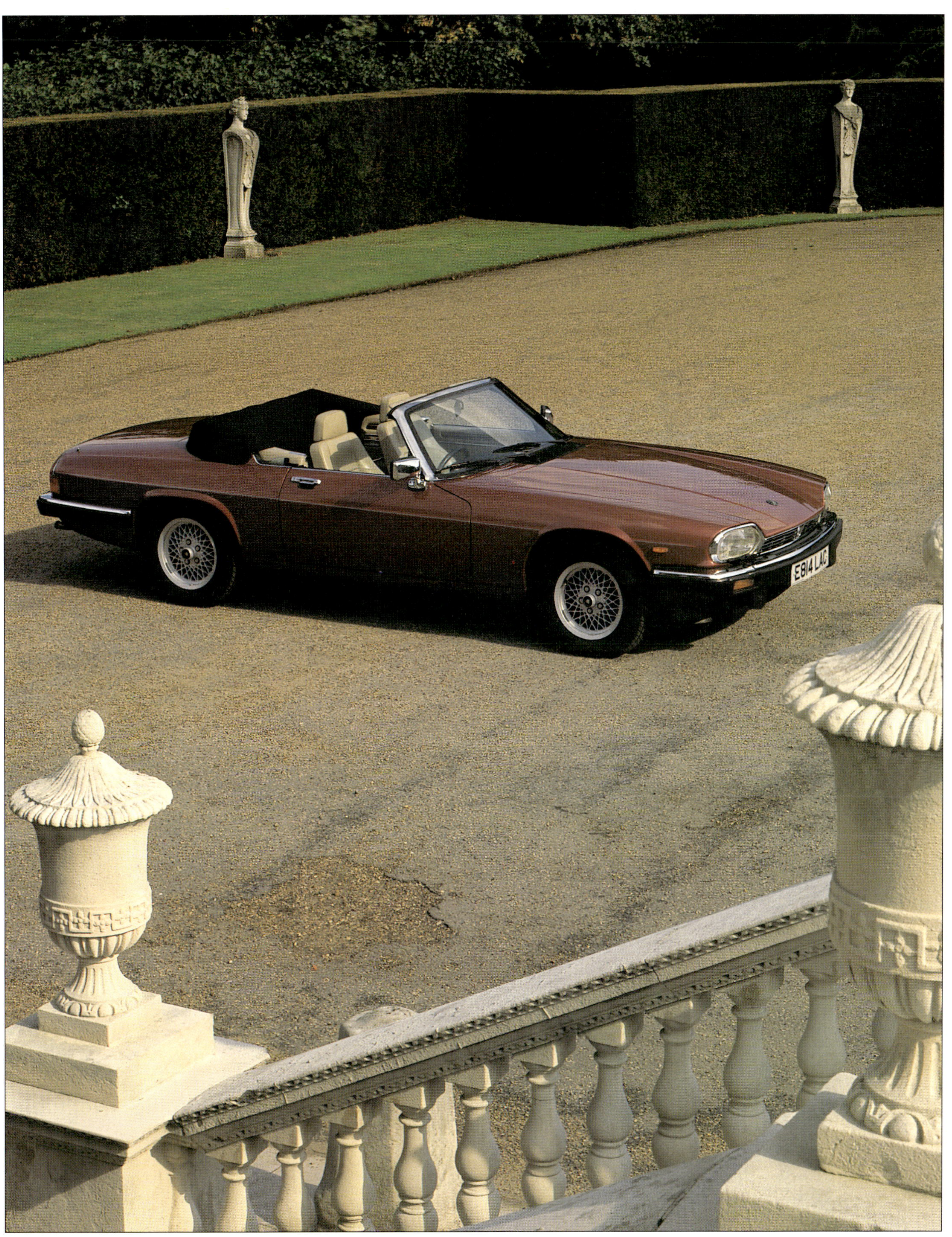

Convertible XJ-S 5.3 of 1988 with its electrically-operated hood down when it could run at 100mph without rustling the driver's hair.

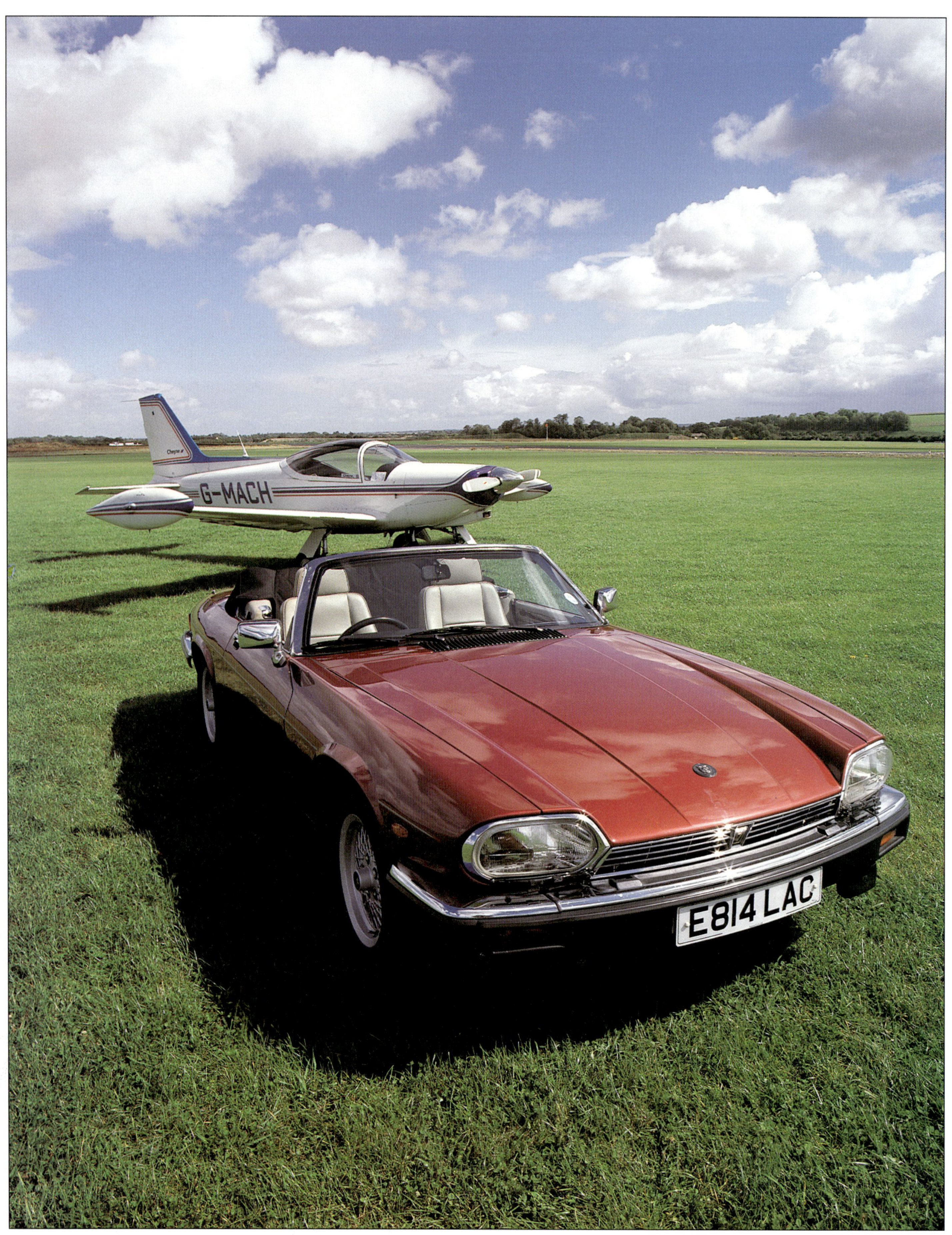

When the sun was out, the top of the XJ-S 5.3 Convertible was soon down and stowed away for fresh-air motoring.

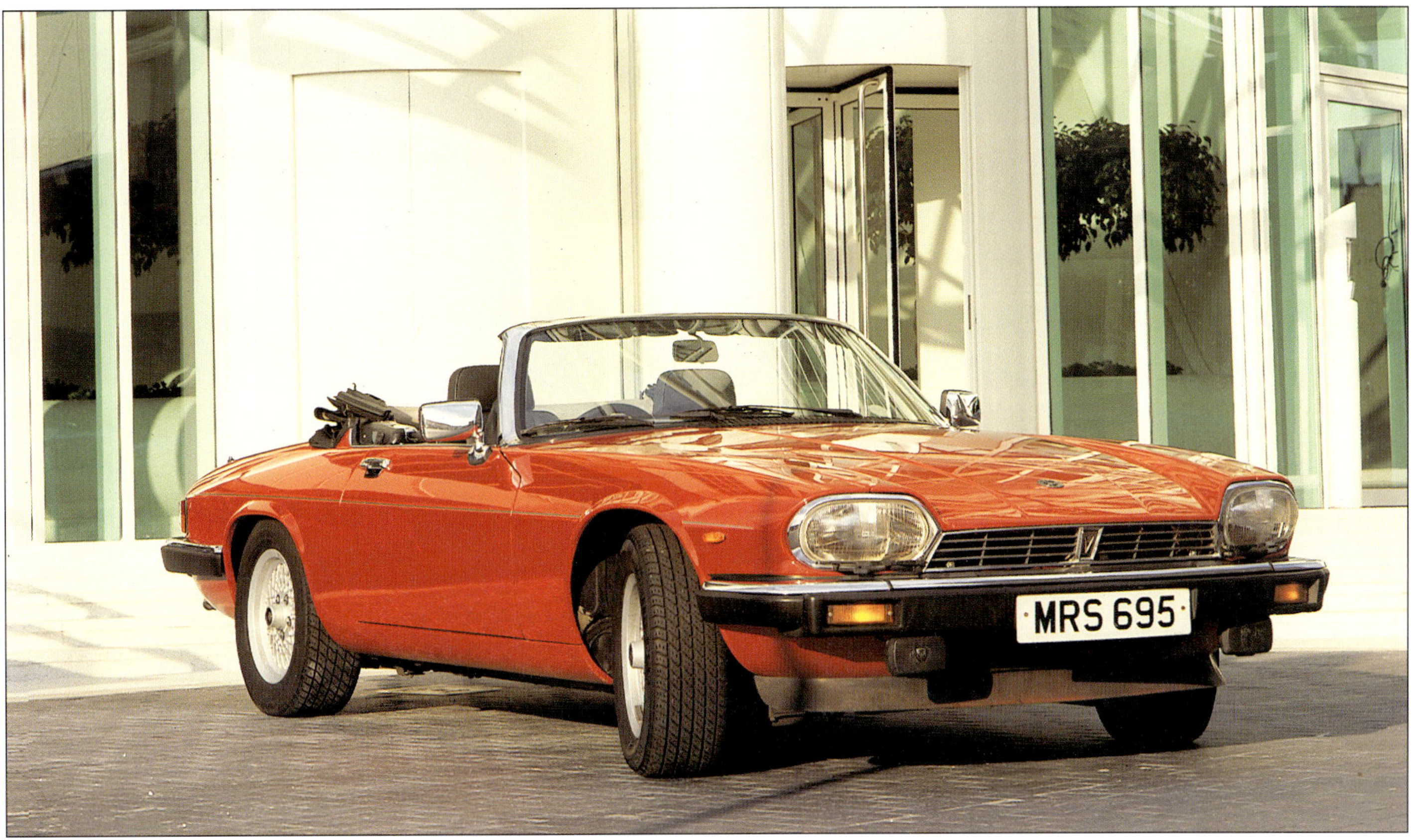

ABOVE: Further example of the XJ-S V12 Convertible from 1989, showing off its sleek lines.
BELOW: The XJR-9 Silk Cut Jaguar that took the 1989 World Sports Car championship and won at Le Mans.

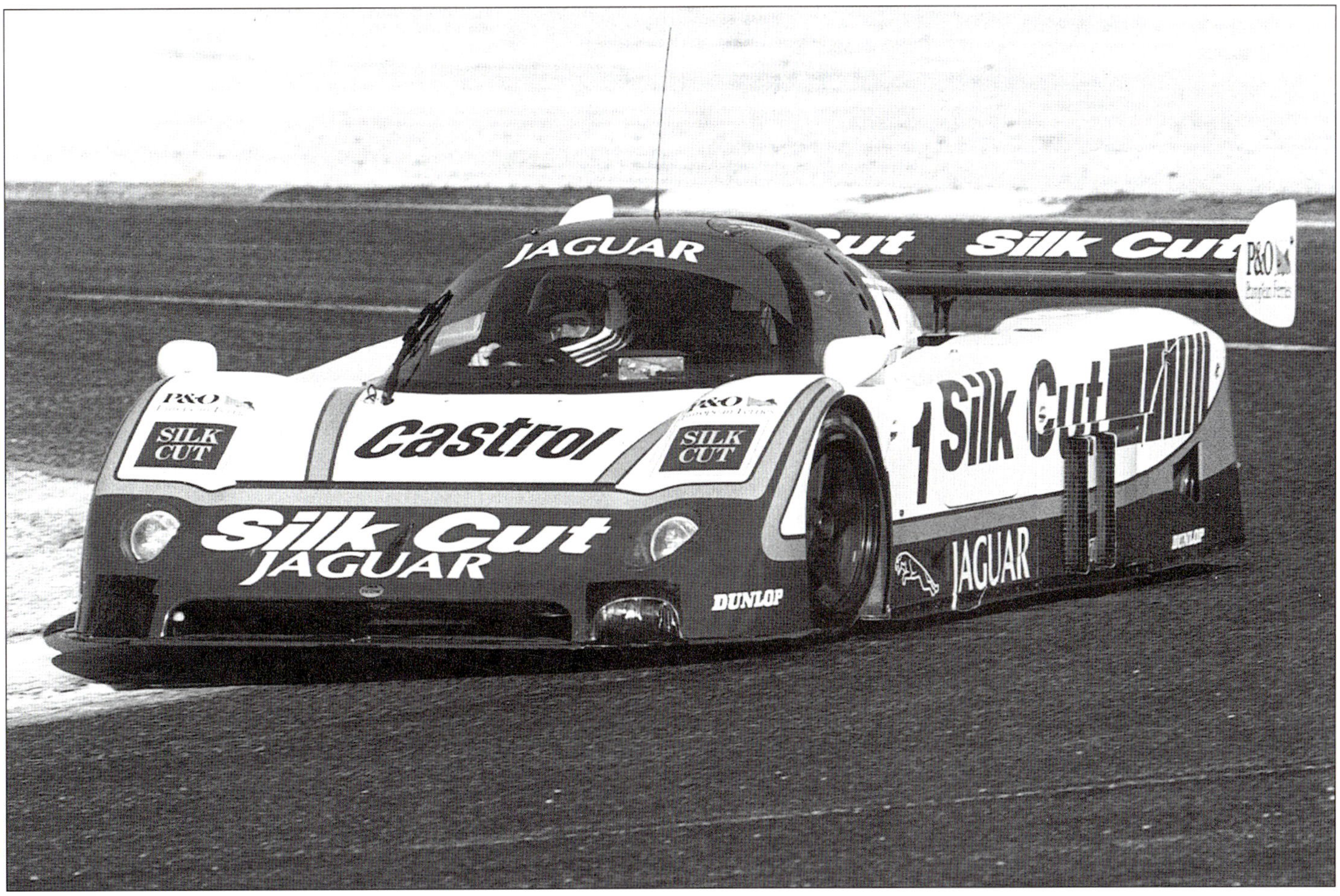

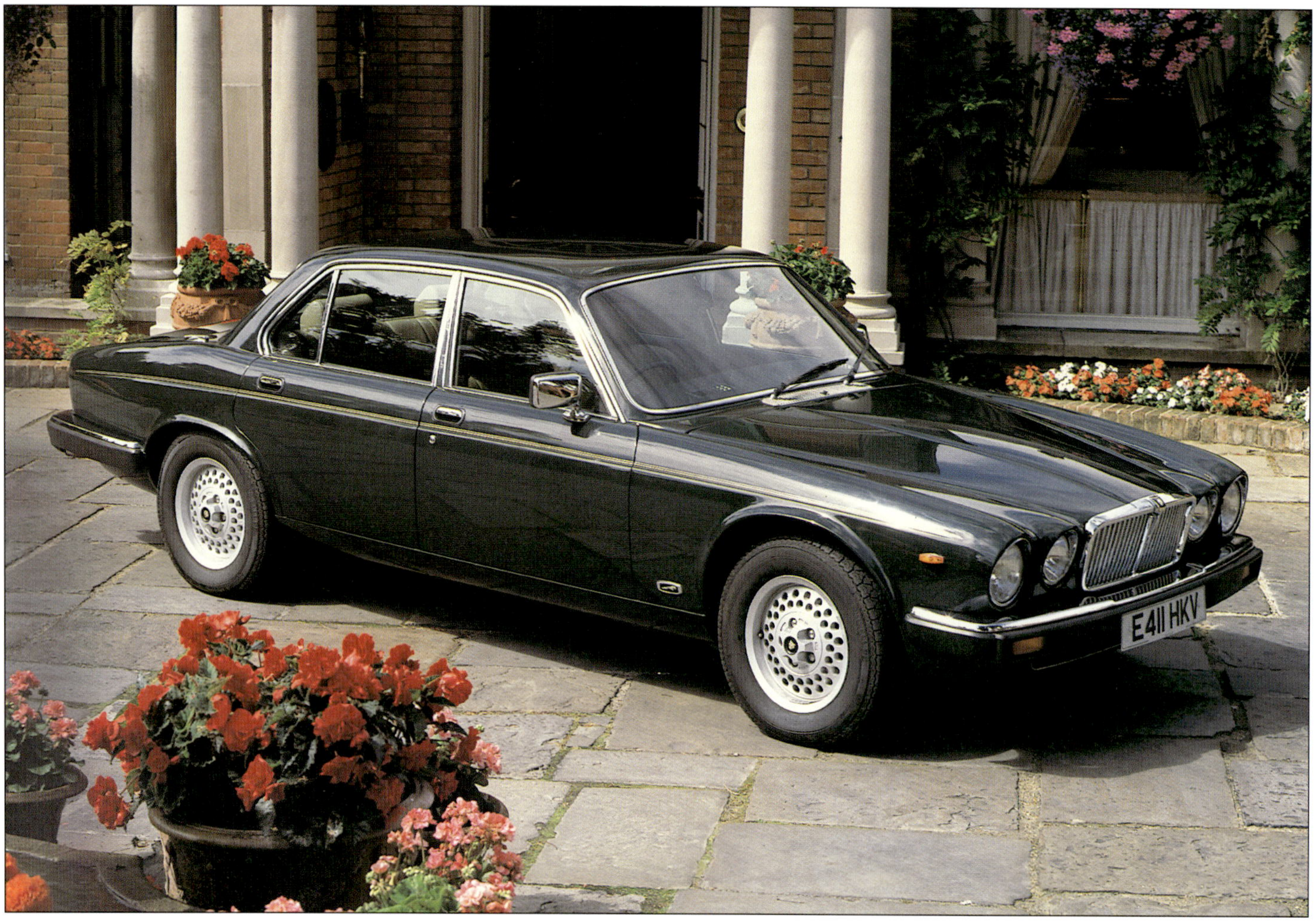

ABOVE: Mighty Series III Sovereign V12 from 1988 with the classic Jaguar saloon body style, and the leaping mascot now a side badge.

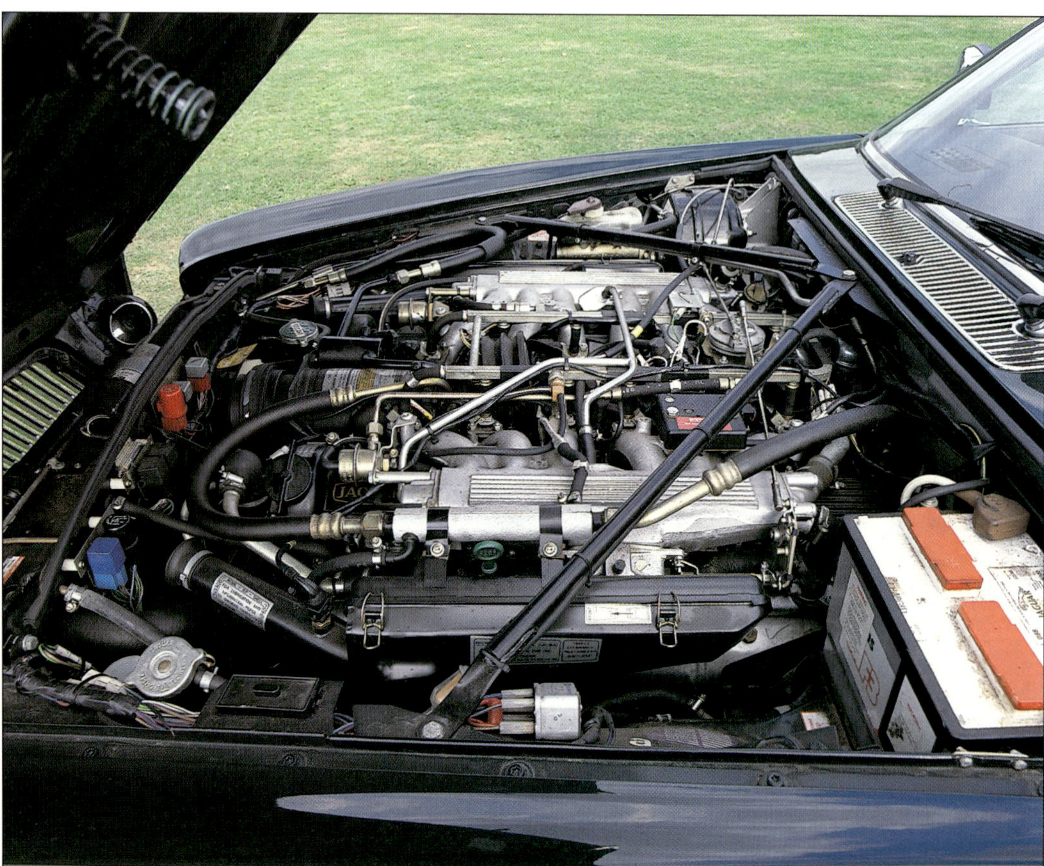

RIGHT: Daunting under-bonnet view of the V-12 engine with its complex array of components somehow fitted in while remaining available for service.

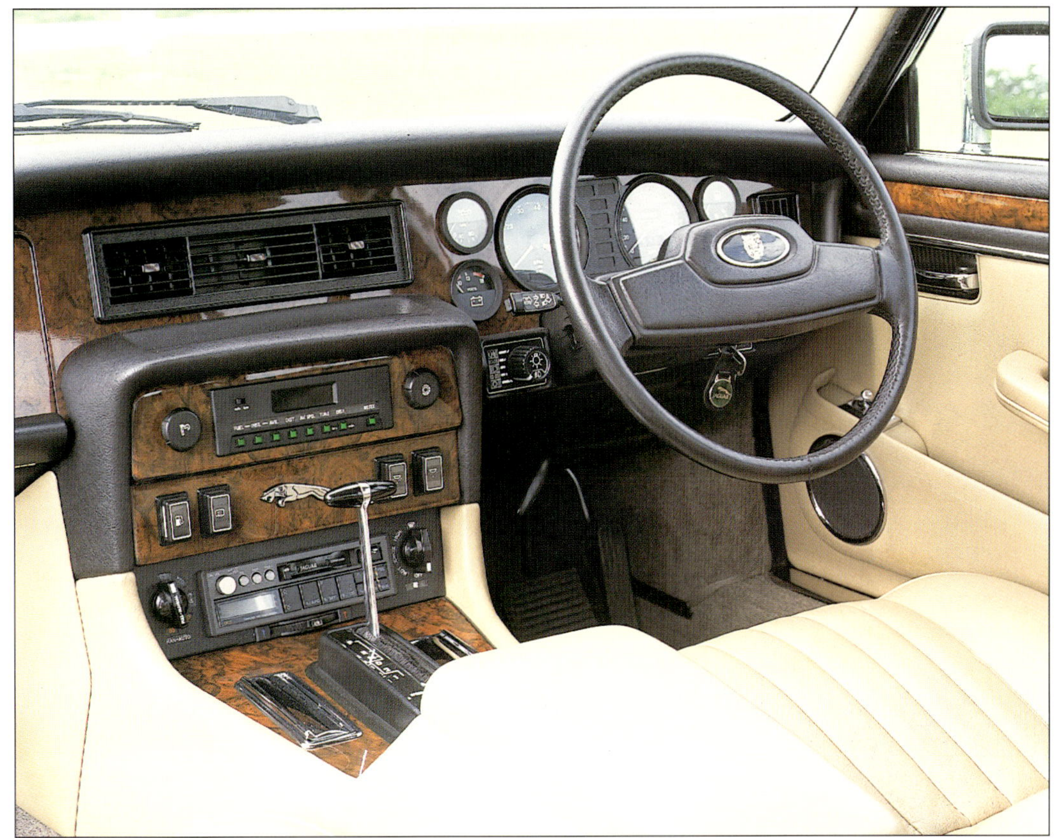

LEFT: Interior of the Sovereign V12 saloon showing the fine fixtures, fittings and finish produced by the Browns Lane factory.

BELOW: Sport version of the XJ 3.2 and 4.0 models that added revised suspension, a lower ride height, special wheels and other features, this a 1996 car.

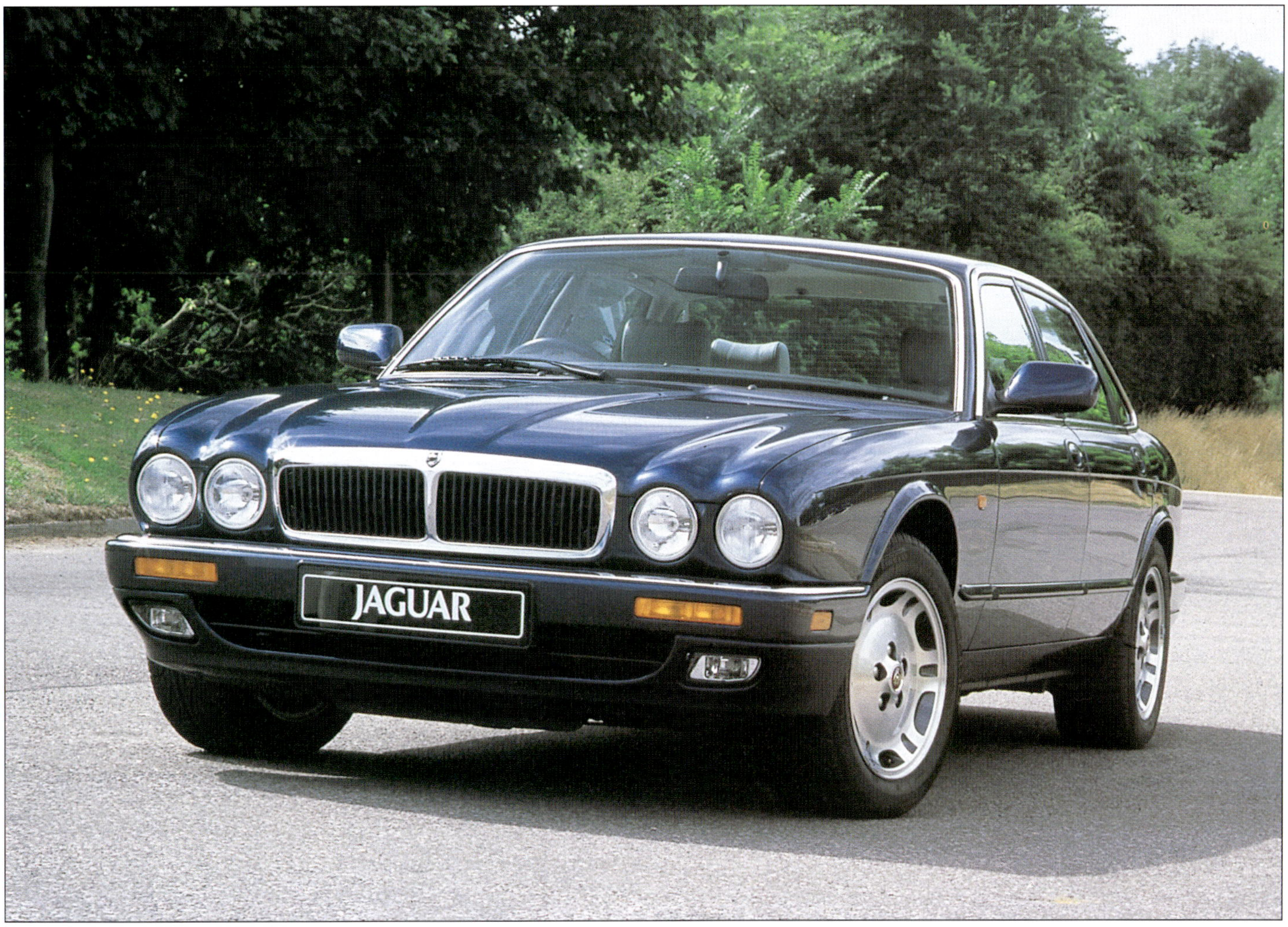

MODERN DAYS WITH FORD

1990-1996

DURING 1990 the firm was taken over by Ford and, at first, Jaguar enthusiasts feared that this would dilute the special nature of the cars. They need not have worried for the factory just carried on building Jaguars but used the Ford money and facilities to improve its product and move on to fresh ones.

The smaller coupé returned for 1992 as the XJ-S 4.0 whose body had a good number of subtle changes involving nearly half the panels. The model, along with others, was available with a dual-mode automatic transmission offering normal

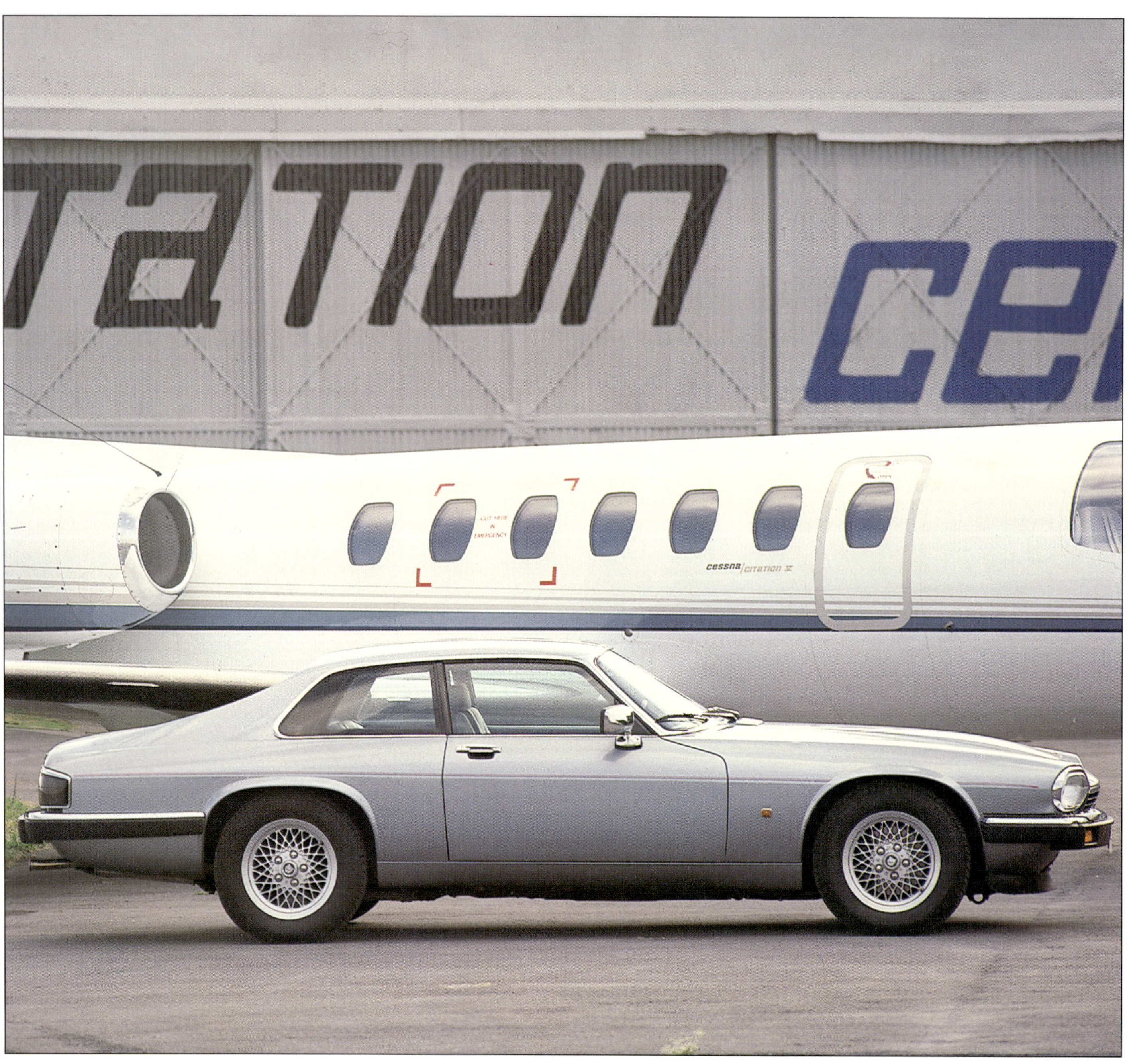

Jaguar coupé for the 1990s, the long-running XJ-S, in this case powered by the 4.0-litre engine.

and sport to suit the driver's mood and road conditions. However this year was the end of the line for the Daimler limousine, it having survived badly for so long in its specialised market. Equally specialised and totally different was the limited edition XJ220, deliveries of this supercar commencing in July.

An XJ-S 4.0 Convertible was added to the line for 1993 when the XJ-S coupé and convertible went over to the 6-litre, V-12 engine. The V12 saloon followed suit for 1994, as did the Daimler Double Six, both available in Majestic form where the wheelbase was increased and the roof line raised to give more space for the rear passengers.

In 1995 Jaguar added the XJR6 to its range, a sports saloon powered by a 4.0-litre supercharged engine producing some 322bhp. The blower was a mechanically driven, Roots type while both manual or automatic transmissions were available. The model was distinguished by diamond-turned alloy wheels among its styling features while a traction control system aided the driver in using the power to the best advantage.

This brought the two marques to 1996 when both had cause to celebrate and produced cars to mark the occasion. For Jaguar it was 60 years since the name

By 1992 the concept XJ220 had reached production and the first few went out to customers in July.

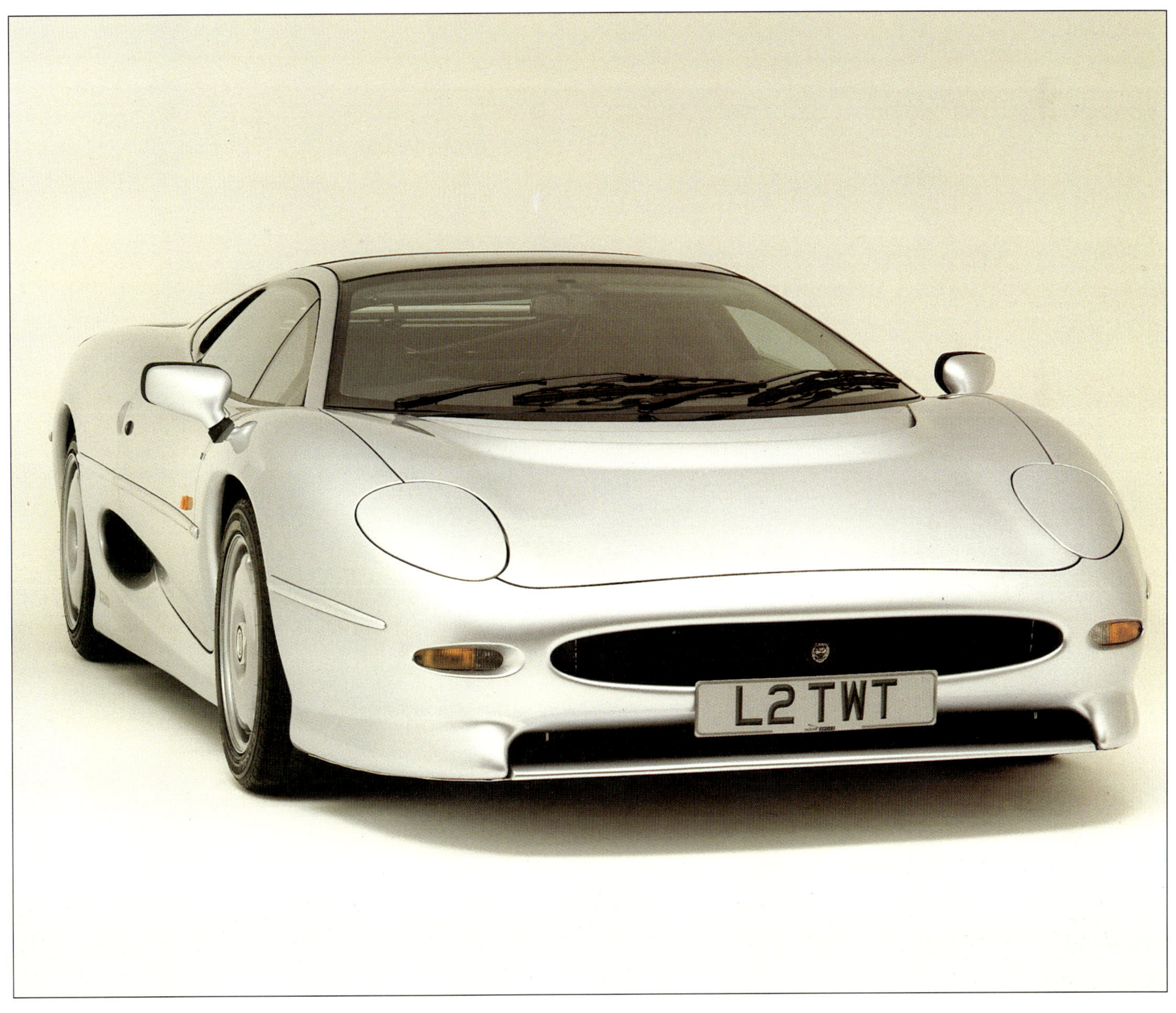

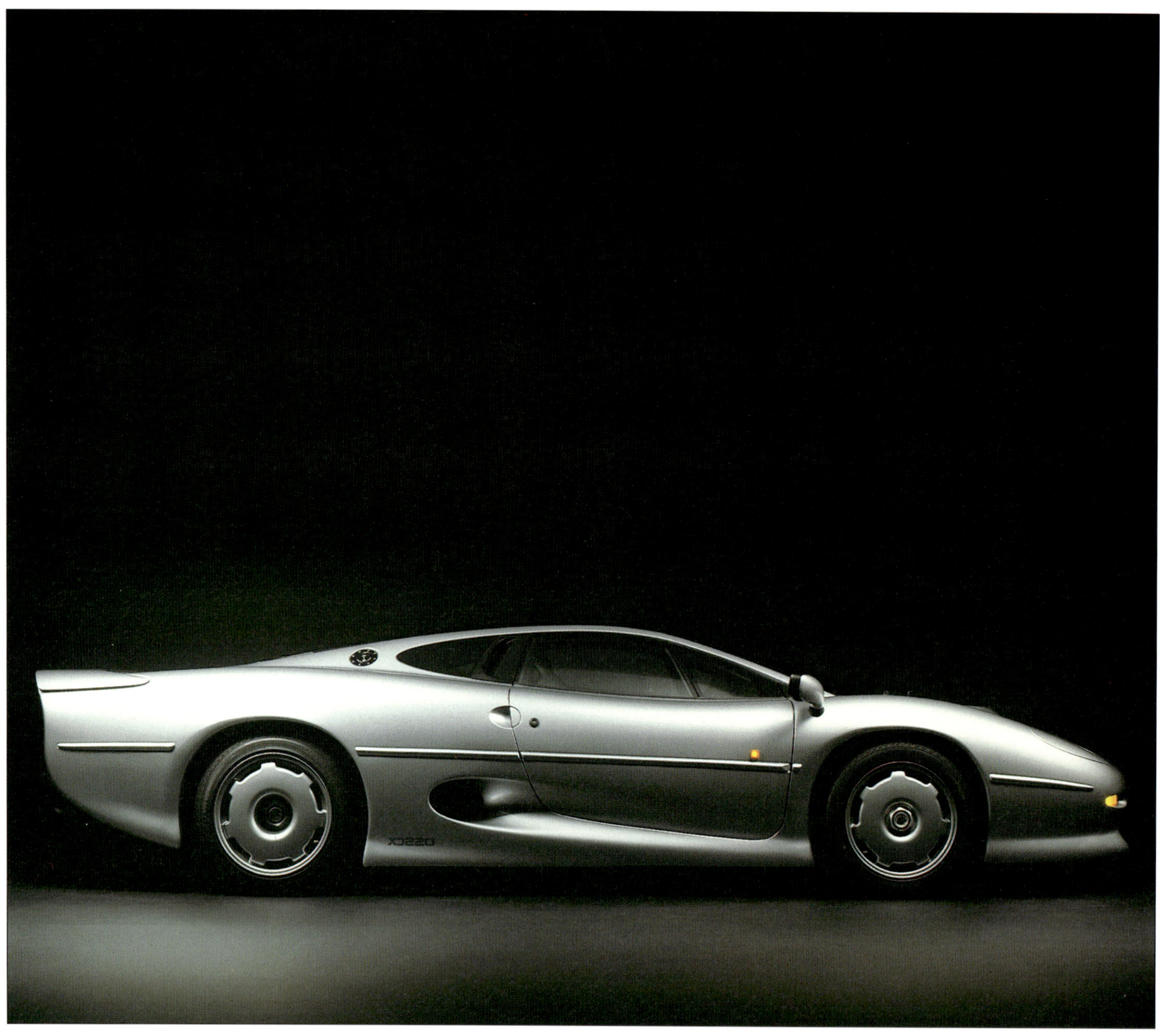

The XJ220 took Jaguar into the realms of the supercar and also reflected the company's further success at Le Mans and elsewhere.

had first been used by the firm and it introduced Celebration editions of the XJ-S coupé and convertible models, the latter stretched to a 2+2 form. Both fitted the twin-cam 4.0-litre engine from the XJ saloon and were suitably equipped and trimmed to highlight the blend of style, quality and performance associated with the marque.

It was 100 years for Daimler, Britain's oldest surviving car marque. So, the Century model appeared, based on the Double Six and offered with either the 4.0-litre six engine or the 6.0-litre V-12. As with the Jaguar, there were discreet trim changes to highlight the series.

Thus, Jaguar stood, set fair to run into the new century with its range of prestigious cars noted for their high standards. Sir William Lyons had wrought well when he set the firm on its way to 'Grace...Space...Pace'.

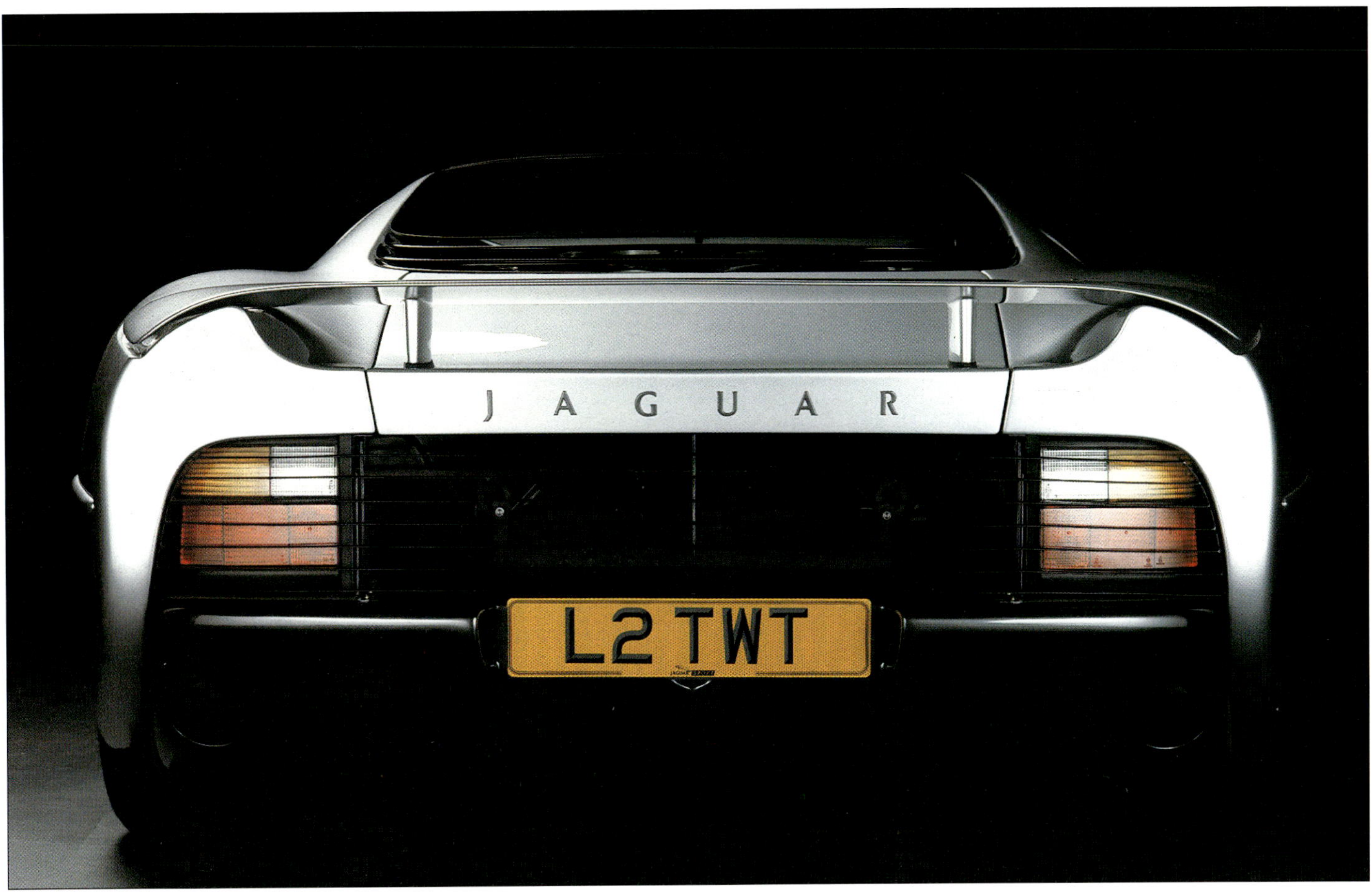

ABOVE: A mid-engine concept was employed for the XJ220, hence the massive ducts aft of the doors and at the rear.
BELOW: Very few people get to sit in these seats, even fewer to drive this XJ220 whose speedometer matches its model code.

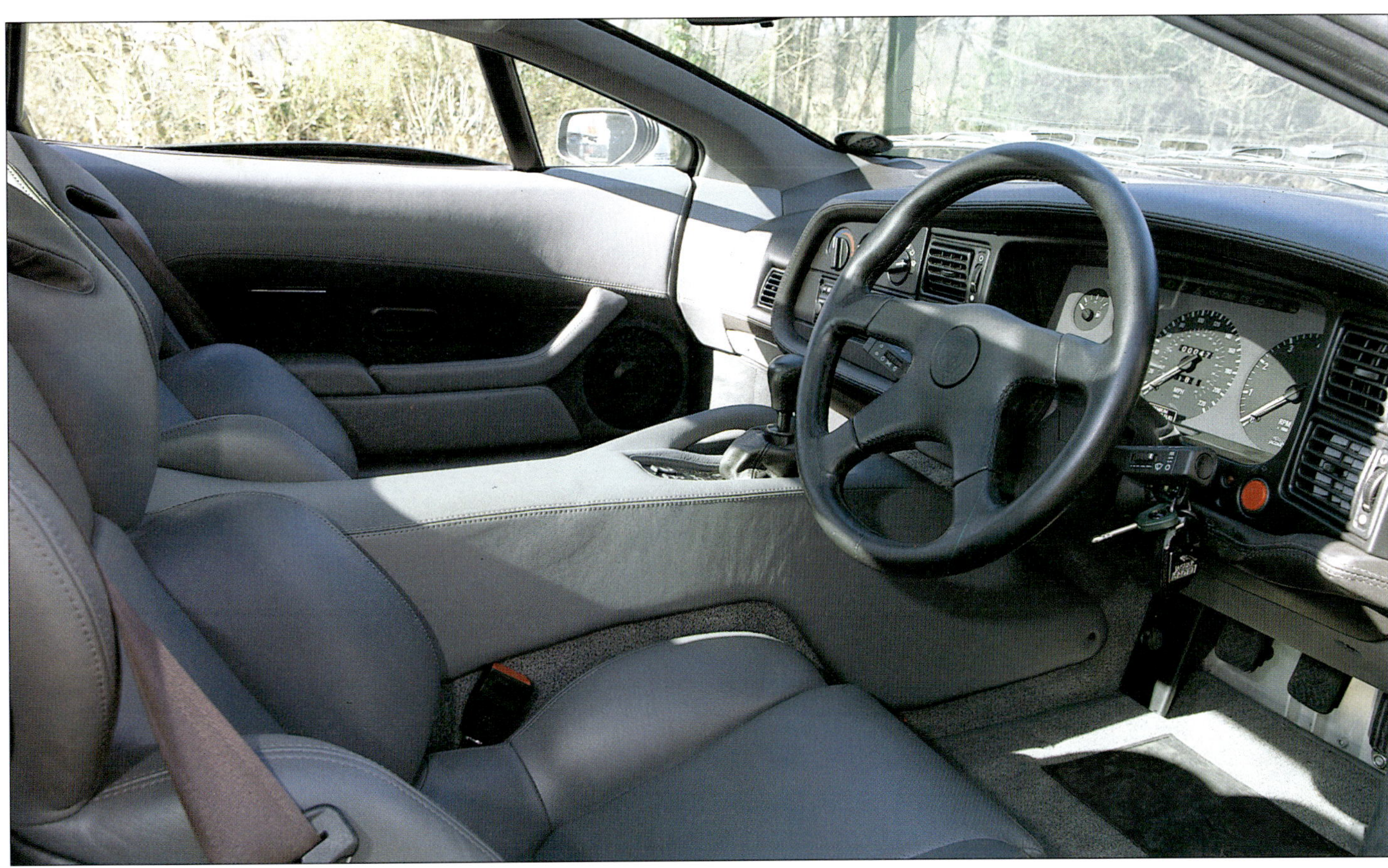

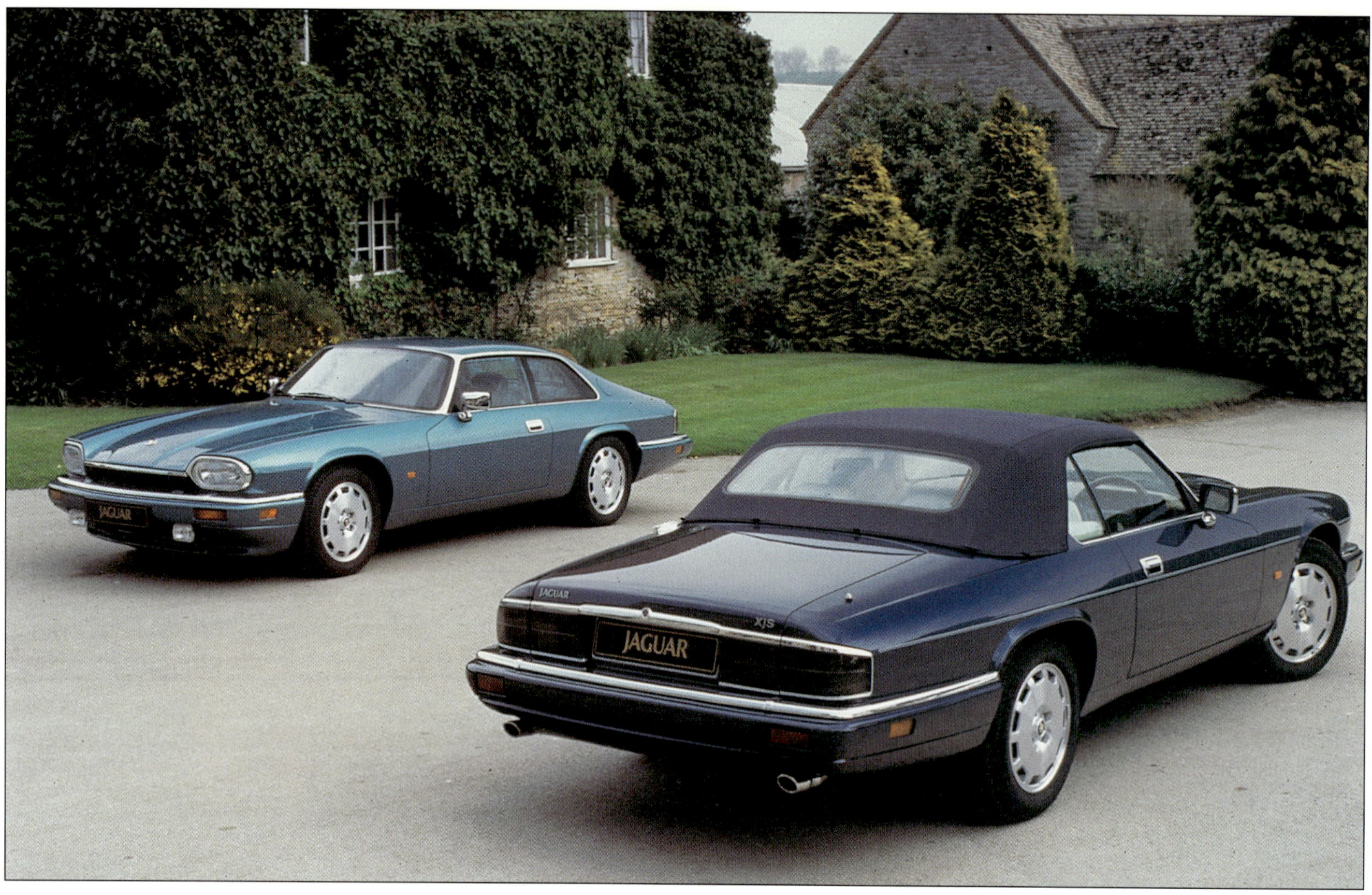

ABOVE: For 1996 both coupé and convertible XJS models were built in a Celebration edition but this pair is from the previous year.
BELOW: The basis of the range remained the four-door saloon with the six-cylinder engine, this being a 1994 XJ6 of 3.2 or 4.0 litres.

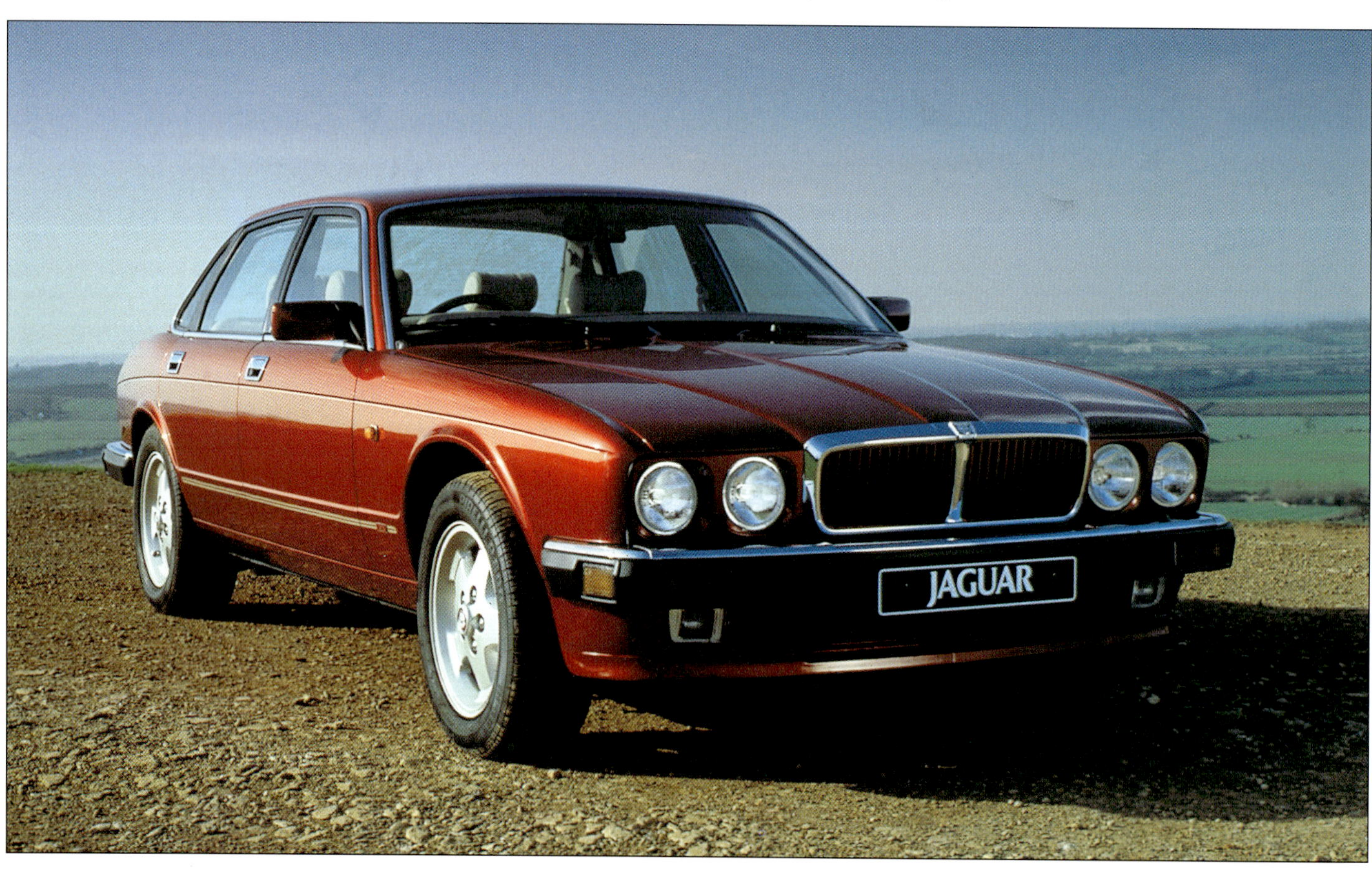

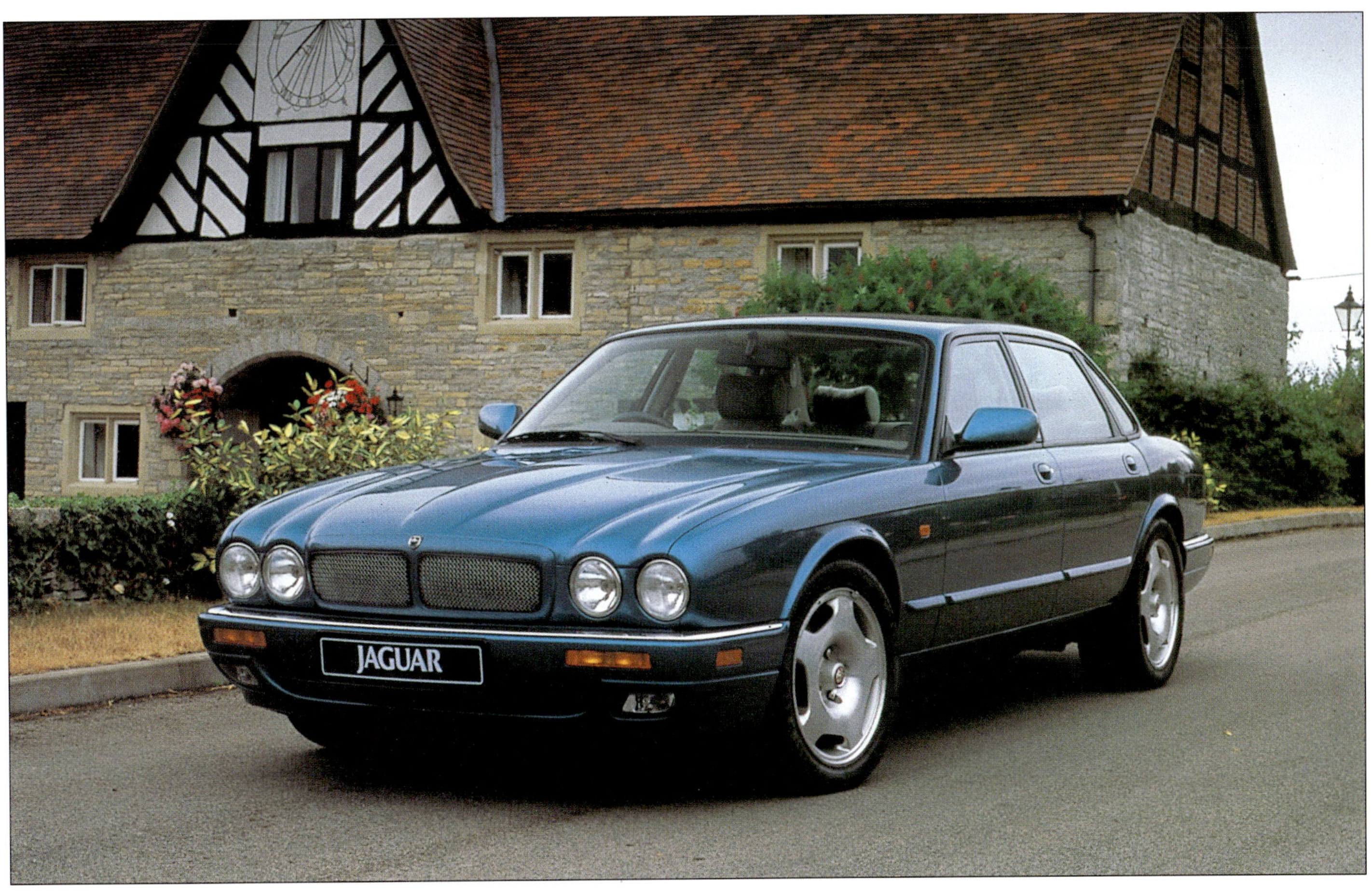

ABOVE: New in 1995, the XJR6 with supercharged 4.0-litre engine had a fresh grill design and offered excellent and refined performance.
BELOW: Celebration model XJ-S 4.0 Coupé of 1996 used the twin-cam, six-cylinder engine and was badged to highlight 60 years of the Jaguar name.

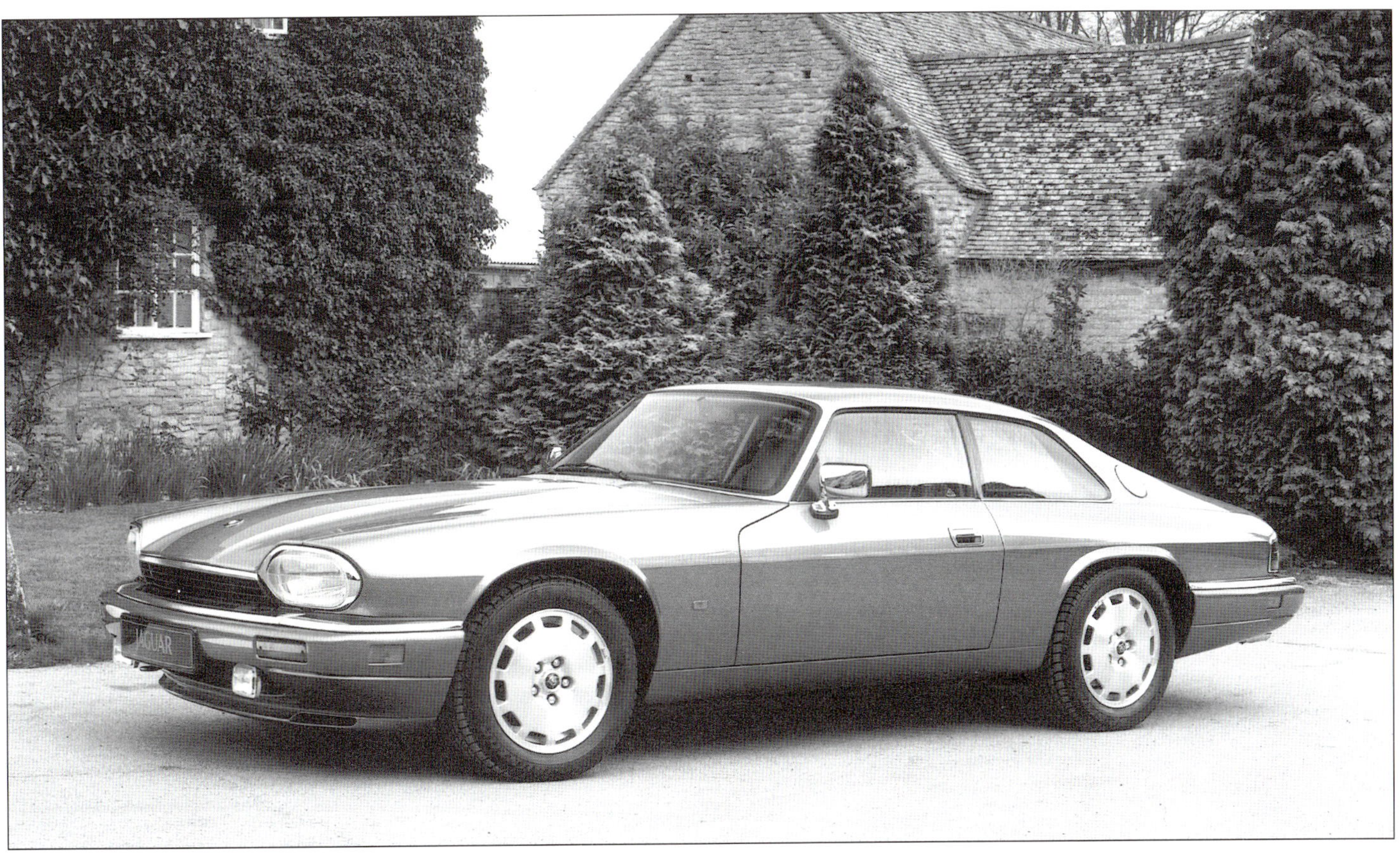

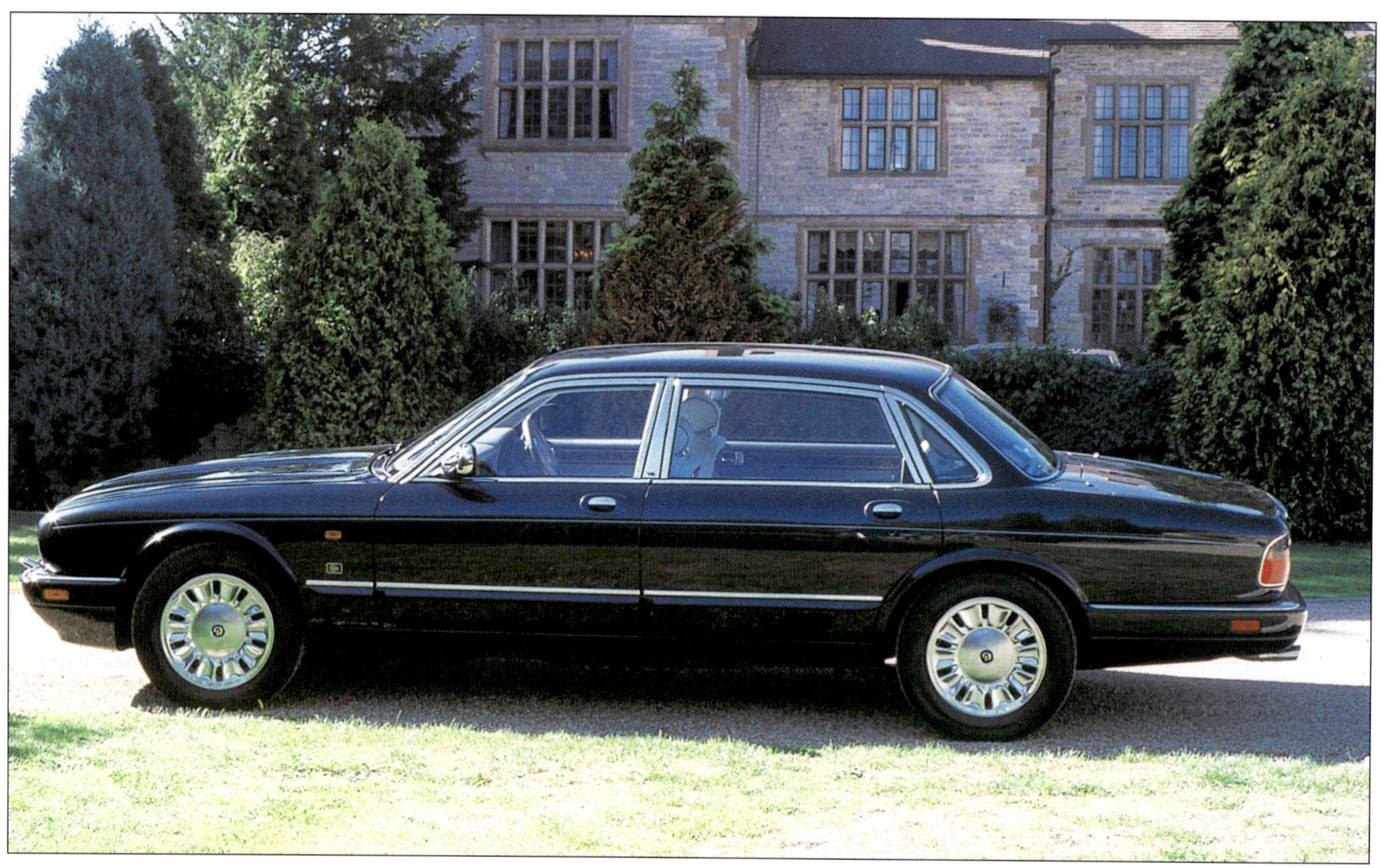

ABOVE: In 1996 Daimler celebrated 100 years of car making with this Century saloon, based on the Double Six but with a choice of engines.
BELOW: One hundred years of Daimler, the old for 1897, the new for 1996.

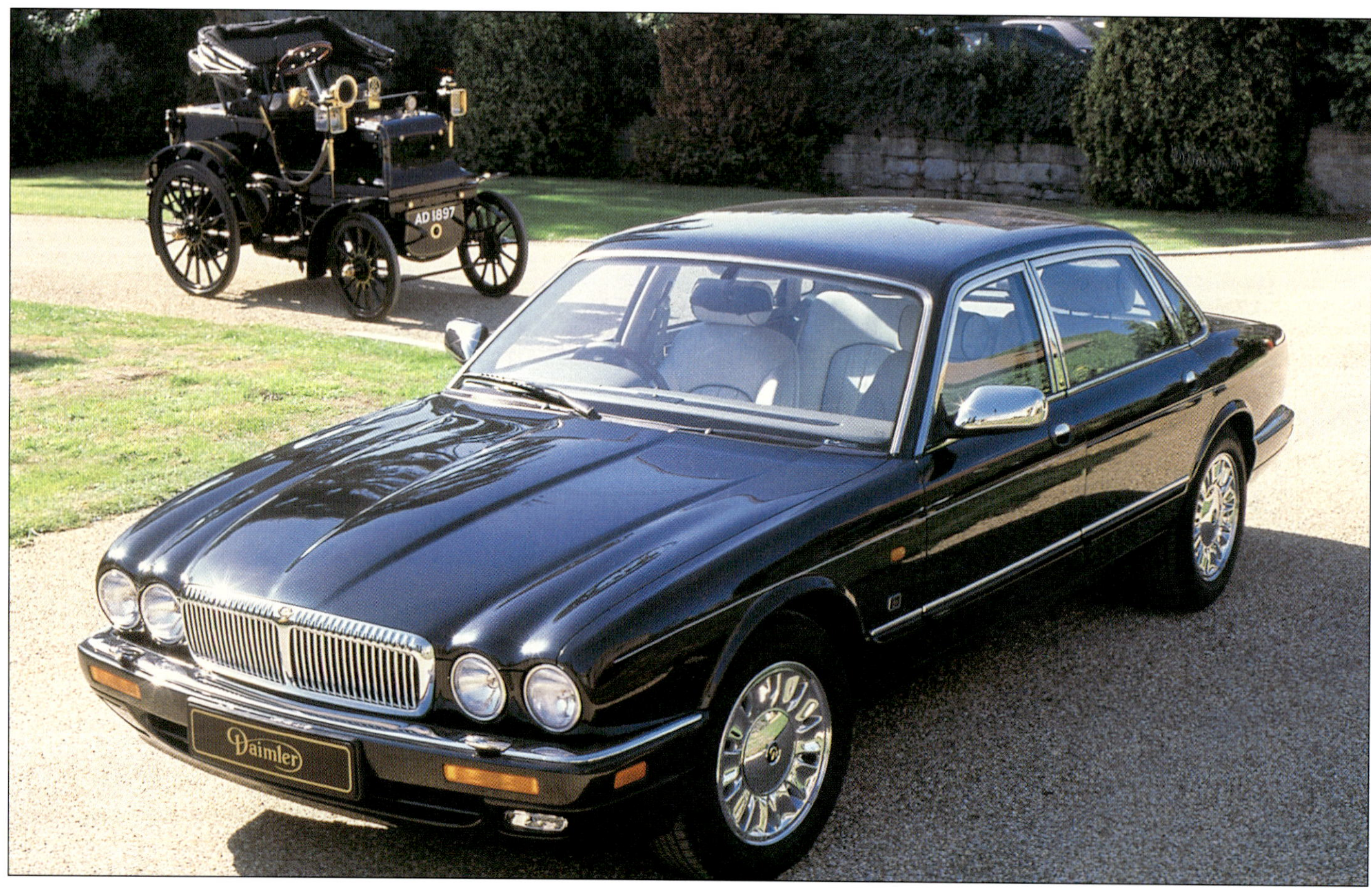

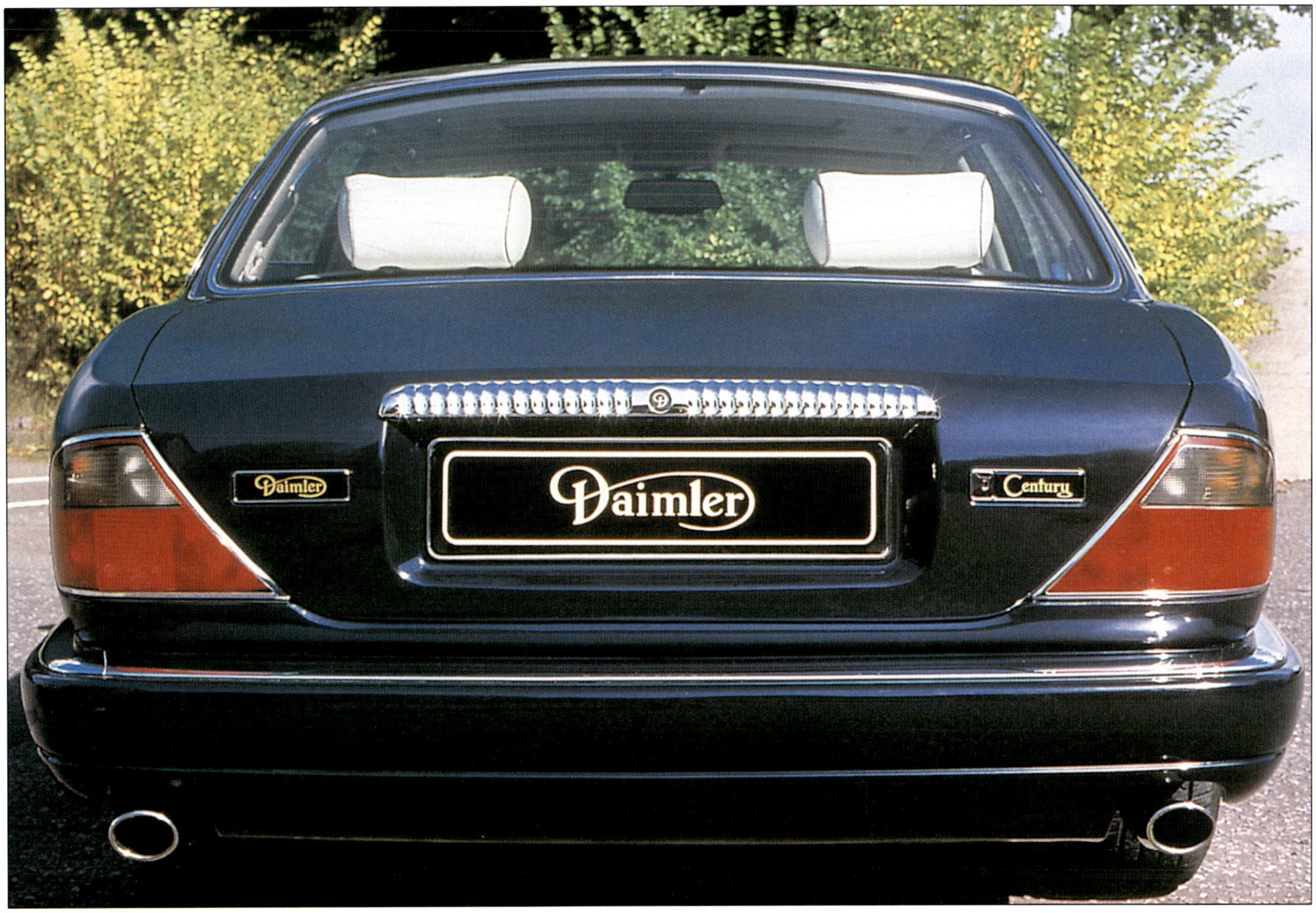

ABOVE: Discreet badges on the rear panel of the Daimler Century saloon to let the world know of the firm's achievement.
BELOW: Long wheelbase version of the Jaguar Sovereign, new for 1996 and available with 3.2 or 4.0-litre engines.

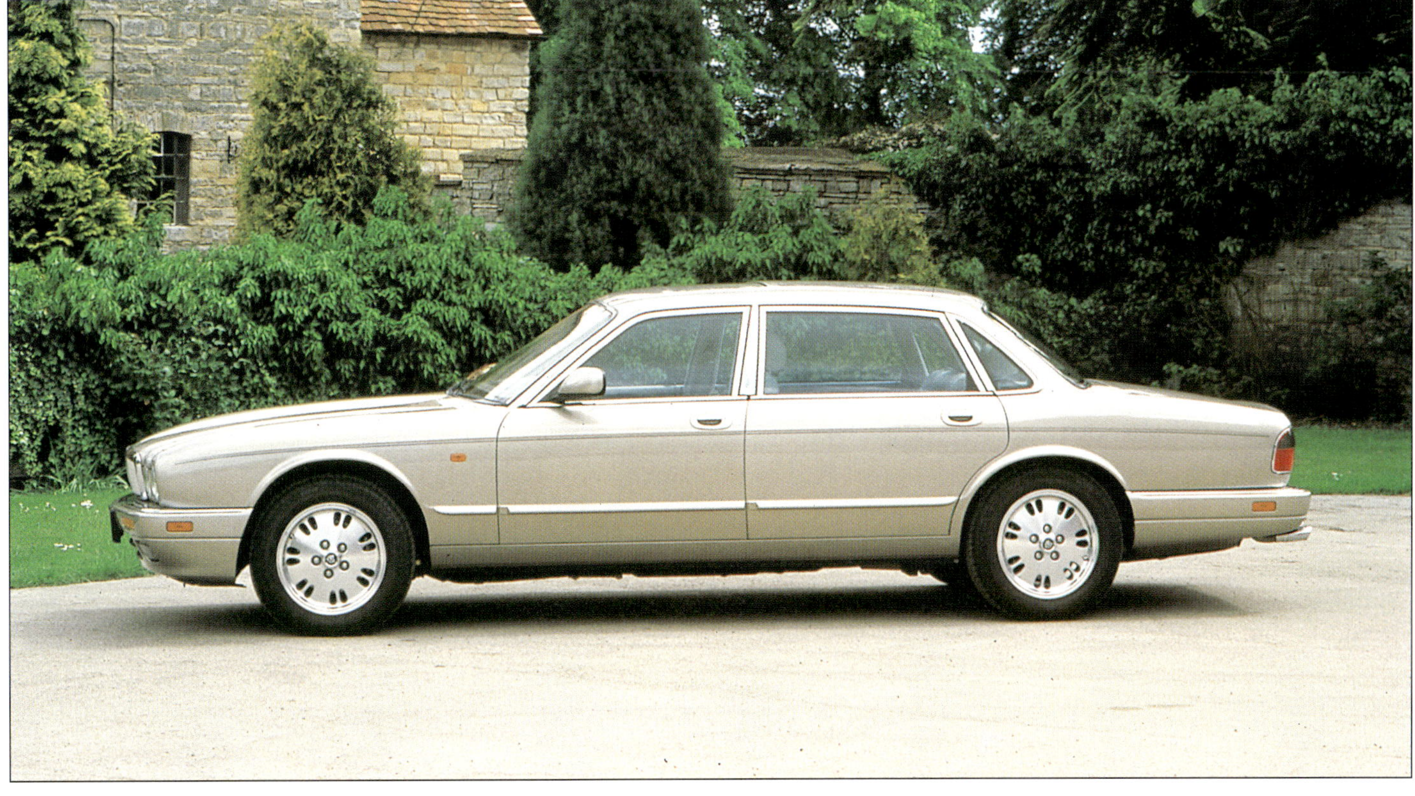

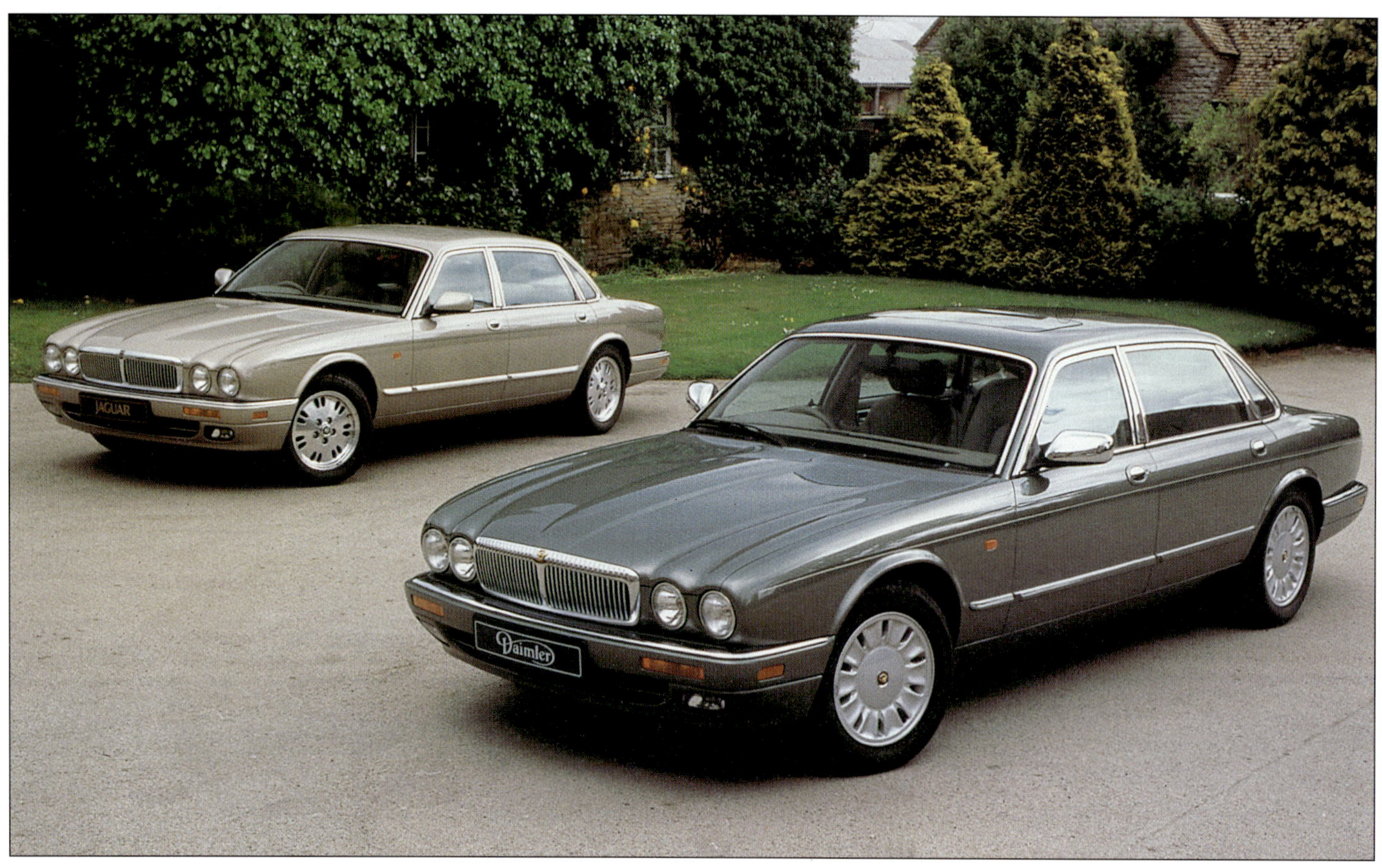

ABOVE: The Jaguar and Daimler long-wheelbase saloons standing side by side, ready to celebrate 1996 and 60 or 100 years respectively.
BELOW: A far cry from the first SS1, these are the optional leather seats for the XJR Jaguar of 1996, highlighting the progress made.

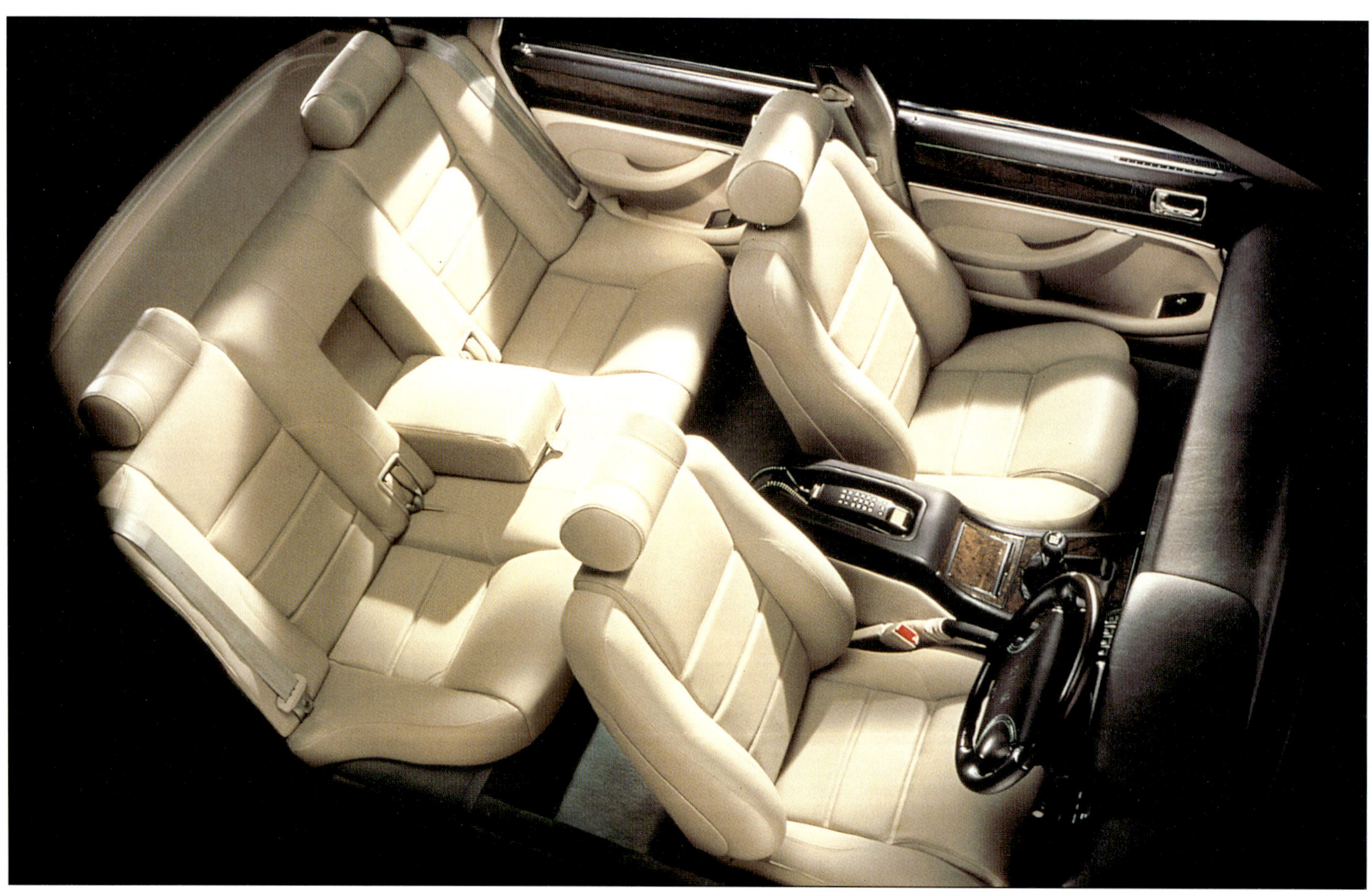

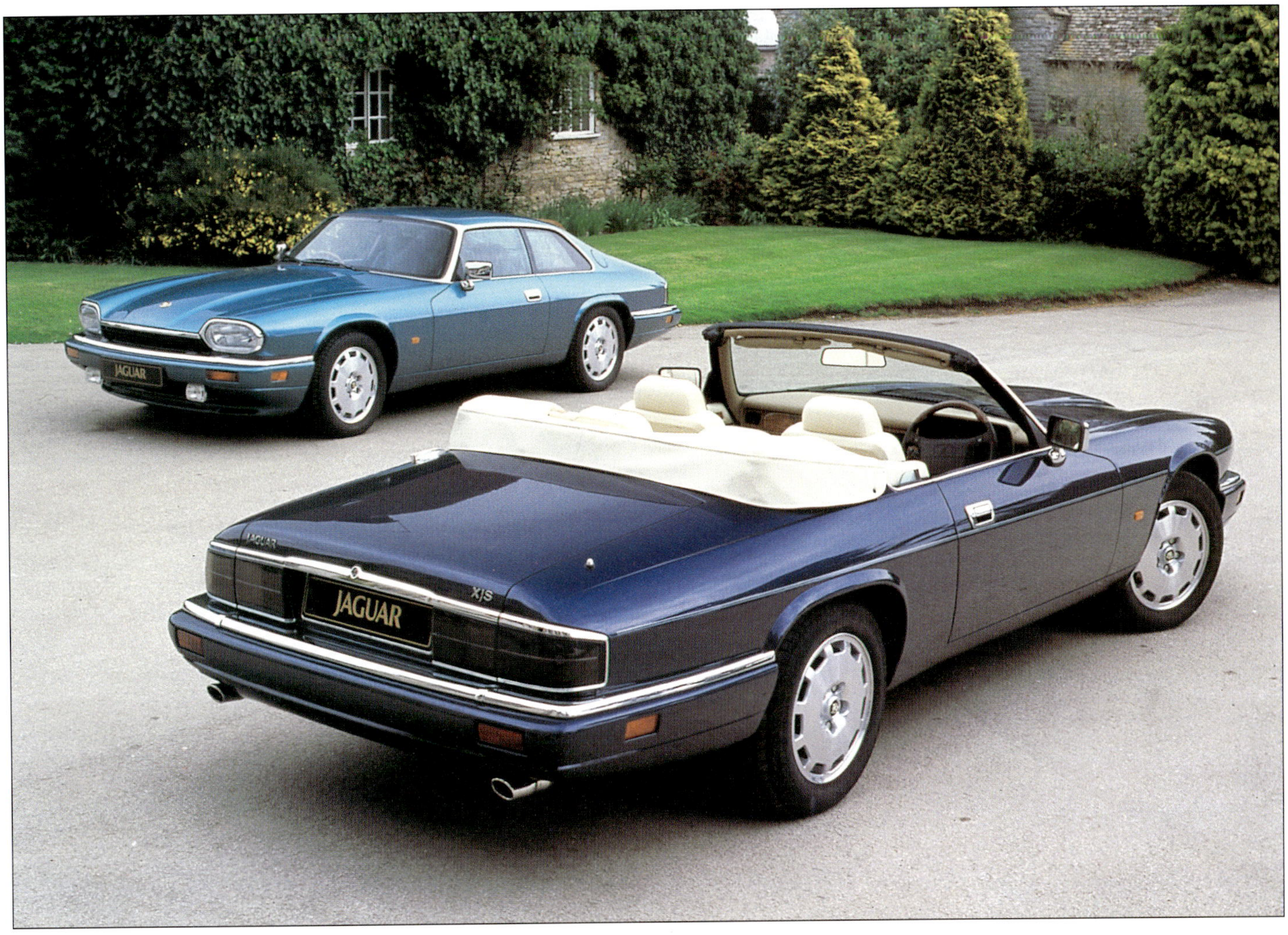

XJ-S Celebration coupe and convertible of 1996 - celebrating 60 years of grace, space and especially pace.

LIST OF JAGUAR & DAIMLER MODELS

SS & JAGUAR

1922-26	Swallow sidecar
1927-32	Austin Swallow
1927-32	Morris Cowley Swallow
1929-30	Swallow Fiat 509A
1929-31	Swift Swallow
1929-32	Standard Swallow
1931-32	Wolseley Hornet Swallow
1932-36	SS1
1932-36	SSII
1935-36	SS1 Airline
1935	SS90
1936-40	Jaguar 1½
1936-40	Jaguar 2½
1936-39	Jaguar 2½ SS100
1938-39	Jaguar 3½ SS100
1938-40	Jaguar 3½
1945-49	1½
1945-49	2½
1945-49	3½
1948-51	Mk V 2½
1948-51	Mk V 3½
1948-54	XK120
1950-54	Mk VII
1951-53	C-type
1954-56	D-type
1954-57	XK140
1955-57	Mk VIIM
1956-59	2.4 Mk 1
1957	XK-SS
1957-58	Mk VIII
1957-61	XK150
1958-59	3.4 Mk 1
1959-61	Mk IX
1960-67	2.4 Mk II
1960-67	3.4 Mk II
1960-67	3.8 Mk II
1961-64	E-type 3.8
1961-64	Mk X 3.8
1964-68	S-type 3.4
1964-68	S-type 3.8
1965-66	Mk X 4.2
1965-68	E-type 4.2
1966-68	420
1966-70	420G
1967-69	240
1967-68	340
1968-73	XJ6 series I
1968-71	E-type 4.2 series II
1971-74	E-type series III
1972-73	XJ12 series I
1974-79	XJ6 series II
1974-79	XJ12 series II
1975-77	XJ6C
1975-77	XJ5.3C
1975-93	XJ-S 5.3
1979-86	XJ6 series III
1979-83	XJ12 series III
1983-91	XJ-S
1986-89	XJ6
1988-89	XJR
1988-89	XJR-S 5.3
1989-93	V12
1989-96	XJ6 4.0
1989-96	Sovereign 4.0
1990-93	XJR-S 6.0
1990-92	XJR 4.0
1990-96	XJ6 3.2
1990-96	Sovereign 3.2
1992-94	XJ220
1992-96	XJ-S 4.0
1993-94	XJS 4.0
1993-96	XJ-S 6.0
1994-96	V12 6.0
1995-96	XJR6 4.0
1996	XJS Celebration 4.0

DAIMLER

1963-69	V8/250
1966-69	Sovereign
1968-92	DS420 limosine
1969-73	Sovereign series I
1972-73	Double Six
1974-78	Sovereign series II
1974-78	Double Six series II
1979-87	Sovereign series III
1979-93	Double Six series III
1983-88	Sovereign 5.3
1986-89	Sovereign
1986-89	Daimler 3.6
1990-96	Daimler 4.0
1994-96	Double Six 6.0
1996	Century 4.0
1996	Century 6.0